Kreuzerkrieg

**Other Books on Naval Affairs by
Edwin P. Hoyt:**

Adult

The Last Cruise of the Emden

For Young People

From the Turtle to the Nautilus
(THE STORY OF SUBMARINES)

The Glorious Flattops

Steamboat Stories

The Tragic Commodore
(A BIOGRAPHY OF OLIVER HAZARD PERRY)

Edwin P. Hoyt

Kreuzerkrieg

The World Publishing Company
Cleveland and New York

PUBLISHED BY THE WORLD PUBLISHING COMPANY
2231 WEST 110TH STREET, CLEVELAND, OHIO 44102
PUBLISHED SIMULTANEOUSLY IN CANADA BY
NELSON, FOSTER & SCOTT LTD.
LIBRARY OF CONGRESS CATALOG CARD NUMBER: 67–24477
FIRST EDITION
COPYRIGHT © 1968 BY EDWIN P. HOYT
ALL RIGHTS RESERVED. NO PART OF THIS BOOK MAY BE REPRODUCED IN
ANY FORM WITHOUT WRITTEN PERMISSION FROM THE PUBLISHER, EXCEPT
FOR BRIEF PASSAGES INCLUDED IN A REVIEW APPEARING IN A NEWSPAPER
OR MAGAZINE. PRINTED IN THE UNITED STATES OF AMERICA

For Chris

CONTENTS

	Introduction	9
One	Eve of War	19
Two	War Plans	38
Three	*Gott Strafe England*	55
Four	Men and Morale	66
Five	Confusing the Enemy	83
Six	Into Action	103
Seven	The Squadron Strikes	116
Eight	Converging	128
Nine	*Dresden*	142
Ten	Search and Destroy	156
Eleven	Two Squadrons Prepare	160
Twelve	The Battle of Coronel	181

7

Thirteen	The Victors Rejoice	214
Fourteen	So Fierce the Hunt	232
Fifteen	Moment of Glory	240
Sixteen	One Last Defiance	248
Seventeen	The Wolves Arrive	255
Eighteen	"Prepare to Weigh"	262
Nineteen	The Last Battle	270
Twenty	"What Is the *Scharnhorst* Doing?" "She Is Sinking."	278
Twenty-one	The Stern Chase	290
Twenty-two	One Boat Was Launched	301
Twenty-three	The Summing Up	304
	Epilogue	311
	Index	325

INTRODUCTION

UNTIL THE LAST QUARTER OF THE NINETEENTH
century one could not really call Germany a sea-
faring nation; the German Empire was scarcely half
a century old and none of its component states
had depended on the sea for a livelihood. Germany
did possess rich agricultural resources, and when the
Industrial Revolution began she found that she had
manufacturing resources, too, so the creation of the
German merchant marine was a slow business, and
the establishment of the German navy did not come
about until late in the 1870s. In 1875 there was no
German navy to speak of, but fifteen years later
Kaiser Wilhelm I could boast a force of four thousand
men and twenty ships.

The German navy came into being because the
Kaiser and Chancellor Bismarck had established the begin-
nings of German empire. The overseas empire began in

Africa, which was ripe for the taking by Europeans in the late years of the century; and once it was established as a series of trading posts, the German traders called for force to protect them and punish the natives who sometimes rose up against the harsh treatment accorded lesser peoples by the colonialists. In the 1880s, when this problem arose, Chancellor Bismarck was not overly concerned with these burgeoning colonies, not nearly so much as the merchants of Hamburg and Bremen, and he was not willing to spend vast sums of the government's money on a navy, no matter how the businessmen howled. Germany's future lay on the continent of Europe and he could see that future clearly. As far as force was concerned what was needed was a huge land army, not a navy.

Yet even Bismarck had to admit that the possession of colonies gave strength to the word *Empire* and that there was value to colonialism above the material, and he was not reluctant to support a reasonable naval force. The youthful German Admiralty arrived at what to Bismarck was an admirable solution to the problem of policing the colonies. The navy men proposed creation of a *Kreuzergeschwader,* a cruiser squadron. The word was to become a household word in Germany because the *Kreuzergeschwader* roamed the world, meting out punishment to those callow natives who dared defy the will of His Majesty the Kaiser. Landing parties disembarked off the East African Coast and went burning and pillaging through the countryside when the natives refused to bring their trade goods to the German post at Dar es Salaam. German naval troops stormed ashore at Samoa to quell an uprising against the German trading company there. German seamen punished the natives of the

Palaus when they refused to do as they were told. Each punitive expedition, each firing of the cannon of the new cruisers, was reported in detail in the German press, and the Cruiser Squadron became famous in less than a year after its establishment.

Late in the nineteenth century the cruiser was a combination of sailing and steaming ship: it was armed with 12 guns, carried a crew of 250 or 300 men, was usually three-masted, ship-rigged, and powered with engines of about 2000 horsepower, attached to a single fourbladed screw—that was the steam concept of the day. The cruiser was the basic ship of the German navy, and of nearly every other navy in the world until 1890. Then the stirrings of the great steel ship idea began to be felt in Europe, culminating in Britain's building of the fearsome battleship *Dreadnought* in 1906, with which Britain created an entirely new class of ships and new naval strategy.

The German strategy in the twentieth century continued to rely heavily on the existence of a cruiser force. The Germans built dreadnoughts, but only enough to present a threat to the British Home Fleet. Outside home waters the German cruisers were still the Empire's main line of defense. No longer was there simply one *Kreuzergeschwader* with responsibilities all over the world; there were a number of cruisers, some in Africa, some in European waters. Still, the soul of the old *Kreuzergeschwader* continued to exist in what was called the German East Asia Cruiser Squadron.

Germany occupied the Kiaochow area of China's Shantung peninsula and its marvelous protected harbor. The Germans took a tiny fishing village called

11

Tsingtao and made it into one of the most important port cities of the East. They spent more than twelve million dollars on the port facilities and created as fine a port as existed, as good in its way as Hong Kong or Shanghai, and better than Weihaiwei in the north.

After the turn of the century, the balance of power in the Far East was a delicate and worrisome matter to all the important nations of the world. Britain maintained her big bases at Hong Kong and Singapore, and had taken a lease on Weihaiwei to make of it a subsidiary naval base after the Germans seized Tsingtao. The French had moved into Indochina and had special concessions in South China that made it common for French ships to be found in China waters. The Russians had been driven back, but only to Vladivostok, by the ambitious Japanese, who controlled the fine port of Port Arthur in Manchuria, and had taken over all of Korea to make it part of the Japanese economy. The military and naval forces of all these powers kept jealous watch on one another, through their naval attachés officially, but unofficially through networks of spies and trading organizations in all parts of the East. No foreigner moved, no ship changed anchor, without the word being passed to half a dozen chanceries at Nanking, the new capital, where the Republic of China governed. In 1913 warlords menaced the capital and the banks of the Yangtze River, China's great central artery, and the ships of several nations were called to the Yangtze to protect the lives and property of the foreign community. Ships representing the German East Asia Cruiser Squadron were there, for this was precisely the type of duty for which they were designed. The old-fashioned cannon of the war-

12

lords were no match for the modern rifled guns of the
steel warships, and soon the warlords were vanquished
or driven away from the river banks.

From time to time in the year since, there had
been incidents, but by and large the China station was
very quiet as 1914 began. The Europeans were used
to cooperating with one another against the Chinese,
and to a lesser extent against the Japanese, who
formed a third force in Asia. Consequently, even when
war clouds began to be seen over western Europe,
there was no overt sign of enmity among the foreigners
in Asia. Englishmen frequented the clubs of Tsingtao,
just as Germans were welcome visitors to the English
clubs of Shanghai and Hong Kong. The tensions at
home were known, and even understood, but halfway
around the world they did not arouse much excitement. So indefinite was the consideration of war that
the German high command had worked out only the
most rudimentary plans for such an eventuality. As
far as Europe was concerned, the men of the military
machine made it their occupation to assess every
known combination of nations that might be engaged
in war, as allies and antagonists, and to assess every
known possibility of action. But as far as Asia was
concerned, Germany simply said that the Cruiser
Squadron was the first line of defense of German
interests in Asia, and let it go at that.

Here the Germans in Berlin were not playing the
fool, they were simply recognizing the cruel fact
that whatever value Germany's colonies might hold
for the homeland in matters of prestige and possibility,
in 1914 the German foothold in Asia could be very
easily dislodged and there was nothing the men in
Berlin could do about it. Except perhaps in Africa,

13

there was not a German colony abroad that was strong enough to defend itself for long against an enemy with modern weapons. In the Pacific and even in Kiaochow the defense installations were made to protect the colony against native uprisings.

In the cockpit of Europe, Germany was struggling vigorously to prevent enclosure by an alliance of Russia, France, and England—the Triple Entente—which threatened Germany's expansionist aims, in Europe and elsewhere. The Russian and German emperors exchanged visits, and German diplomats tried to woo Russia away from the Entente. It was a difficult matter because the Hapsburg Empire of Austria-Hungary was expanding in the south, and had taken territory claimed by the Slavs of Serbia. The Serbians were then strong and growing stronger, in terms of Balkan power, and the Austrians feared that the Serbs might dominate all southern Europe, take Albania, and somehow destroy Hungary. The Germans tried to ignore all this action that was being watched so carefully from St. Petersburg, and to divert the Russians with promises of riches in Persia that could be obtained through German-Russian cooperation. They even hinted at riches for the Russians in Constantinople, although here the Germans had to tread softly; the Turks were theoretically their friends.

By 1912 it had become apparent that the German overtures to Russia had failed and could not be counted on to help Germany. Then the Germans turned to Britain, attempting to woo England to a position of neutrality. To do this the Germans would have had to renounce all their ambitions insofar as naval strength was concerned. The army men were willing to let Britain rule the sea, but the colonialists

14

and the navy men were not. In the spring of 1914 Britain and Germany did draft agreements on the matter of the Portuguese colonies and a Baghdad railroad system, but France and Russia conspired to make the British suspicious of the Germans, and the tentative agreements were forgotten. The strength of the Triple Entente was restored. How strong it was became apparent in two ways. First, the Germans had arranged with the Turkish government to send General Liman von Sanders to Turkey to take command of the Turkish first army corps and, using that as a basis, to reorganize the Turkish army along German lines. But so much pressure was brought by the Triple Entente powers that von Sanders was deprived of his command and remained, only saving face, as inspector of the Turkish army, a post without power. Meanwhile a British admiral became Admiral of the Turkish fleet, to reorganize that fleet along British lines, as part of Turkey's attempts to modernize and Europeanize her way of life. Second, the German Prince zu Wied took over the state of Albania as a sovereign principality in the spring of 1914, but was unable to hold it because of the objections of the Greeks and the Italians.

Even so, in the spring of 1914 the Germans still retained hopes that they might woo Britain away from the Triple Entente and much was done to that end everywhere in the world.

But if war were to come—and this was inherent in all that was thought and done in Berlin—then the farflung Germans in the colonies would have to shift for themselves. As far as German might was concerned, the Cruiser Squadron and the colonial troops were already written off. There lies the crux of this

15

story. It was expected that the East Asia Cruiser Squadron would remain in China waters and defend Kiaochow colony as long as it could withstand the onslaught of the enemies who might mass against it. Berlin never considered that the Cruiser Squadron might strike a vital blow at the enemy, or that for a period of months this handful of ships would terrorize all British shipping everywhere simply by its existence. How and why all this happened is the tale to be unfolded in these pages.

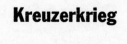

Kreuzerkrieg

1

EVE OF WAR

IN THE LAST FEW YEARS BEFORE THE TURN OF
the twentieth century the German Emperor of the Hohen-
zollerns began to develop overseas colonies, as the French,
British, and Portuguese were doing so successfully. It was a
time of imperialism. Even the immature, self-contained republic of the United States was casting about for overseas possessions, so there was nothing sinister or unusual in the German
policy; the Germans were acting in the fashion of the important powers of those times.

The Germans made their first colonial acquisition in 1883
in Southwest Africa. Two years later they established a pro-
tectorate over East Africa. They annexed the Marshall Islands
and the Solomons that same year. Before 1900 the German
Empire had expanded far and wide into the Pacific and onto
the mainland of Asia, where the colony of Kiaochow was
established on the Shantung peninsula. In the Pacific, parts of

Samoa and the Marianas Islands also came under German imperial control.

Establishment of a far-flung oceanic empire meant that for the first time in their history the Germans must become a sea power and compete with France, England, and a growing Japan. In terms of the balance of naval power Germany stepped in to take over the place vacated by Czarist Russia after the stunning debacle at the Battle of Tsushima Strait, where the naval power of Russia was crushed by Japan. Germany began building naval bases in her colonies.

At first the small German Admiralty was regarded by the army general staff and the crown as a minor part of Germany's defense mechanism. The officials of the Empire, so long bemused by land warfare, were slow to realize that in establishing overseas colonies they had committed themselves to a strong naval policy. The results of the commitment were some time in coming.

The early policy was strictly a landsman's dream: Prince Otto von Bismarck and his advisers believed they could get along with the building of a few gunboats for each colony, and then dispatch capital ships to the colonies if need arose. A number of school ships were built by the navy, and these were also sent frequently to foreign stations for the dual purpose of showing the flag and giving the young sailors experience.

Before 1900 it became apparent that the gunboat theory would never serve Germany's purposes. The Imperial General Staff was not willing to sink huge sums of the country's defense budget into creation of navies to serve in foreign climes. The ships would seldom be seen in the German homeland—perhaps coming home once every ten years. To those accustomed to thinking of Germany's problems as the problems of land and frontiers, it was wasteful to talk in terms of foreign battleships. Begrudgingly, the army men were persuaded to let the navy build small armed sloops to deal with problems that arose abroad—such as the nearly disastrous encounter with the United States over Samoa, and the unpleasantness of the Boxer Rebellion in China.

More and more often the capital ships of the German navy were forced to travel halfway around the world to visit the colonies. China was particularly troublesome because of her three great rivers that must be policed by foreigners seeking trade and influence.

The first permanent vessel of what was to become the German East Asia Squadron was the gunboat *Iltis*, successor to a brave ship that had gone down off Shantung in 1896 with most of her crew. The new *Iltis* would earn a reputation of her own in the bombardment and capture of the Taku forts during the Boxer Rebellion of 1900. Cruisers and the new torpedo-boat destroyers were occasionally sent to aid the *Iltis* in some moment of crisis, but most calls at the growing port of Tsingtao were made by training ships.

The first major concession to the new need for naval power had been made in 1882 when a loose squadron was formed under a commodore to be responsible for *all* German colonial possessions, from West Africa to Kiaochow. More strength was needed, so the squadron was augmented by several light cruisers—the logical development of the old sailing frigates—and instead of putting control in the hands of a simple captain with commodore's duties, a Rear Admiral was appointed to command. *Kontreadmiral* von Blanc was one of the most distinguished of these leaders.

Four years later a regular system of rotation and relief of ships and crews was established to serve the Pacific and East Asia stations and it soon became apparent that there was need for a special East Asia Squadron, because the bigger ships were constantly being called for service in the rough waters of the Pacific Ocean. The squadron could not always be called into action in China. In the 1890s there were constant troubles in Africa, and the squadron was called to put down rebellions in East Africa, in the Cameroons, and to show German naval strength off the coast of Chile during the civil war of 1891.

In 1896 the existing cruiser squadron was diminished by designation as a *Kreuzerdivision*, and its sphere of activity was removed once again to the Asian coast. The men soon found that the new title was a downgrading. Again the general staff was trying to keep the cost of colonial expansion low.

The futility of the attempt to cut costs became apparent in 1897 with the occupation of Kiaochow as a *permanent* German colony. Admiral von Dieterichs became successor to *Kontreadmiral* Tirpitz, and a second cruiser division was sent out from Germany under *Kontreadmiral* Prinz Heinrich von Preussen to strengthen the force.

Little by little, the East Asia Cruiser Squadron grew. During the Boxer uprising, men from the Squadron took part in Admiral Seymour's ill-fated expedition to try to relieve Peking.

Until 1906 the Cruiser Squadron consisted of two divisions of cruisers and two admirals, but then it was reduced once again as the Germans began to feel a bit pinched by the demands of their various colonies for naval force. But at least the Squadron secured more modern vessels, and ships of the Hansa class were assigned to the Far East, when that modern cruiser came into service in 1900. Other changes came too, in the wake of the speedy development of naval warfare. Three dispatch boats were added, with strong wireless telegraph equipment. Several torpedo boats were assigned (in days before the submarine was truly tested as a naval weapon). Then, in 1908, came the *Panzerkreuzer Scharnhorst*, and three years later her sister ship, that other large armored cruiser, *Gneisenau*. The Squadron had suffered its ups and down, but in 1911 its force was fixed at two heavy cruisers and three light cruisers, plus such supporting vessels as might be necessary from time to time.

When *Kontreadmiral* Maximilian Graf von Spee took over the command of the East Asia Squadron in the autumn of 1912 it consisted of the two heavy cruisers, plus the light cruisers *Emden, Leipzig,* and *Nürnberg;* the torpedo boat *S-90,* and the torpedo boat *Taku,* which had been taken from the Chinese during the Boxer troubles; and a small, lightly armed steamer named *Titania,* which was used as an escort vessel and dispatch boat, much as destroyers were to be used later. These ships actually comprised the Squadron. For administrative purposes, several other vessels were within the admiral's command, although strictly speaking they were not part of the Squadron, for it was almost inconceivable that they could be gainfully employed except in Chinese coastal waters. These vessels were the heavy gunboats *Iltis, Jaguar, Luchs,* and *Tiger,* and the river gunboats *Vaterland, Tsingtau,* and *Otter;* the last three were stationed on the Yangtze River near Canton.

Because *Kontreadmiral* von Spee commanded a squadron did not mean that the full Asiatic might of Germany could be found often in one place. Quite the contrary. The vessels were usually scattered around the German possessions in the East, from Ponape to Tsingtao. It was useful to have so many vessels of such disparate sizes, for the light unarmored cruisers could go into harbors where the big ships must stand outside, and the cruisers were not very comfortable when they were forced by circumstance to make shows of force in such places as the confined waters of the Yangtze River. By and large the gunboats did very well in these rivers, and in the bays of the mainland; the big ships should be sent to quell trouble where large parties of armed men were needed.

Admiral von Spee was appointed to the command of the Squadron on September 19, 1912, and immediately made

23

preparations to go to Tsingtao, where he arrived at the end of October aboard a North German Lloyd steamer. He took control of the Squadron on December 4 in Shanghai. There was trouble along the Yangtze that fall and winter and it was the Squadron's responsibility to protect German interests and act in concert with the other ships of foreign powers to keep the Chinese warlords under control.

In the spring of 1913 the relief ship came to Tsingtao, and all the ships of the Squadron reported there in June for the happy event. It was German naval policy to replace about a fourth of the crew of the Squadron every spring, since even with extra pay and the perquisites of the white man in the Orient the sailors found life very lonesome in the Far East. That spring and summer the admiral and his heavy ships were scheduled to make a duty voyage to the German possessions in the Pacific. They planned the trip for spring, and had actually embarked on the voyage to Sunda when the word was flashed that a new revolution had broken out against the government of President Yuan Shih-kai in China. The heavy cruisers were ordered back to China station duty for the summer while *Emden* went off on the Pacific cruise.

The next year, 1914, *Emden* was to stay on guard duty at Tsingtao, while *Scharnhorst* and *Gneisenau* made the South Seas trip. *Nürnberg* was on station that spring on the west coast of Mexico, protecting German interests against mistreatment by government or insurgent troops in the revolution that was ravaging that country. Times had not changed so very much from the old days: the East Asia Squadron was still called on to police far too much territory because the German government simply did not have enough warships to do the job otherwise. *Nürnberg* was foul in the bottom and badly in need of a refit after too many months at sea, and the admiral planned that she should come back to Tsingtao by way of Honolulu and the German colonies in the South Seas, then to

24

go into drydock in the inner harbor at Tsingtao for a leisurely and thorough overhaul. The admiral's plan called for *Seine Majestäte Schiffe Leipzig* to take the position of SMS *Nürnberg* off the Mexican shore, since it would be most impolitic to leave that coast unguarded in these perilous times. It would be done as soon as the relieving steamer arrived in Tsingtao and the crews could be transferred.

Patricia, the relief ship, came into the great protected harbor on June 2, and the replacement of crews began with German thoroughness. Each replacement was handed a card before he left *Patricia.* On the card were listed his ship's name and number, his action station on the ship, the place in the boat to which he was assigned, and his task and division of the ship.

The officers of the warships came aboard *Patricia.* Each officer collected the men assigned to him; took them aboard the cruisers; showed them where to sling hammocks and the clothes press they were to use; told them where and how to get their food, where and how to eat it, and the bounds of the ship. Hundreds of cases and bales were shipped off *Patricia* by gangs of Chinese coolies who strained under the loads along the narrow gangways, and by cargo nets and hoists. Just five days after the docking of *Patricia* at the long Tsingtao pier, SMS *Leipzig* was ready to weigh anchor and set course for the west coast of Mexico. She and her crew, half experienced and half green as a monsoon sea, were on their own. They would forego the niceties of fire drills and gunnery practice and action-station exercises while in port. Training would be conducted at sea while the *Leipzig* was on the way to her new station. It was not the best way, even the admiralty agreed to the justice of complaints, but this was peacetime and a few corners could be cut. By the time the *Leipzig* would arrive on station, *Fregattenkapitän* Haun could be expected to have ship and men well in hand again. He had already

25

commanded *Leipzig* for more than a year and he knew what she and he could do, and what could be expected of officers and men, even green ones just out from the fatherland.

So at one o'clock on the afternoon of June 7, a Sunday, SMS *Leipzig* set out, band playing and flags flying, for her rendezvous, her hold jammed with coal and provisions stacked so tightly on her decks that the deck officer, *Leutnant* Walter Schiwig, said she looked like a seagoing pushcart.

Out they went, past Cape Yatau, and then past the Chalientao lighthouse which stood on an island outside the bay. The islands of Japan were to be the first port of call, so the course was set for the Strait of Shimonoseki, and on June 9 they approached the straits and took on a Japanese pilot. At eight o'clock the next morning they passed the Yokosuka naval base where most of the powerful Japanese fleet lay at anchor, and then they, too, anchored in Yokohama harbor. *Korvetten-kapitän* von Knorr, the naval attaché at the Tokyo Embassy, came aboard to confer with Captain Haun, and soon it was announced that there would be shore liberty. At two o'clock in the afternoon the party boats were moving back and forth to the ship, and the watch was reduced to skeleton; after all, this was peacetime and they were in a friendly port.

Friendly? The officers went ashore with *Korvettenkapitän* Knorr who showed them the sights and then took them to dinner at a private house. Over the cigars the talk turned to politics and Knorr warned that if there were a European war, Japan would join it on the side of France and the other members of the Triple Entente. She would also attack Tsingtao, he said, for this would be her major reason for entering the war. He had told the German diplomats just this much, and they had not believed him; they had even warned him not to continue such talk. They had, in short, told Knorr to mind his own business.

Oddly enough, as the *Leipzig* lay at anchor in Yokohama

harbor, paying and receiving compliments in calls among the fleet, the British China Squadron commander, Vice-Admiral Sir Thomas Jerram, arrived for a visit in Tsingtao aboard the heavy cruiser HMS *Minotaur*. There was long and friendly association between the men of the British China Squadron and the German East Asia Squadron. Twelve naval officers, 2 doctors, and 430 enlisted men had formed the German contingent in the ill-fated Seymour Expedition to Peking; 4 officers, 1 doctor, and 85 men had gone on the final Peking relief expedition; and 5 officers, 1 doctor, and 242 men had fought at Taku and elsewhere around Tientsin as members of the Third Sea Battalion during the Boxer troubles.

On hearing of the coming of the British, Admiral von Spee may have had (his officers most certainly did have) feelings of mild annoyance that the British had chosen this most unfortunate time to arrive. Coming so soon after the arrival of the relief ship, the *Minotaur* caught the Germans in the middle of preparations for sea. There was a great deal of work to be done, in shipping supplies, coaling, and especially in training the new crewmen. Admiral von Spee would have liked to have been out on the high seas, conducting exercises in seamanship and gunnery, rather than cooped up in port entertaining dignitaries. Also there was talk in the wardrooms that it was a very odd time for the British to come, unless they were snooping on the preparedness of their host.

Of course, as it turned out, snooping was part of the British reason for the courtesy call. It was the responsibility of the British China Squadron to keep track of the whereabouts of the various ships of the other navies in the Far East. Admiral Jerram's intelligence officers were coming to do their duty.

The unloading of the *Patricia* had scarcely been completed, that pleasant ship had hardly been sent back to the homeland with all the honors Tsingtao could bestow on her,

27

when the British came in sight. On the morning of June 12 *Minotaur* arrived, and at ten o'clock she was pulling alongside the long pier of the inner harbor. *Scharnhorst* and *Gneisenau*, which usually anchored in deep water, were ordered into the quay to lie alongside the visitor.

Flags flying, and her trim and deck as spic and span as a warship can be, HMS *Minotaur* came slowly in, guided by the harbormaster himself and a pigtailed Chinese carrying a brand-new landing flag to mark the point on the pier opposite which the visitor's bridge should lie.

Then the visits began. Visits were exchanged by the British and German admirals. Visits were exchanged by the captains of the *Minotaur*, the *Scharnhorst*, the *Gneisenau*, and the *Emden*. Admiral von Spee gave a dinner for the British senior officers aboard the *Scharnhorst* on the first night. Governor Meyer-Waldeck gave a ball at the great stone governor's palace on the hill overlooking the harbor. The officers of the *Gneisenau* held an open house and dancing party for the visitors and residents of the colony. For this occasion the quarter-deck was scoured with sand and pumice, potted plants and bunting were brought out and scattered around, and electric lights were strung along the rails. Canvas curtains were hung from the sides of the quarter-deck, to protect the ladies from the cool night air of Tsingtao's spring, and soon the quarter-deck was turned into a very respectable dancing salon. The officer's mess, on the other side of the exterior bulkhead, became a dining room in which a resplendent buffet was set out before nightfall. Roast beef, ham, cheeses from Germany and from Manchuria, fishes, and salads were laid out on stiff white linen amid shining silver service, and the wine of Germany was chilled.

The bar for the men was located on the rear upper deck. Here bamboo chairs and tables were spread about and white-coated Chinese boys stood ready for the slightest motion of a finger by one of the officers. The saloon, behind the officers' mess, was given over to tables for the older people, particularly the civilians, who would play cards while the younger guests and the naval officers danced, literally beneath the muzzles of the 8.2-inch guns of the after turret.

It was a pleasant and exciting evening. The ladies from Tsingtao appeared in their long silk dresses and their dazzling jewels. The officers in their dress uniforms and the civilians in their mess jackets looked every inch the gentlemen. There was much bowing and smiling and stiff courtesy as befitted gallant men of action, but there was also much laughter and gaiety supplied by the ladies who made the men of war forget their calling for a few hours.

On the morning after the party the *Gneisenau* moved out to her customary anchorage in the roadstead, near Arkona Island. She had to vacate the pier because merchant ships were clamoring for the space to unload their cargoes. *Scharnhorst* was primarily host ship to its opposite number, the flagship of the British squadron.

For four days the festivities continued, aship and ashore. There was a 1200-yard race of whaleboats, a polo game between officers of the *Scharnhorst* and the *Minotaur*, boxing matches between sailors of the two ships at every weight, gymnastics and jumping contests, and a football game. It really made no difference who won, except for discussion in the messes, but the English went back to their ships congratulating themselves on winning the football, and the Germans congratulated themselves on victories in most of the other contests. To the British the football victory showed the importance of teamwork. The Germans gloried because they had won more victories in more contests than their opponents, showing that the Germans favored versatility over preciosity. In all other ways the occasion showed the equality of the British and the Germans, from the ranks of their officers down to their reminiscences of past cooperation in international affairs and exercises in the Pacific. Admiral von Spee had received his promotion to Vice-Admiral since his coming to the Squadron, and the ships were much the same—*Minotaur* weighing perhaps 3000 tons more than *Scharnhorst* and slightly outgunning her. So equality and friendship were the order of the day, with each nation's representatives thinking privately that the others were quite good fellows, but not quite up to the mark of their own.

On June 13, as the festivities were just getting under way at Tsingtao, the *Leipzig* left Yokohama on the longest leg of her trip east, the 3400-mile journey to Hawaii. Mount Fuji stood high and silent and beautiful above the landscape as the ship pulled away from the harbor, and the officers and men could look back and see the sacred mountain above the horizon for many hours. But by noon the mountain, too, was below the wave level and the ship was on the high seas, out of sight of land. Now there were drills and practices, the *Leipzig*'s captain striving to get his ship up to expectations before she reached Honolulu. It was not possible, of course, to take a crew that was 25 per cent greenhorn and make them perform as well as old sea dogs who had been working together for a year, but the captain tried.

The purpose of the *Leipzig* was not to follow the steamship routes to Honolulu but to get there in the quickest possible time, so the captain steered a great circle course for the islands. During the first few days, just outside Japanese waters, they encountered a number of steamships, but then they were off the normal steamer route, and alone. This suited Captain Haun very well indeed because it allowed his officers to concentrate their fullest efforts on practice in gunnery, fire control, damage control, and seamanship. The officers stood watch and watch, four hours on, four hours off, with the captain taking his own watch on the bridge in the first division, as was the

German custom among *Kleinekreuzers*, or light cruisers. *Ober-leutnant zur See* Schiwig, for example, was the youngest officer on the ship in point of service, having been aboard for only one year. So he was, as he put it, "maid of all work." He was torpedo officer. He stood daily deck watches. He was adjutant, and he was in charge of the wine mess, among many other duties. He accepted these responsibilities cheerfully, knowing that the moment a more junior lieutenant came aboard he would be able to shuck many of them, and that he could look forward to greater responsibility and less onerous duty as he progressed up the naval ladder.

All the officers were much amused on this voyage by Staff Doctor Protz, whom they had embarked at Yokohama for the trip to Honolulu. The doctor was on his way home for leave, and would take ship at Honolulu for America, and then cross that continent to sail for Germany from the other side. The *Leipzig* being a warship without extra accommodations for passengers, Dr. Protz slept on the bridge in the charthouse, on a little couch usually reserved for the captain's use—this was as much of a cabin as the room aboard the light cruiser permitted. Dr. Protz slept very little on the fortnight's voyage, preferring to stay up in the warm evenings and clear starry nights of the Pacific spring and early summer, spinning yarns with the young officers of the watch.

The *Leipzig* had a pleasant voyage. The work was hard— but that was to be expected. On June 26 the island of Kauai was sighted. That night the *Leipzig* passed into the channel between Kauai and Oahu. On the morning of June 27 they were in touch with the port authorities by wireless, and at nine o'clock the ship was at the mole in the harbor of Honolulu.

For the next few days the crew relaxed, and the officers who did not have duty spent many happy hours lying on the beach at Waikiki, and celebrating with the doctor until he left them to sail to the United States on the steamer *Korea*.

Meanwhile the British cruiser *Minotaur* had left Tsingtao on June 16 bound for her summer base at Weihaiwei, the British squadron's anchorage, and an impatient Admiral von Spee was free to do the work necessary to carry out his summer mission. The *Scharnhorst's* band played as the British cruiser moved away from the quay; when she arrived at the outer roadstead, Admiral Jerram signaled his thanks to SMS *Gneisenau*, which was still lying there, and in an hour *Minotaur* had disappeared over the horizon. Preparations for the three months cruise of the South Pacific waters could begin.

First there was gunnery practice. Life at sea was to accustom the new men of the Squadron to their ships and their routine. The admiral had hoped for a week or so of this practice, but the visit of the English had changed his plans, and so gunnery was cut down to two days. One by one the ships also reported on minor repairs that were needed; it was decided that *Gneisenau* had the most important deficiencies, so she went into dock first. The others came along for supplies and coaling, a task that was always onerous on the steam-driven warships until fuel oil came into use, but one that was less burdensome at Tsingtao than anywhere else the China Squadron traveled. Scaffolding was erected at the fore and aft ends of the ships, and walkways were built to connect the companionways that led to the coal holds with the go-downs or warehouses where the large-lump and clean-burning Shantung coal was stored.

In the center of the *Gneisenau* the boat crane was used to lift heavy baskets of coal onto the deck, and then down into the holds. From the water side, the crew of the *Gneisenau* worked from flat-bottomed scows, carrying coal up the gangways and down into the hold. Normally, all the coaling would be done by Chinese coolies, but the admiral was in a hurry to get to sea, and so the *Gneisenau* was coaled by her crew, and then was made ready for sailing. The urgency was not quite so great for the *Scharnhorst*; the admiral was staying on a few days in Tsingtao to finish up his paperwork and to make sure that the needs of the *Emden* and the men of the Squadron would be met by the civil authorities during his absence.

At eight o'clock on the morning of June 20, to the usual strains of band music, half inspirational, half saddening *("Wenn Gott will Rechte Gunst erweisen, den schicken er in die weite Welt")*, the *Gneisenau* pulled away from the quay and glided into the calm waters of Germany's finest Asiatic harbor. At the horseshoe reef the last message was passed to a harbor boat; at the entrance that separated inner and outer roads there was a last look at the lighthouse; at Arkona Island there was a last signal with the shore; then the *Gneisenau* set forth on her own, her men thinking of the adventures ahead and the return to Tsingtao in September. When they returned, nearly all the officers of the ship were destined to be replaced, for they had been aboard *Gneisenau* for two long years, and they were promised a trip across the Trans-Siberian Railway and through European Russia in time to be home for Christmas with their families. Soon the mountains that surrounded Tsingtao faded from view, the craggy Laushan last of all, and then they were alone on the breast of the sea. No one had time for much philosophizing as the ship cleared the outer roadstead, however, for the first task of every man aboard was to clean the ship for sea. Two days of coaling had left her filthy, from the rims of her bulkheads to the floor of the ward-room, and every nook and cranny must be searched for the telltale grime of coal dust. The paintwork was scoured. The woodwork was washed. Hoses were brought out and half-naked men scrubbed and swept the dirt away from the whitening decks. The men sang as they splashed barefoot through the sea water, wielding brush and mop, and they laughed in anticipation of the wonders that would soon unfold for them. It was Saturday, and the next day, Sunday, would be the easiest day of life aboard the peacetime warship, with skeleton watches and only the most necessary work. This Sunday it would be necessary to scrub up the brightwork on the ship, but that was not a vexing task, particularly when the course was set for Japan.

By way of Quelpart Island, south of Korea's peninsula, two days after sailing from Tsingtao, *Gneisenau* slowed and entered the entrance to Nagasaki port on the west of the main island of Japan. At the pilot station she was queried as to name and nationality and told to await the coming of the port authorities for inspection. Doctor and pilot arrived and the ship was brought into harbor while the delighted men made ready for shore leave. Nagasaki was a particularly pleasant leave port, not only because of the Japanese city that lay beyond the quay, but because it was a deep-water port, which meant that the *Gneisenau* could be moored to a buoy in the middle of the fjord, and still be as safe as she could possibly be in any kind of weather.

Disappointingly, there was to be no time for shore leave on this voyage. Captain Maerker of the *Gneisenau* was cutting matters fine, but he could not cut them so fine as to arrange shore leave. The purpose of the *Gneisenau's* visit was really to pick up the mail, which had been posted here according to orders issued earlier, before the English had come to Tsingtao. The mail service was quite good, considering everything; from Germany it took not more than fourteen days to receive a letter. This was approximately the same time it took for mail to get to Tsingtao or Taku, or any point above Shanghai. Of course it was a day or so earlier at Port Arthur, and several days shorter at Vladivostok, but the Squadron had seldom any occasion to be visiting either Port Arthur or Vladivostok. Fourteens days, via the Trans-Siberian Railroad, was a very short time in the first few years of the twentieth century, before the development of air mail. The old way, by sea, had meant a five-week lag between letters posted in Europe and their arrival in East Asia.

The mail arrived on the day that the *Gneisenau* came to Nagasaki. *Gneisenau* topped off her coal bunkers with four hundred tons of fine Japanese coal, and in a pouring rain the next morning she slipped her buoy and set forth for the East China Sea, on a course that led her along the coast of Kyushu Island, through the Colnett Strait, and north of the Ryukyu Islands into the Pacific Ocean proper.

The weather was fine, and it continued so, although each day the red ball of the rising sun rose higher and hotter above them as they headed into the southern seas. On June 26, even as Admiral von Spee and the *Scharnhorst* made ready to sail from Tsingtao, the *Gneisenau* crossed the Tropic of Cancer at longitude 140 degrees east and entered the tropics. Awnings were spread over the decks for protection from the fiery sun, and straw hats were broken out for the men, who were punctiliously instructed by *Oberstabsarzt* Dr. Nohl and his medical staff in the dangers of exposure to the tropical sun.

On June 27 *Kapitänleutnant* Waldemar Born, the chief navigating officer of the *Gneisenau*, was pleased to announce to the captain that he had made his landfall, right on schedule. It was Urakas, the most northerly of the Marianas Islands, and the cruiser passed close by it so that the new men of the crew could have their first look at a tropical island.

The Marianas are a volcanic chain, and Urakas is not one of their most imposing representatives. The men looked out to starboard to see a wild desert island popping out of the ocean, the great brown crater of the lifeless volcano rising to a thousand feet, with no greenery to be seen on its rocky shores, and only a busy swirling coating of seabird life to give it the semblance of anything on earth. The *Gneisenau* then moved down the long chain of islands, ever southward, coming in close, by day, for looks at the shores, but moving out to a

35

healthy distance by night, for these were not well-charted waters, and there was not a single beacon to guide them away from coral reef or rock.

On Sunday, June 28, the *Gneisenau* reached Pagan, site of an unfortunate accident in the year just past. In 1913 the two heavy cruisers of the Squadron had started out on their tour of the south and had come this far before being recalled to guard the interests of Germany in North China waters. At Pagan a party of lieutenants had gone ashore one day for a look at the tropical vegetation and animal life. They had hiked up the side of one of the two volcanoes. One youngster had strayed from the group and had not returned with the others. That same night two hundred men, led by Captain Brüninghaus, had scoured the scrub vegetation and had found him, dead in the midst of a patch of bushes, apparently overcome by fatigue and the hot sun. This year veterans of that sad experience recognized the landmarks of the disaster as they came up to anchor. There was new cleared land along the mountainside, the result of a fire set by a rocket which was shot off to recall others of the crew after one landing party had found the young officer.

Pagan was not a proper harbor for a ship of His Majesty's Cruiser Squadron—the reef was difficult—and the *Gneisenau* anchored outside the coral on the afternoon of June 28. That day several boats went ashore to visit the little settlement of huts and cocoanut palms. One boat capsized on the way back to the ship, running afoul of the heavy surf at the edge of the reef, but no one was lost or injured, and the accident was regarded as a good joke on those who had an unexpected bath.

That evening, after darkness swooped down (as it does in the Tropics), the men assembled on the cool upper deck to sing and talk and smoke, and the officers sat on the quarter-deck, playing chess or smoking quietly and looking out to the dimming silhouette of the island. As darkness became complete the Southern Cross shone down brightly from directly over head, and Venus made ready for her transit across that sky. It was as peaceful a night as any man of the sea might wish for.

As officers and men slept, the sailors on watch in the wireless room put together the night's news reports for the morning reading of the officers in the wardroom. This night the wireless men put down the startling news that the Archduke Franz Ferdinand of the family Hapsburg, heir to the crown of Austria-Hungary, had been assassinated at Sarajevo. Next morning even the least politically minded of the officers read the news with a start, for it was known that the Serbs—Slavs—of Sarajevo were a troublesome lot to the Austrian Empire. It was known that there had been many arguments about the status of the Slavs within the Hapsburg Empire. It was known that the Czar of the Russias took a strong interest in the problems of these Slavs. It was known that Austria-Hungary and Germany were bound together with Italy in the Triple Alliance whose natural enemies were the Slavs and Russians. Startled is a simple word to describe the emotions that began to surge through the breasts of the officers of SMS *Gneisenau* as they learned the news.

The other ships of the Cruiser Squadron had the news as well. Admiral von Spee and the men of the *Scharnhorst* received the news while they were at sea, heading for rendezvous with *Gneisenau*. The men of the *Leipzig* received the news from the wireless station at Honolulu, as they steamed away from the islands after their brief stay. The men of the *Nürnberg* received it in their vigil off the coast of Mexico. None knew exactly what the news meant, but all, from *Vizeadmiral* Maximilian, Graf von Spee, down to the lowest *Matrose* in the forecastle, knew that this information threatened to change their lives.

2

WAR PLANS

ADMIRAL VON SPEE RECEIVED THE NEWS OF THE
archduke's assassination while on the high seas, bound for the
Marianas, where the flagship *Scharnhorst* would rendezvous
with her sister ship, *Gneisenau*. Admirals do not confide their
hopes and fears to the officers of their ships or even to the staff,
but von Spee was as much at sea as was his ship at the
moment. It was almost unbelievable that there could be a
war. The economic relationships of the European nations
seemed inextricably entangled, and never had all of them
prospered so much as now. And yet the admiral, like the
German Admiralty, was always prepared for war—or rather
for many different wars—for that was his reason for being in
uniform.

He had a plan for war against Japan. He had a plan for
war against Russia. He had a plan for war against England,
one for war against France, and one for war against any combination of these powers. Yet at the moment there was nothing

to be done but watch the trend of events in Europe. Nothing was to be gained by guessing the possible course of the future. It would be more profitable to spend the time counting the dolphins that played around the bow of his flagship.

From the admiral's point of view, the news did serve one useful purpose: it snapped his officers and men to an attention to duty that had not been seen in the Squadron since the troubles along the Yangtze the year before. During battle drill every man was conscious of the importance of his task, each man put into the job that little extra effort that made it all seem ridiculously simple, for no man could be quite sure that the next call to action stations would not be made in all seriousness.

The two big ships were now scheduled to call at Saipan, the seat of government of the German colony of the Marianas. They anchored at the west of the island, again in deep water because the settlement of Garapan could not properly be said to have a port. There were social calls back and forth between ship and shore. The governor came aboard with the colony's doctor, and the naval officers went ashore to call on the leading inhabitants. The Marianas' population was of four strains: the original Chamorros, the Carolinians, the Samoans, and the foreigners. They all lived separately, and each group entertained the officers of the cruisers.

Gneisenau left Saipan on July 2, to stop off at the island of Rota where the officers might have a bit of sport in a goat hunt. *Scharnhorst* was two days behind; they would meet at Truk, the marvelous port in the middle of the Caroline islands. On the way both ships ran afoul of a typhoon which was devastating the seas to the north of them. Fortunately the cruisers caught only the outer edges of the storm and were not seriously delayed, although they spent many hours in heavy seas, and *Gneisenau* had to heave to outside the atoll on the night of July 5, rather than chance the heavy weather

39

for the entrance. She awoke on July 6 to a blustery day and steamed carefully into the northeast passage into Truk. The men who had not before seen it were fascinated with the first sight of the great reef, forty miles long, which encircles Truk atoll, for it stood straight out of the water like a cliff and the waves broke against it so fiercely that the line of the reef could be seen for miles by the thread of foam that edged it. The passage was always a difficult one; it was best made on a sunny day with the sun behind the ship so that entrance and shallows stood out sharply. There was no hope of sun on this day, so *Gneisenau* waited for a lull in the storm and then moved through the entrance, and an hour later anchored in Eten harbor, between Toloas and Eten islands. It was a dream anchorage: twenty fathoms of water under the hull, a coral bottom where the anchors would not foul, and protection from the worst weather by the long circle of the reef.

The next morning the flagship arrived and anchored alongside her sister ship. In the evening came the *Titania*, the Squadron's dispatch ship, escorting the Japanese collier *Fukoku Maru*, which had been chartered for the long voyage into the Pacific possessions of the German Empire. The logistics of this voyage gave some indication of the strengths and weaknesses of the German position in the Pacific, militarily speaking. The strength lay in the precision planning of Admiral von Spee and his staff. *Fukoku Maru* had been sent on June 18 from Tsingtao to meet the warships at Truk, and so careful had been the planning that she arrived within eight hours of the time that the much faster flagship dropped her anchor. But the need for bringing along colliers showed a basic weakness of Germany's position. All the coal that the Germans would use in the Marianas, the Carolinas, Samoa, and the rest of the farflung empire that had been acquired in the South Seas, must be shipped from coal-producing Tsingtao colony or from coal-producing Japan or Korea, or from Manchuria. The pleasant Pacific isles were useless as fuel producers. Admiral von Spee's big cruisers seemed to travel with the wind, and seemed to be quite strong enough to hold their own under any conditions, but the fact was that they were totally dependent on easy access to supplies of coal, and the faster they steamed the more alarmingly they ate coal. For this trip the admiral had chartered the *Fukoku Maru*, the German collier *Elsbeth* would meet the ships later, and the *Titania's* hold was filled with coal for the warships' use. All this was done to make sure that the Squadron did not eat up the slender supply of coal in the various colonies.

Gneisenau had coaled on June 22, and she had not steamed at more than ten knots (her best cruising speed for low fuel consumption) all the way from Tsingtao, and here two weeks later her bunkers were low. *Scharnhorst's* situation was even more demanding: leaving four days after *Gneisenau* she had put on steam to catch up, and she must now have coal if she was to be prepared for an emergency. In the international atmosphere of July 1914 there was no room for carelessness in such matters: coal meant survival to the warships.

So they coaled. The admiral and those who could escape the task went ashore, and the younger officers who could find some excuse fled to the *Titania* to sit on the quarter-deck with Captain Vogt, drink beer, and watch the proceedings with the interested eyes of lucky men who have escaped a disagreeable task. Coaling, like so much else aboard the warships, was the responsibility of the first officers, *Korvettenkapitän* Alfred Bender of the *Scharnhorst* and *Korvettenkapitän* Hans Pochhammer of the *Gneisenau*. They put on their oldest uniforms and their bravest smiles and set out to do the dirty job in the shortest time possible. For once, because so many of the members of both crews were youngsters, the job was accomplished with a will. Many of the sailors had never coaled before from a steamer, so the novelty sustained them for the first few hours.

41

Coaling began early in the morning before the sun had risen high. The *Scharnhorst's* boats were run out and dropped down and rowed to both sides of the *Fukoku Maru*. The men climbed ladders and made ready to go into the hold. The *Scharnhorst* and the *Fukoku Maru* were brought together, rubbing gear was dropped over the side of the cruiser to protect her paint and plating, and the steam hoists of the collier were fired up. All morning and all evening, with a respite in the middle of the day when the temperature was in the 90s, the crew of the *Scharnhorst* and the crew of the *Fukoku Maru* loaded coal into sacks in the dirty hold of the collier, dumped the sacks into cargo nets which were then transferred to the bunkers of the *Scharnhorst* where other sailors emptied the sacks. Within an hour the fine black dust covered every corner of the ship again. It would be removed only by the usual arduous cleaning.

When *Scharnhorst's* great maw was filled the crews of *Gneisenau* took over the collier and repeated the process under the light of large electric lamps and the ship's searchlight. And as *Gneisenau* coaled, *Scharnhorst* cleaned, so that by dawn both ships would be filled and spic and span once again.

During the next few days the admiral went ashore to attend to affairs of state, the crew had frequent liberty, and the younger, more curious officers begged various of the ships' boats from the first officers and sailed them in and out of the tiny islands that dotted the harbor.

The admiral went ashore in state, accompanied by most of the twelve officers of his personal staff, aboard the *chefboot*, the admiral's launch, a vessel some thirty feet long with a single stack placed well forward and tall enough to keep the smoke and soot away from the open stern, where the admiral chose to sit in a deck chair in clement weather, the great naval ensign of Imperial Germany streaming out behind him.

Ahead of the open stern cockpit was a glassed-in cabin for heavy weather. The launch would easily accommodate some twenty passengers, and it took half a dozen sailors to operate her to the satisfaction of the fleet; she was really as large as a little inter-island cruise boat.

On the second day at Truk the native chiefs and their nobles came to the *Scharnhorst* in their great ceremonial canoes. They clambered up the sides on ropes and rigging, and arranged themselves around the quarter-deck on matting made of cocoanut fiber, and then one group after another, each representing a separate tribe, gave a performance for the admiral and his staff. There were war dances, including a group who danced with long slender warclubs which they pounded on the deck and waved at one another. There were girls in fiber skirts, necklaces of mussel shells, their hair filled with flowers.

Admiral von Spee was delighted with the performance, as was the crew of his ship. Dressed in their tropical whites, the crew members clustered anywhere on the ship they could sit or stand and gain a view of the dancers. The admiral smiled and nodded and pulled at his Vandyke beard. He greeted every individual chief and talked about them with the governor of the island, and he applauded as happily as any young sailor at the dancing of the pretty girls.

The show lasted until evening, when the natives took to their canoes and returned to the land, lighted back through the darkness by the *Scharnhorst's* searchlight.

Following the assassination of Archduke Franz Ferdinand the Austrian authorities quickly discovered that the assassin was one Gavrilo Princip, a Bosnian revolutionary who was acting for the Serbian nationalist society called Union or Death, or, sometimes, The Black Hand. Union or Death had been founded in 1911 to carry out agitation against the Austro-

43

Hungarian Empire, and to work for the creation of a Slavic empire in the West. In 1913 the Austrians had forced the Serbs to evacuate Albania, which they were then occupying. Because of a series of Balkan wars, territories in that region of the world had changed hands a number of times, and Russia and Austria-Hungary both had aspirations. Following the assassination, the Austrian prime minister sought the support of Germany in taking a strong stand, which would mean war with Serbia, to settle territorial matters once and for all. The Germans did not believe that the Russians (who were allied with Serbia by treaty) would risk a war. So on July 5, as the two German battlecruisers were approaching Truk, the Austrian and German leaders were meeting in Berlin to plan action against Serbia. At the moment much of world opinion was sympathetic to the Austrians, and it became more so as it was learned that the Serbian government had known of a plot against the life of the archduke, but did nothing about it.

Would there be war or would there not? Who could tell? In all the messages that came for the admiral there was no definitive note. He was kept informed by the Tsingtao wireless station of rumors and messages as they came across the world from Berlin, but he did not *know*, and not knowing he could not act. All Admiral von Spee could do was prepare his ships for action in case war did come, and this is what he did.

In the second week of July, as the various officials of the Austro-Hungarian Empire argued among themselves about the line to be taken with Serbia, the cruisers were making ready for maneuvers at sea. On July 15 they steamed out of Truk's harbor just after four o'clock in the afternoon, to practice night maneuvers, and especially to brush up on their searchlight procedures. The next day the admiral sent *Scharnhorst* and *Gneisenau* out for gunnery practice, while he took the big white *chefboot* and his staff for a visit to the uninhabited Oroluk atoll near Truk. The admiral was a nature lover, and he wished to record for the German people his findings at the atoll. Also, it was very good form for him to let his captains work out their kinks alone during these early days of gunnery practice, and the astute admiral knew that he could win even more respect by appearing to be blind to the mistakes that were inevitable with the untrained crewmen so recently out from Germany.

At the atoll, however, instead of prowling around looking for new species of crabs and birds, the admiral was rocketed to attention by the discovery of a Japanese schooner, which busied itself with fishing when he approached, although the Germans could swear that fishing was not its major occupation until that moment. It was to be expected; just as the British visit to Tsingtao had been a part of the British navy's "keeping an eye on things," so the Japanese were watching the movements of the Cruiser Squadron's heavy vessels. The Germans were doing the same. Each night into the wireless rooms of the *Scharnhorst* came coded messages from Tsingtao, telling of the movements of the major British, French, Russian, and Japanese vessels in the Far East. Such information was a lifeline to any naval commander; unless he knew the strength and disposition of his enemy he might be surprised at any moment and wiped out without a real chance to defend himself.

As the admiral searched for turtles and found Japanese sharks instead, his captains were hard at work. First *Gneisenau* towed a pontoon target for *Scharnhorst*, and the flagship limbered up her big guns. Then the process was reversed and the *Gneisenau* had a chance to practice her shooting.

Two days later the admiral inspected his two fighting ships and said that he was pleased with what he saw. The awkward youths who had come out on the *Patricia* had been taken neatly in hand by their more experienced mates, and were beginning to shape up as members of a fighting team.

The two cruisers exhibited their marksmanship and the speed with which they could move from relaxation to readiness, and the admiral smiled.

On that same day, July 17, the two cruisers bore down on the island of Ponape, their landfall in the Carolines and most important island in the group. The weather was dirty enough that the doors and windows of the afterships had to be closed to prevent soaking from the following seas, but as they came in sight of the island, Ponape appeared wreathed in bright sunshine, although the waves were so high that it was difficult to make out the white circle that represented the island's protective wreath of coral reef. It took considerable skill in navigation and maneuvering to manage the entrance to the harbor that day, but the captains of the two cruisers were skilful sailors, and there was no trouble as they slipped through the passage and into the calm waters of the lagoon.

Scharnhorst anchored off the island of Langar. *Gneisenau* anchored under the Djokadj rocks. Neither ship seemed secure enough for its captain, and during their entire stay in the Carolines steam was kept up and double anchor watch was maintained. Even so, the weather stayed dirty, and *Scharnhorst* moved her anchorage to a point farther out in the basin, where she pitched and rolled incessantly. There was no comparison—except unfavorable—between the harbor of Ponape and that of Truk.

The wireless chattered incessantly. Hour after hour *Funkentelegraphie-Meister* Lutz stacked up messages for the admiral. Many of them were no more than repetitions of the latest rumors. The Austrian crown council had met on July 7 and decided on war, said one. The envoy who had gone to investigate the assassination had found no evidence of Serbian government complicity, said another. The Austrian crown council had met and had agreed to declare war on Serbia, said a rumor that came out on July 14, and was transmitted to

Tsingtao, then to the admiral at sea. Everyone, it seemed, was talking about arming and maneuvers. There was still nothing to be done except sit still, and that was what Admiral von Spee proceeded to do. The crews of both vessels were given shore leave at Ponape. Officers organized expeditions into the interior to visit such odd relics as the ruins of Metalinim, city of an ancient society that built buildings with thick walls of basaltic rock. They visited Djokadj Rock, a peak on a neighboring island which had been a stronghold during the native rebellion of 1910 against the German Empire. Dutifully the sailors paid their respects to a wooden cross erected in memory of a German warrant officer who had fallen in the final assault on the rock, Admiral von Spee leading all the others on the steep ascent, although it made him puff considerably, for the admiral had been putting on weight around the middle. The admiral was making the trip, of course his chief of staff, *Kapitän See* Fielitz, would make it, and so would all the ship's commanders and senior officers. If he accomplished no more that day, the admiral struck a blow for good health among his senior officers, for nothing else could have persuaded them to so much exertion for so little reason. The admiral was a man with a sense of history and a sense of destiny. He had brought with him on this voyage a carved stone memorial which commemorated the Germans who had fallen in the campaign to bring peace and German rule to the islanders. He took it to the churchyard with proper ceremony, and surrounded by most of the ships' companies and the civilian population of Europeans, and escorted by the local police corps, he dedicated the memorial to the men who had lost their lives fighting for the fatherland. It was an impressive little service, and it was remembered by the men of the Cruiser Squadron who witnessed it. The air was growing heavy with patriotism that July.

It was a quiet, anxious period. On July 23 the Austrian

government issued an ultimatum to Belgrade, demanding punishment and reparations. Confidentially the German government told its servants that Germany would support Austria in the affair. On July 24 the Russians said they would not stand for any annexation of Serbian territory by Austria. The next day tension seemed to ease as the Austrians assured Russia that they had no intention of taking Serbian territory.

Tension did ease, but it did not end. The officers busied themselves with more trips to historic sites, and, led by the admiral, bathed in the deep pools of the rivers that rushed down the volcanic mountains. These swims were perhaps the most enjoyable of all entertainments to the men of the Cruiser Squadron; on board ship, fresh water was a precious commodity and not to be wasted on such frivolity as bathing. Here at Ponape was an illustration of the difficulties of life at sea. As the officers disported themselves in the streams, the men were busy with the ship's boats, carrying fresh water from a small creek on the shore, storing it in buckets and vats, and moving it into the fresh-water tanks between the double decks of the ships.

Among them, the two cruisers and the *Titania* boasted many boats, and they were all in use these days, including the admiral's white launch, now christened *Swan of the East*. The large motor launch of the Squadron was in more use than the admiral's launch, for the Squadron's launch could carry ninety men ashore, and with unlimited liberty the men could be ashore any time they were not on watch. There were rowing launches, rowing pinnaces, and two steam pinnaces to do the work of liberty boats and work boats.

All this freedom came to an abrupt end. On July 27 Winston Churchill, Britain's civilian naval chieftain, ordered the British navy not to disband after maneuvers that had been concluded that week. It was an ominous sign to Germany. The next day, July 28, Austria declared war on Serbia, and Admiral von Spee's flagship hoisted a signal in the blue Pacific sky ordering his ships to make ready "for drill." Under peacetime regulations, "drill" meant an absolute minimum of expenditure. Every shell, torpedo, mine, and bullet must be accounted for. Every piece of pipe and railing on the ship must be written down. "Drill" did not mean the dismantling of the fire hazards that the peacetime ship could allow, the wooden bulkheads in the messes, the paneling in "officers' country," the thousands of items of bric-a-brac with which officers and men alike loaded their little cubicles to give themselves the feeling of having a place of their own in the great steel monster in which they lived.

"Drill" meant a thorough overhaul of the guns and of every firearm on the ship. It meant inspection of the armor, proper stowing of the paints and other fire hazards, a thousand little precautions against disaster and for efficient movement.

It was not unusual that an order for drill should be issued; although the preparations at this period were usually carried out in such times as when the entire Squadron was assembled for maneuvers. The men were excited, however, and they turned to with a will. They worked from dawn on July 28 until nightfall, and when they were finished Captain Schultz of the *Scharnhorst*, Captain Maerker of the *Gneisenau*, and Captain Vogt of the *Titania* were ready for inspection by their chief. At least a part of Germany's East Asia Cruiser Squadron was ready for action that day, but two heavy cruisers, a dispatch ship, and two colliers did not make a squadron. Admiral von Spee's problem was to assess the political situation and decide what he could do to best serve the Kaiser.

At the moment, his light cruiser, *Nürnberg*, was on her way back to join the Squadron, *Leipzig* having replaced her on the Mexican coast. *Leipzig* had arrived off Cape St. Lucas, the sentinel of Lower California, and had anchored in Mazatlán harbor on the same day, July 7, just after lunch. *Nürnberg*

49

was in the harbor too, having just arrived from Panama. No time was wasted in turning over the Mexican station, because *Nürnberg* had been on station since the middle of 1913 and the men were eager to be back with the squadron, and then to go home as soon as possible. Only a few hardheads and pessimists really expected war.

Captain Haun and the men of the *Leipzig* were not long in learning the restrictions of their station. First was the matter of coal. There simply was not enough coal available and no way of assuring enough political stability on the mainland to keep a supply there.

The trouble had begun in 1911 when Porfirio Diaz was overthrown as President by a revolutionary government under Francisco Madero. In turn, Madero was overthrown and killed by Victoriano Huerta, who claimed the presidency. But soon so did another Mexican general, Venustiano Carranza, and the country was plunged into civil war early in 1913. The civil war was the reason for the coming to Mexican waters of "gunboat diplomacy"—the enforcement of the rights and privileges of the citizens of the great powers by gunboats and larger vessels. In the nineteenth and early twentieth centuries "gunboat diplomacy" was accepted practice.

As *Leipzig* arrived on the Mexican coast, the revolution was becoming chaotic. In April the United States had gone farther than any other power and had occupied Vera Cruz on the east coast of Mexico. Mexicans had not liked that action, and the occupation had helped weaken the Huerta government. Even as *Leipzig* came into the Gulf of California, forces were at work that would lead to the fall of the Huerta government, and a week after *Leipzig's* arrival that government would collapse.

Obviously, in such a changeable political climate the one way for *Leipzig* to assure herself of a coal supply was to bring it in from abroad. *Nürnberg* had made a contract through the

San Francisco consulate for a coal supply. A British firm had agreed to give the German navy charter of a collier named *Citriana*. She was an old tub, as the men of *Leipzig* saw when they came into harbor, so old that several members of the warship's crew swore that the owners sent her to Mexico in the hope that she would be lost through an act of war or would founder, and that they could then collect the insurance money. *Citriana* carried 900 tons of coal—but what coal! It was crumbly and dusty and it burned with a yellow flame and a black smoke that could be seen when the ship was far down beyond the horizon. Coal was stored at Guaymas, Mazatlán, San Blas, and Manzanillo—the German Admiralty had not been so lax as to leave all to chance and the local judgment of the naval commanders. But how to get at it? At best, it meant the coal must be shipped onto coal cars—as the 250 tons stored at Manzanillo had been. Then it must be taken off onto lighters and brought to the ship. All this presupposed no one was shooting at the men working the coal, and in July 1914 who could guarantee that kind of peaceful atmosphere in northern Mexico? Carranza was fighting Huerta, and Pancho Villa, Carranza's lieutenant, was getting ready to fight Carranza.

What might happen was illustrated by the beer situation in Mazatlán. Through the foresight of the German colony ashore a supply of beer had been set aside at the local brewery for the *Leipzig*, and a good thing it was, too, because by the time *Leipzig* arrived, the rebels outside the city had control of the brewery's water supply. And as for food, there simply was no supply of food available for the *Leipzig* in the town or from the surrounding countryside. She would have to depend on supplies brought from abroad by steamer, or would have to leave the station long enough to find supplies.

On the night of July 7, the officers of *Leipzig* had mingled with the officers of *Nürnberg* and they had exchanged tales of

51

their adventures since last they met. Captain Haun had met with Captain von Schönberg of the *Nürnberg*, and they had discussed the political situation here on the Pacific coast and that at home. Since the coal problem was so serious, Captain Haun detached his commissary officer, and sent him back to San Francisco on the *Nürnberg*. He was to arrange for shipment of 200 tons of coal. At the same time a wireless message was sent to Berlin asking that a German collier be sent to Mexico with another 3000 tons.

As for food, the men of the *Leipzig* had not been entirely unprepared. They had brought with them an extra food supply; at Yokohama they had bought five big pigs who were kept in crates on deck. They had also turned a portion of the deck into a henhouse, with dozens of chickens who supplied eggs and would supply meat for the table. They had added more tinned and fresh supplies at Honolulu. So the food problem was not pressing.

On July 8, the *Leipzig* had taken her first coal from the *Citriana*, and several German members of the crew had their baptism of fire. *Leipzig's* steam pinnace had been towing a *Citriana* boat to the far side of *Leipzig* so the coaling could be speeded. In towing, the steam pinnace made a broad circle and passed quite close to land, at a point where the rebels of Pancho Villa maintained a post. Without warning, bullets began flying through the air, and the Germans ducked. Soon they discovered that the shots were not aimed at them but at Captain Minister, the master of the *Citriana*. He was most unpopular in Mexican waters because the *Citriana* had been involved in carrying Americans during the occupation of Vera Cruz.

That evening *Citriana* sailed for San Francisco, for *Leipzig* and *Nürnberg* had exhausted her coal cargo in one coaling. *Leipzig* sailed for Guaymas, to settle a problem that was quite typical of the extraterritorial disputes of the day. Guaymas was beleaguered by Pancho Villa's men. The government defender, General Tellez, was nearly desperate for munitions and money to pay his troops. He had received some help from the large German community, but now he was being very insistent about a "loan" and the Germans sent word to Captain Haun that they needed help.

Leipzig steamed into Guaymas' port on July 10 and found the German colony very nervous. On the arrival of the warship the demands of the government general ceased abruptly, but that was not the entire problem. The rebels were fast approaching Guaymas in force and the Huerta forces were ready to evacuate the city. Five steamers and two old sailers had been brought into the port for this purpose. On July 12 hundreds of soldiers streamed into Guaymas' main square accompanied by their wives and children. Most of them were Indians, fleeing the rebels. They were disorganized, but not totally so; they still had a band with them and a drum and bugle corps.

Two days later the government gunboat *General Gueraro* arrived to lead and protect the exodus. Using barges and lighters and every boat in sight, the refugees clambered aboard the steamers and the sailing craft. On July 14, when they were ready to leave, fifteen hundred soldiers were crowded aboard the ships, armed with machine guns and light weapons, along with three thousand civilians. The Red Cross flag was raised over one of the steamers, which was also to be used as hospital ship, and the loading was completed. The next morning the flotilla set out to sea.

On July 16 the rebels marched into town, shouting "Viva Carranza." The rebel general came out to the ship, accompanied by a German soldier of fortune, Major Maler, who had trained as a hussar in Torgau. Friendly relations were established, and the rebels promised to protect the property of the Germans. The *Leipzig* remained in harbor for several more

53

days, along with the American warships *Raleigh* and *Annapolis* which were guarding American lives and property. Germans and Americans exchanged visits to the benefit of both. The Americans had a movie projector aboard the *Annapolis*, and the Germans had liquor, which was strictly forbidden on American warships. But soon the worsening revolutionary situation brought a call for *Leipzig* to return to Mazatlán, and on July 23 she did so. There she joined a squadron of foreign warships. The United States was represented by the USS *California*, flagship of Rear Admiral Howard, the cruiser USS *Albany*, and three transports. A British warship, the *Algerine*, was in the harbor. A Japanese heavy cruiser, *Idzumo*, lay not far away. For a week these warships would lie at anchor as the angry words of statesmen buzzed through the air of the world. On July 28, the *Idzumo* quietly disengaged herself from the international squadron and went to La Paz, ostensibly for coaling, but the Germans also thought she went for instructions and to take a position that had been predetermined in case of war.

Leipzig sat and waited, her crew growing more edgy every day. She needed coal again, and she was waiting for the return of *Citriana* from San Francisco, with Dr. Reimer aboard, for he was to return on that collier after having made arrangements in San Francisco for a continuing supply of coal.

Nürnberg, meanwhile, had arrived at San Francisco on July 21. There she had coaled and had gone immediately to Honolulu to coal again. From the harbor at Ponape, Admiral von Spee had called *Nürnberg* to come to him without the slightest delay, and she was responding. *Nürnberg* arrived in Honolulu on July 27, coaled, and left the same day bound south and east. Admiral von Spee was making his plans.

3

GOTT STRAFE ENGLAND

ON JULY 29 ADMIRAL VON SPEE WAS STUDYING
his war plans as the word came that Russia had announced
mobilization against Austria. This was threatening news, but
it did not clarify the situation. Still, the German war plan was
being put into effect, because the German situation in Asia
was so precarious that no time could be lost.

The defensive portion of the plan, which did not bring
danger in case the threat disappeared, called for the protection of Tsingtao and other German colonies, evasive action
by the Cruiser Squadron so as not to be caught and blockaded
in Tsingtao, and the provision of coal at various points in the
overseas empire so the cruisers could continue to operate even
if away from base.

Early in June Admiral von Spee had explained the war
plan to Captain Karl von Müller, commander of the light
cruiser *Emden*, when it became apparent that von Müller
would be left in charge of Tsingtao's defenses during the

absence of the admiral and the bigger ships of the Squadron.

Now the German gunboats were called in from the Yangtze River and from other parts of China. All supply steamers and German merchant steamers were warned that they must seek either German or neutral ports. They understood that this meant to get out of Russian, French, and British waters. On July 30, as acting chief of defense of Tsingtao, Captain von Müller called a meeting of all the senior officers in the colony.

In the Carolines, Admiral von Spee ordered his captains to make their ships ready for action, but he gave no further information. On the night of July 30 he received the message that war threatened between Germany and several of the large powers. The next day the German ships at Ponape were truly cleared for action. This clearing was more than routine; it involved the removal of every unnecessary item from the ships. In the case of the Squadron ships at Ponape all the personal belongings and luxuries would be stored with the Jaluit Company at Langar and could be recovered there when the emergency ended.

Lighters came alongside *Scharnhorst* and *Gneisenau*. The cranes loaded cargo nets filled with cases and trunks belonging to the officers and men, awnings, railings, supports, booms, and extra deck supplies. All wooden wardrobes were ruthlessly removed. The admiral's silver and the pictures, chairs, settee, and carpets in his quarters were removed. Like the deck officers, he was to have one wooden chair and one wooden table, and all else of inflammable nature must be thrown out.

The officers unloaded their dress uniforms and their extra clothing, and all the treasures they had acquired during their service in the Far East.

In Tsingtao the *Emden* was a day ahead of the rest of the Squadron; all these preparations were carried out by

July 31, and the little cruiser coaled and went to sea, obeying Admiral von Spee's orders that she was not to be caught inside Tsingtao harbor in case of war. On July 31, *Emden* accompanied the collier *Elsbeth* on a southeast course toward the Pacific islands all day long, taking her out past the normal cruising line of the various European fleets that ranged up and down the China coast. At 2300 hours *Emden* left the collier and laid a course for Quelpart Island off the coast of Korea, intending to wait on the high seas until the war situation was resolved. On August 1, *Emden* waited, and although Germany declared war on Russia that day, Captain von Müller did not learn of it until nightfall. Then von Müller turned northeast, toward Tsushima Strait. He had an enemy—Russia—and he was most likely to find Russian ships in or near that strait on their way to Vladivostok or coming out of that Siberian harbor toward Japan.

Captain von Müller was the luckiest of captains of the East Asia Cruiser Squadron, because he had specific orders and was in a position to take action. Admiral von Spee must wait through more anxious days, the pages of the war plans before him, until the total situation was resolved. On August 2 he knew of the war against Russia, and the next day of the war against France, but what could he do? *Nürnberg* was on her way to him; he must wait for her.

Early on the morning of August 3 the admiral ordered the word of war passed to the officers and men of the Squadron. Later in the day he assembled the men of *Scharnhorst* on the quarter-deck, announced the Kaiser's mobilization order, and Captain Schultz called for three cheers for Germany's emperor. *Hoch der Kaiser, Hoch! Hoch! Hoch!*—rang the cheering throughout the ship. Now Admiral von Spee boarded his barge, stern and erect, and, accompanied by his staff in their summer whites, was piped aboard the *Gneisenau*. He went stiffly to the quarter-deck and stood between the elevated guns of the after turret. He was unsmiling, his bristly gray hair hidden by his cap, his bushy gray eyebrows meeting in the center with his frown, and his Vandyke bristling as he spoke. He gave the news. Cheers were again called for, and the men responded with a will. Patriotism was brimming.

"At the moment," the admiral continued, "only Russia and France are our opponents; England's attitude is still uncertain, although unfriendly. Consequently we must also regard English ships as enemies." He knew of the European treaties of alliance and he was certain that war would be general within a few days.

Having spoken, the admiral turned on his heel and, followed by his staff, marched off the quarter-deck of *Gneisenau* and back to his barge. He had much to do in the next few hours. He returned to his cabin on the *Scharnhorst*, to his papers and to the unceasing flow of messages from the wireless.

The Squadron faced, or soon would face, very strong enemy forces, particularly if Great Britain entered the war, as the admiral had every expectation she would, within a matter of hours. Here was the breakdown of forces in the Far East as best as German intelligence had been able to assemble it on that August day.

Russia: Two armed cruisers, one gunboat, two minelayers, fifteen destroyers and torpedo boats, eight submarines; there was also a reserve squadron of four torpedo boats and three submarines of older design, plus eighteen small gunboats on the Amur River. This Russian fleet was not really a serious threat to the Squadron as a whole. Russia had not recovered from the Russo-Japanese War, and the German East Asia Squadron was far superior in guns and modern design. A Russian cruiser, such as the *Jemtschug*, might overpower one of the admiral's light cruisers, such as the *Emden*, but that was a matter for von Müller's lookout at the moment.

France: Armored cruiser *Montcalm*; armored cruiser *Dupleix*; one armored gunboat, one destroyer, four river gunboats.

England: Battleship HMS *Triumph*; heavy cruisers *Minotaur* and *Hampshire*; light cruisers *Newcastle* and *Yarmouth*; eight destroyers, four torpedo boats, three submarines, and one tender; sixteen sloops and gunboats; and ten river gunboats. This was the Far Eastern force of Britain. Besides this force, in Australian, New Zealand, and East Indian waters there were the battleship *Australia*; the battleship *Swiftshire*; ten armored cruisers, one light cruiser, and a number of supporting craft.

Besides this, if Japan came into the war, there was the entire Japanese fleet.

Against such a considerable array of fighting craft, Admiral von Spee could muster only the East Asia Cruiser Squadron: two heavy cruisers and three light cruisers.

Scharnhorst and *Gneisenau* were sister ships, although they varied slightly in performance and operation. *Scharnhorst* carried a bit more coal than her sister ship and she managed 1.3 knots more at full speed (23.8 knots). Each ship weighed 11,600 tons. Each carried eight 8.2-inch guns and six 5.9-inch guns. Each was protected by armor 6 inches thick on sides and deck. Each was 143.8 meters long and 21.6 meters wide, drawing 7.5 meters. Each carried 18 deck officers and 5 engineering officers, plus other specialists, a total complement of 764 officers and men. *Scharnhorst* also carried the Admiral von Spee and his staff. The two big German cruisers had both been launched in 1906, which made them quite modern in terms of the navies of the day.

Of the three light cruisers in the Squadron, the oldest was *Leipzig*, launched in 1905. She was also the smallest, only 110.6 meters long, 13.2 meters wide, and displacing 3250 tons. *Nürnberg* was built in 1908 and she was slightly larger:

59

116.8 meters long and 13.3 meters wide, displacing 3470 tons of water. *Emden* was the newest and best of the three, at 118 meters long, 13.5 meters wide, and displacing 3650 tons. All three light cruisers carried ten 4.1-inch guns. *Leipzig* and *Nürnberg* could attain a speed of 23 knots. *Emden's* newer boilers could bring her up to 24.5 knots.

Matched against enemies of their own class, these fighting ships could be expected to do the Kaiser proud. Their morale was good, their armament was good, their shooting was good. Admiral von Spee's principal task on the eve of war was to be sure that he was not outclassed and that he was not surprised.

On August 2 German civil authorities in Australia informed von Spee that if hostilities broke out between England and Germany, the big 17,000-ton battleship *Australia* and half a dozen of those Australian and New Zealand cruisers could be expected to divert to China waters to be placed against the German East Asia Squadron, in addition to Admiral Jerram's China Squadron, and perhaps the British East Asia Squadron as well. This information was important to the admiral, coming as it did, and it helped him to make his plans.

It was as yet impossible to make any final war plans because the admiral had to know what course England would follow. As one of the *Gneisenau's* officers put it, "against France and Russia it would have been a merry war, for which we were perfectly ready, even in these remote parts." But what would England do? That was the key question.

On August 3 Captain von Müller in the *Emden* moved into the west channel of the Tsushima Strait, off the Korean coast, looking for Russian ships, and hoping not to run into the heavy cruiser *Askold* for which *Emden* was no match at all. Von Müller half hoped to run into the Russian cruiser *Jemtschug*, against which *Emden* might stand a real chance of victory. She was running in heavy weather. Her wireless operators reported any number of code conversations and thought they could recognize the signals of some of their English and French acquaintances.

On the opposite shore of the Pacific Ocean that night, *Leipzig* was lying to on the inner side of Magdalena Island, just off the Pacific side of Baja California, accompanied by her English collier *Citriana,* ready to coal. *Leipzig* had been through a long and arduous adventure in the past few days, and it appeared that more adventure was on the horizon.

After the Japanese warship *Idzumo* slipped away, ostensibly to coal at La Paz on Baja California, the remainder of the fleet of western European and American warships had undertaken the defense and evacuation of Mazatlán. They had landed armed men and removed the Europeans and several hundred Chinese who wished to seek safety from the Mexican revolutionaries. On July 31 *Leipzig* had taken forty civilians aboard, and had then moved outside the harbor with the other ships, concluding the evacuation. All *Leipzig's* passengers were either German citizens or people of German descent.

On July 31 *Citriana* had returned from San Francisco, whence she had been sent some days earlier for more coal for SMS *Leipzig.* Commissary Officer Reimer was aboard, bearing the good news that he had bought the 2000 tons of coal authorized. He also brought newspapers dating from July 23, which told of the agonies suffered to that date in the chanceries of Europe.

On the afternoon of August 1, Captain Haun of *Leipzig* had learned by wireless of the German declaration of war on Russia, and he had called his officers to his cabin to read to them from the sheaf of cables in his hand. No one knew, of course, what England would do, and they had an English collier on hand, captained by an officer of the Royal Naval Reserve. They could not, obviously, expect any cooperation from Captain Minister of the *Citriana* if war were to come

61

between England and Germany. At seven o'clock that night Captain Haun had appealed to the American admiral to take his forty passengers, pointing out that he must coal at La Paz, for he had been ordered to return to Tsingtao because of the outbreak of war with Russia.

But the *Leipzig* did not go to La Paz. Outside that port she was in touch by wireless with the German steamer *Alexandria*, bound for Portland, Oregon, and persuaded that ship to take Dr. Reimer again to San Francisco, to buy more coal. Captain Haun had sealed orders that covered war situations: the order in case of hostilities was for *Leipzig* to secure as great a coal supply as possible from neutral America, and then to head back for the Squadron, accompanied by and followed by a succession of coaling steamers.

Of how much more use to *Leipzig* the *Citriana* was going to be remained very much in doubt. Captain Haun must be prepared for war with Britain and the necessity of dealing with Captain Minister as an enemy.

The tempo of the wireless traffic increased that night. At midnight came the word that Germany was at war with France. The tension on board *Leipzig* grew very strong, and many anxious glances were cast across to *Citriana* which was following them so docilely, honoring its charter, and also quite aware of the *Leipzig*'s heavy and light guns, which had been run out for practice several times in the past twenty-four hours.

Shortly after midnight the two ships stood in to Magdalena Bight, and *Leipzig* began to coal greedily from the collier. Captain Minister went off that night on a moonlight shark- and turtle-hunting expedition.

By five o'clock in the morning the cruiser had 822 tons of coal in her hold—her capacity. She had taken all she could swallow and must leave 300 tons in the collier, a fact much lamented by Captain Haun because he did not know what was going to happen next—until the middle of the coaling. Then the message came: war had been declared by England against Germany.

It was discovered that the English Captain Minister had learned of the declaration, too, and that he had managed to destroy his code books and other documents while ostensibly out fishing quietly for sharks.

At about two o'clock on that morning in Tsushima Strait, Captain von Müller in *Emden* scored the first naval stroke of the war when he captured the Russian mail steamer *Rjasan*. He put a prize crew aboard her and took her back to Tsingtao.

On the morning of August 4, as *Nürnberg* steamed swiftly and steadily toward Ponape to make contact with the Squadron, *Scharnhorst* and *Gneisenau* put out to sea for target practice. There was no further restriction, except that of good sense and the admiral's orders on the firing of ammunition. The peacetime regulations had gone out the window with that first declaration of hostilities. Yet the Germans were careful to keep their military activity well out of sight of land, for in the harbor lay the Japanese *Fukoku Maru*, their chartered collier. It was much the best to be rid of *Fukoku Maru* without delay, and also to avoid arousing her suspicions. Fortunately the collier did not carry a wireless.

A German civilian was sent aboard the *Fukoku Maru*, ostensibly to accompany her to Samoa on business. It had been agreed that she would leave after the Squadron fueled and wait in Samoa—all this was part of the trip planned in peacetime. The admiral's great care was lest *Fukoku Maru* attempt to stop somewhere and make rendezvous with other Japanese ships, or in some way warn Germany's enemies where the major ships of the German Squadron were located at that moment. If *Australia*, for example, and two or three of the heavy cruisers came up at Ponape, the East Asia Squadron might never really get into action.

At the time that *Scharnhorst* was last coaling from *Fukoku Maru* (making allowances for the international dateline) so was *Leipzig*, across the sea, taking on one last little bit of coal from *Citriana*. On that night of August 4, Pacific Time, when Captain Minister had discovered the true state of affairs between his country and Germany, no time had been lost by the Germans in assuring his silence, at least on the wireless. *Citriana*'s wireless was dismantled and taken aboard *Leipzig*. Then *Citriana* was allowed to go on her way, one last gesture of goodwill by *Leipzig*.

On the afternoon of August 5, Asia time, Captain von Müller learned of the British declaration of war. He was then on his way back to Tsingtao, as rapidly as he could go with the *Rjasan* to look after. He knew what he must do—it had all been laid out for him with the Admiralty's thoroughness. He must coal, and then he must make his way as rapidly as possible to the Squadron. Where he would join his admiral was something he expected confidently to learn when he returned to Tsingtao harbor.

At Ponape that afternoon, the admiral was making ready for sea, waiting for *Nürnberg*, which had been rerouted from a rendezvous point at Samoa to come posthaste to Ponape. His captains were tearing down the last of the luxuries of the ships. In the officers' messes the woodwork and tapestry, which warded off heat and cold alike, were stripped from the walls and thrown into the sea, to the delight of the natives, who came out in their canoes to dive for bits of wood and cloth. At the end of that day, nothing was left of the fine wardrooms but red striped steel walls and bare decks. They had tables and chairs and the *Gneisenau* had her piano, from which she refused to be parted. The one decoration that remained on the wall of that ship's wardroom was the Kaiser's picture.

Hoch! Hoch! Hoch!

In the afternoon, while the work of destruction was proceeding, the Catholic missionary priest of Capuana Mission came aboard the two warships to give confession to the Catholic sailors and officers of the ships. Black as they were from coaling, the men went to services. No one minded.

Ave Maria. Gott Strafe England!

4

MEN AND MORALE

THE MAN WHO NOW SET FORTH TO LEAD HIS squadron into glory and to destroy all he could of Britannia's rule at sea was a pleasant, sharp-eyed professional naval officer and a titled member of the German nobility. *Vizeadmiral* Maximilian Johannes Maria Hubert Graf von Spee was fifty-three years old, born on June 22, 1861, at Copenhagen, where his German parents had been living.

The young count had enjoyed a noble childhood, learning to ride and hunt—and to chop down boors with icy glance or cold remark. In the spring of 1878, when von Spee was not quite seventeen years old, he chose the sea as his career and became a cadet in the *Kaiserliche Marine*. He was a tall youth with bushy brown straight hair, a strong chin, a longish face, deepset eyes, and already the suggestion of heavy brows.

Four years later he became *Unterleutnant zur See*.

Holidays in this youthful period were spent where he had grown up, at his father's castle at Heltorf in the Rhine province, not far from Düsseldorf, or in another of his parents' houses, in Lucerne, Switzerland.

As a sea cadet, Maximilian von Spee served on the school ship *Vineta*. After his promotion to *Unterleutnant* he was transferred to the gunboat *Moewe*, where he became a deck officer.

On a trip to Southwest Africa he was stricken with a disease diagnosed as "joint rheumatism" and had to take a nine-month leave from the service to recover his health. He went home to Germany during this period, but after his recuperation he became harbor commander at the port of Cameroon. He occupied this post in 1887 and 1888. Then he went back to sea, aboard the training ship *Moltke*, as an instructor.

In 1889 he married and began to raise a family that would comprise five sons. He was promoted by this time to *Leutnant zur See*, and it was believed in the Admiralty that he would be one of the nation's most promising young officers—if his health held up.

Von Spee progressed steadily up the ladder. He became *Kapitänleutnant* in 1892, and learned gunnery aboard the cruiser *Bayern*. He was adjutant. He learned the intricacies of coastal defense. He learned the art of mine laying.

In 1899 he was appointed *Korvettenkapitän*. In 1904 he was promoted to *Fregattenkapitän*. In 1905 when he was forty-four years old he made the huge leap (in peacetime) to *Kapitän zur See*. His break had come in 1897. He was adjutant and flag lieutenant to *Kontreadmiral* Prince Heinrich of Prussia, when that admiral took over command of the newly formed Second Division of the Cruiser Squadron. Von Spee was brought favorably to the attention of the Kaiser, and his future was assured.

He had been not only a staff man, however. He had spent some time as first officer of the battleship *Brandenburg*. During the Boxer rebellion he had been in command of the light cruiser *Hela.* In 1901 and 1902 he had engaged in that most dangerous of occupations, minesweeping, as commander of the sweeper *Pelikan.* All this endeared him to his line officers. Then, for four long years he had been buried in Berlin, as head of the Reichsmarine division of coastal defense.

He had enjoyed nearly every variety of experience that the navy could offer, at least all those deemed important in these years. It was as a staff officer that he had received his flag in 1910, when he was chief of staff of the North Sea naval district—but it was not forgotten in Berlin that he had also contributed considerably to the development of German gunnery tactics in three previous years as commander of the battleship *Wittelsbach.* Two years after his appointment to the North Sea he was chosen for the very important job of East Asia Squadron leader. In a way it was the most independent position in all the Kaiser's navy, because sheer distance made it impossible for Emperor Wilhelm or anyone else to read clearly the tactical, or even strategic signs, and in almost any argument the commander in the field would have his way.

There was little of value that Berlin could ever do for Tsingtao, and practically nothing that could be done on short notice, except to give the Squadron its head. At the outbreak of war, for example, an extra 10,000 tons of good German coal was shipped to Tsingtao, but of course shipment then meant that the ships would actually never see the coal. The last real contribution of the Reichsmarine to the East Asia Squadron had come in June, when *Patricia* had unloaded her stores and men.

Berlin had given Admiral von Spee his pick of officers and good stout men who were loyal to Squadron and to country. His chief of staff, *Kapitän zur See* Otto Wilhelm Henry Fielitz, was eleven years younger than the admiral, an excellent age difference, for it eliminated feelings of envy or competition between the two men. Fielitz had achieved his captaincy when he was forty-two, two years younger than von Spee had been when he was so promoted, and so the chief of staff could look forward to a distinguished career of his own. There was no call for competition.

The captains of Admiral von Spee's five cruisers were all vigorous and sound men in their middle forties. Commanding the flagship *Scharnhorst*, Captain Felix Hermann Albert Schultz was senior in naval experience and, although his looks belied it, the oldest, forty-five. He sported a mustache and Vandyke as did all of them but Captain von Müller of the *Emden*, who was clean-shaven. But where Chief of Staff Fielitz's mustache was brushy, turned up on the ends, and grew to lengths that would please a Coldstream Guardsman, Captain Schultz wore his dark mustache close-clipped along his downturned upper lip. It gave him a much more stern appearance than Fielitz' rather puckish look, but then Schultz had the most difficult job of all von Spee's captains: in addition to the responsibility of command he had two men senior to himself aboard his own ship, both experienced seamen, and an entire admiral's staff of younger men who were theoretically junior to Schultz, but who considered themselves responsible only to the admiral. Schultz was an East Prussian, and, as might be expected, he was a stern taskmaster and a good officer of the old school.

Kapitän zur See Gustav Otto Julius Maerker was an easier man to know by far than Captain Schultz, perhaps because he was born in Herford in Westphalia rather than in Prussia. He was a slender man, similar in this respect to von Müller, and in spite of a heavy mustache and Vandyke that gave him a ferocious look, he had gentle and humorous eyes, deepset and dark, and he parted his hair rather carelessly in the middle, sweeping it back on both sides. *Gneisenau*, his command, was as tight a ship as *Scharnhorst*, but there was never as much

69

tension aboard her as on the flagship. Maerker was a tough commander but a resilient one; he had learned much of his seamanship in the hard school of gunboats, where junior officers face command and diplomatic problems that might tax an admiral. Like Chief of Staff Fielitz, Maerker was new to his command, both having come out that summer on *Patricia* to join the Squadron.

Another young-looking captain was *Leipzig's* Captain Johannes Siegfried Haun, and among the captains he was junior in rank, holding only the rank of *Fregattenkapitän*, as did von Müller of the *Emden*. Haun had held his rank only a year; he was considered very fortunate to have so important a command, and so much responsibility as to be sent off to guard the American station by himself.

Oddly enough, the oldest-appearing of all the captains was the second youngest: *Kapitän zur See* Karl Franz Christian von Schönberg, a Saxon, born in 1872. He had been captain of the *Nürnberg* since the end of 1913, and had received his promotion to *Kapitän zur See* while racing back from the American station in July. He was a big, graying, corpulent man who had won eight medals and liked to wear them when he had his picture taken (unusual among the captains). One reason he had come up so rapidly in the service was that he had considerable skill in navigation and had spent some time ashore in Berlin in the Reichsmarineamt navigation department.

The sole bachelor among the captains, and at forty-one the youngest of them, was *Fregattenkapitän* Karl Friedrich Max von Müller of the *Emden*. Like all the others he was a career naval officer, having come up through the ranks from cadet. He had held his command longer than any other captain in the Squadron except Haun in *Leipzig*. *Emden* was one of the happiest ships in the Squadron, too, because von Müller was an understanding and just man, though the son of a

70

disciplinarian father who had been a general in the Prussian army.

These were the men who would do the Kaiser's work in the Pacific Ocean, or, for that matter, in nearly all of Asia's waters. With such an inferior force of ships it was ridiculous for a logician to consider that these men could exert any particular influence on the course of the war that had just begun, but not one of them considered affairs in this light. They were dedicated men, setting out to *win* the war for Germany.

The admiral's first task was to assemble the Squadron, or as much of it as he could hope to bring together. *Leipzig* was to stay on the American station. The news from her was good enough: she had been able to purchase coal in San Francisco and there was no reason that she should not be quite effective as a raider, doing the business of a light cruiser, capturing and sinking enemy ships along the North American coast— with particular attention to the big ships of the Canadian Pacific Line, which sailed up and down the coasts and to the Far East.

Nürnberg turned up outside Ponape harbor at dawn on August 6, having nearly exhausted her coal supply in rushing from Honolulu as quickly as she could, keeping in touch with the German wireless station at Yap on her trip. *Nürnberg* now had to strip for action as the larger cruisers had done, and she had very little time. The admiral was eager to be gone from Ponape; he had been there too long. Japan was certain to come into the war on the side of Great Britain, living up to their treaty of alliance. It was entirely possible that the Japanese already knew the whereabouts of the major ships of the Squadron; the admiral remembered that innocent fishing boat not far from Truk. Von Spee issued a terse order which caused Captain von Schönberg of the *Nürnberg* to gasp a little in his cabin. *Nürnberg* and the rest of the Squadron must

71

be ready to leave Ponape by nightfall, and that meant coaled, stripped, provisioned, and ready for action.

It could not have been done had not the officers and men of the *Scharnhorst* and *Gneisenau* turned to, but with the combined efforts of three crews it was possible. There was no question of laying off the onerous work of coaling at midday on August 6. The work had to be done, so it was, and even without the old familiar protection of awnings, for the awnings had been stripped away as fire hazards.

It was a busy day. The mail clerks warned the officers and men, and most managed to scribble hasty last lines before the sacks were sealed and taken ashore. The butchers slaughtered pigs on every ship to prepare the meat supply for the voyage, for who knew what weather might lie ahead?

All the boats of all the ships were used until late afternoon, when the last cask of water was brought to *Nürnberg* from the pleasant little fresh water creek. Then the admiral ordered that the surplus boats be left behind—yes, even including his handsome white barge. He would get along using the gig of the captain of the *Scharnhorst* when there was a call to pay. Two jolly boats, the rowing pinnace, and the motor launch were collected from *Scharnhorst* and the same from *Gneisenau*, and they were put ashore in the care of the harbor master.

In the afternoon two sick men were taken ashore from *Gneisenau*. Admiral von Spee preempted Captain Schultz's gig and came round first to *Nürnberg*, where he collected his son Otto, the eldest of his boys, who was serving as a *Leutnant zur See* aboard the *Nürnberg*. Then the pair came to the *Gneisenau*, where they picked up Heinrich, the second son of the admiral, who was a lieutenant on that cruiser. The tall portly admiral and his tall slender sons then went ashore at Ponape to make their confessions in the Roman Catholic church.

All afternoon boats of the harbor and ships continued to ply back and forth, the harbor boats bringing civilians and colonial officials to have a last drink on the ships and say goodbye to the officers. At four o'clock, as ordered, SMS *Titania* hoisted anchor, made her final signals to the port, and steamed out of the harbor. Even as she went the harbor master's men were out in launches, removing the buoys that marked the entrance to the channel. The German warships knew the way, and the port authorities had no other friends who might be in so great a hurry that they could not wait for a pilot.

The admiral and his sons had come back to their ships, and at five o'clock *Scharnhorst* broke out her departure flags, *Gneisenau* followed suit, and in half an hour the two big ships were outside the reef. Last of all came *Nürnberg*, an hour later than the others—given that much time to finish up the junking and the stowing and to make last goodbyes to people she had met only that morning. Then *Nürnberg*, too, was moving slowly toward the entrance through the late afternoon stillness, through a dozen small boats jammed with natives and settlers from Germany, who waved handkerchiefs and flags in an ever-slowing solemn farewell to men they knew they might not see again.

Outside the reef, the Squadron assembled: *Scharnhorst* in front, *Gneisenau* second, *Nürnberg* third, and *Titania* trailing behind as befitted her station. The course was set northwest, for Pagan, 1020 *Seemilen* away, where the ships would meet with *Emden* and other vessels at a secret rendezvous. The Carolines were too dangerous. Japan was not in the war, and even if she came in within the next few hours, she would not expect the Germans to be sitting on her front doorstep.

The evening of August 6 fell, a warm, delightful tropical night in store. The ships moved steadily along on course in the long ocean swell. The curtain of night dropped suddenly as always, and then the orders began to ring along the decks of the Squadron.

"Larboard watch, mask lights" came the instructions from the admiral to the captain to the officer of the watch. Admiral von Spee was taking no chances this first night of war at sea that his men would forget that most obvious of safety devices, the night blackout.

It was wartime, and the easy ways of peace were put away. In peacetime on the big cruisers life was really very easy, with the officers and crew divided into four watches so that a man stood a watch only four hours in every twenty-four, and some specialists did not stand watches at all. But during war the entire ship was divided into starboard and larboard (or port) watches, with the exception of the engine room. At night guns and searchlights were manned at all times and so were the boats. In daytime an officer occupied the crow's nest atop the foremast from dawn until dust, straining his eyes on the horizon for sight of smoke or a telltale stick of mast.

On the night of August 6 the larboard watch was on, the starboard watchmen slept, officers in their bunks and men in their hammocks, fully dressed and ready for the call to action. Early on the morning of August 7 the entire ship's companies were mustered to the quarter-decks of the cruisers, and there the captains read the latest wireless reports and issued the general orders of the day.

The daytime hours were spent in the usual occupations of cleaning ship from the coaling of the day before, chipping paint, plus checking ammunition, cleaning guns, and inspecting torpedoes and their tubes. All hands were mustered at 1400 hours for battle drill; for two hours the guns were run out, the damage-control parties ordered to simulated danger spots and various problems in enemy attack played out. There was even time for some gunnery practice with live ammuni-

74

tion. At 1600 came a coffee break, then the guns were cleaned and the ships were battened down for the night.

Back in Tsingtao, August 6 was a day of furious activity. Two days earlier, while on the high seas following his captive *Rjasan*, *Fregattenkapitän* von Müller in the *Emden* had been searching for more Russian ships. On August 5 he had received the word from Tsingtao that Germany and England were at war, and on that same day had coded orders from Admiral von Spee directing him to proceed from Tsingtao without delay to meet the Squadron at Pagan in the Marianas Islands. So as fast as *Rjasan* could travel, which was very nearly twenty knots, captor and captive made their way toward Tsingtao, *Rjasan* ahead, under temporary command of *Oberleutnant zur See* Julius Lauterbach, a tubby, good-natured merchant captain in peacetime. When they reached home waters *Emden* took the lead, like a watchful lioness shepherding her cub, wily in her lookout for enemy ships that might be lurking on the outskirts of Tsingtao. No enemies were to be seen, so *Emden* and her prize speeded into port. They reached the edge of the mine field at dawn, and were escorted through by a patrol boat. At six o'clock on the morning of August 6 the *Emden* glided through the calm waters of the inner harbor and pulled straight up to the coaling pier. Arrangements had been made ahead of time by wireless, and a gang of coolies was on hand to do the heavy work without delay.

Captain von Müller turned the ship over to his first officer for loading and provisioning and hastened to the office of Governor Meyer-Waldeck to report on his change of orders. Later in the day he called a meeting in his sea cabin of the senior officers of the navy ships in harbor, and instructed the captain of the old gunboat *Kormoran* to take his guns onto the *Rjasan*, change the name of the Russian steamer to *Kormoran*, and make of her an auxiliary cruiser. This was the designation during World War I of any number of different ships which had been passenger or freight carriers during peacetime. Usually they were big passenger ships, like the *Rjasan*, capable of nineteen or twenty knots. With the addition of several guns, fore, aft, and amidships, they made a special kind of warship. Against a real warship of anything above the gunboat class they might be in trouble. A destroyer could outmaneuver, torpedo, and sink an auxiliary cruiser, of course. But no navy had so many warships that it could patrol the entire sea world, and so these auxiliary cruisers came in very handily for both sides. Against an ordinary passenger ship they were formidable warships, even if they had but one gun. So equipping *Rjasan* as an auxiliary cruiser was serious work. She would be a valuable weapon in Germany's war against her assortment of enemies.

In his orders to Captain von Müller, Admiral von Spee had indicated that as many steamers as could be brought quickly to Pagan should be loaded with coal either to accompany or to follow the *Emden*. One 9000-ton passenger ship, the *Prinz Eitel Friedrich*, was converted that day to an auxiliary cruiser with the installation of deck guns. A fast collier, the *Markomannia*, was told to follow the *Emden* to Pagan. Of the other ships in the harbor, none was fast enough or had enough coal capacity to be useful to the Squadron.

All night long on August 6 the men of the *Emden* worked to ready their ship for an extended voyage. Ashore, Governor Meyer-Waldeck heard from *Korvettenkapitän* Knorr, late host to the men of the *Leipzig*, that indeed his worst fears were realized. Japan was already moving men from Manchuria who would attack the German colony of Kiaochow, reported the naval attaché, whose superiors in the embassy at Toyko had scoffed so heartily at him for this belief only a few weeks earlier.

Coaling was completed late on the afternoon of August 7, and shortly before 1800 hours *Emden* was ready. Exactly on the hour Captain von Müller gave the order, the boatswain piped his signals, and *Emden* began to move. Hundreds, thousands of people—Chinese, German, White Russian, Japanese—lined the pier waving flags and shouting as the warship pulled away from the dock. The garrison band played patriotic and sentimental songs, ending with *Die Wacht am Rhine,* and slowly the *Emden* moved out to the end of the outer roadstead, where she stood, waiting for the old torpedo boat *S-90* which would lead her and the two passenger ships through the mine field, *Markomannia* and *Prinz Eitel Friedrich* in line behind the coal-streaked little cruiser.

The *S-90* preceded them to Cape Yunnuisan, traveling enough ahead so that she could check on the presence of enemy warships outside the harbor and warn the flotilla if they were there. None were. At the cape, the pilot descended into his little boat from the *Emden,* and the three ships separated for tactical reasons, to travel alone across the wide ocean. *Prinz Eitel Friedrich* was to follow one course and steam as quickly as possible to Pagan. *Markomannia,* much slower, was to steam to the Ryukyus and wait there for the *Emden,* which would steam quickly on a zigzag course, looking for prizes. Even though the admiral had said to come with all haste, Captain von Müller had to wait for *Markomannia* anyhow, so why not try to get in a little action in behalf of the Kaiser?

So the ships of the East Asia Squadron steamed on for their rendezvous at Pagan. On August 8 the wireless operators of the *Emden* learned of the swift German victories on the western front, and the ship's crew cheered the war. On August 9, Captain von Müller conducted church services. In the body of the Squadron, the captains also conducted services, except aboard the *Gneisenau,* where they were celebrated at 11:20 in the morning by *Evangelischer Marinepfarrer* Rost, the squadron chaplain who had been embarked on that ship.

It was so hot that day, reported the *Gneisenau's* first officer, that it was impossible to keep one's hand on the steel parts of the ship, but both watches turned out, the officers in their caps and the men in straw hats, to stand on the quarter-deck beneath the blazing sun, while the chaplain in white surplice without a gown conducted the service and assured the men that God was on Germany's side.

The only ship of the Squadron not heading for the rendezvous at Pagan was the *Leipzig*, still ordered to remain on station on the west coast of the United States, and to provide a threat to British shipping. Coaled, laden with fifty tons of deck coal too, the *Leipzig* was heading for San Francisco to carry out her orders, which were to secure a proper supply of coal for her raiding activities, and then work up and down the coast. On August 7 Captain Haun learned from a news broadcast that there were several British ships located along the American West Coast. The broadcast named the Canadian cruiser *Rainbow*. It also named the British sloops of war *Algerine*, which he had encountered off Mexico a few days earlier, and *Shearwater*. Also, the broadcast claimed, two British submarines were in the area, submarines just purchased from the government of Chile.

They also learned that the German steamer *Alexandria* was in San Diego harbor. Captain Haun might have used the *Alexandria* as a coal ship—having the right, now that Germany was at war, to commandeer any civilian vessel for his purposes. But he was very wary as to why the *Alexandria* was in San Diego at all. Had she fled into the port to avoid one of her enemies? If she had, that enemy might be lurking about. It was not Captain Haun's responsibility or right to seek engagement with the British in force; his purpose, as enunciated by the war plan, was to harry British shipping and cause as much trouble to the British Admiralty as possible--

not to get himself sunk chasing after German steamers that ought to be safe in neutral water.

On the evening of August 7, as the *Leipzig* turned north and began steaming toward San Francisco, Captain Haun ordered First Officer Kretschmar to ready the ship for war. As with the others, this meant the dismantling of the awnings, carpets, furniture, paneling, and all the artifices of civilization that made the warship more pleasant in peacetime. There was no place for *Leipzig* to store these furnishings, so they were thrown into the furnaces, and for four hours no coal at all was consumed, because the wood and paintwork burned very nicely. The *Leipzig* set course for the Farallone Islands off San Francisco in weather that was turning heavy and cold. Two days later the tempo of work was reduced aboard the *Leipzig* when the men began falling seasick in the heavy Pacific seas. It grew so cold that one deck officer was willing to wager that they had overshot their landfall and were approaching the Bering Straits.

On the morning of August 11, as the crew of the *Leipzig* froze and cursed in the pitching seas off northern California, the Squadron's flagship *Scharnhorst* led *Gneisenau*, *Nürnberg*, and *Titania* toward Pagan, and just after dawn the officer in the crow's nest of *Scharnhorst* sighted land. In an hour all could see the twin volcanoes of Pagan Island. Close in to shore they also saw a large black hull, and for some time there was concern aboard the flagship. It was quite within the capacity of the *verdammenswert Englanders* to have set a trap for them outside their own territory. What if the battleship *Australia* and several cruisers were lying in wait for them, using the black ship as bait?

But no, these were idle fears. The black hull belonged to the German Lloyd steamer *Yorck*, as the Squadron discovered when the ships drew closer to land. They moved in and

79

anchored near her. No enemy had been reported anywhere in the area. They were undetected.

All day long on August 11 other German steamers arrived in Pagan, whence they had been ordered by the radio stations at Yap and Tsingtao as they reported in once war with England was declared. The *Mark* came, followed by the *Holsatia*, the *Prinz Waldemar*, the *Gouverneur Jaeschke*, the *Longmoon*, and the *Staatssekretar Kraetke*, once the pride of the China run, which had been the ship of *Oberleutnant sur See* Julius Lauterbach, prize officer of the *Emden*.

These ships brought coal, supplies, water, and parts to the Cruiser Squadron. Admiral von Spee had called for every German ship in the area, for when war had been declared so suddenly, he realized that the Cruiser Squadron was in deep trouble. He could not return to Tsingtao, it was too dangerous an undertaking. He could not arrange for supplies, except what he could find with friends. The call had gone out then, and this was the response. There was little time for pleasantry. The unloading began that morning, unloading of everything the Squadron could use from the merchantmen. There was a heavy swell outside Pagan, but nothing could be done about that. A party of 150 men was sent from the *Gneisenau* to the *Staatssekretar Kraetke* to begin unloading coal, and in spite of the swell the steamer was brought alongside for unloading.

The merchantmen were brought up to the warships. They carried live cattle, pigs, chickens, potatoes, flour, fresh vegetables, salt meat, and hundreds and hundreds of tins of foods. The admiral and his staff examined the bills of lading and the lists and took those things they needed—the lightweight items and the foods that would save—for they expected to be a long time at sea, with few friends and many enemies around them.

On August 11 the *Markomannia* was supposed to appear at the rendezvous with the *Emden* and the *Prinz Eitel Friedrich*. Then the three would proceed in consort to join the

Squadron. The *Emden* arrived on August 10, and found the auxiliary cruiser already there—but no *Markomannia*. Well, it was to be expected that the freighter would be slower than warship or converted passenger ship. They waited. On August 11 they occupied the day with target practice, the auxiliary towing a canvas target for the *Emden* while the gunners limbered up the ten 4-inch guns. Still the *Markomannia* did not arrive. Finally they had a mysterious message from her—she claimed to be at the rendezvous. Obviously she was not at rendezvous point. So where was she? For a time Captain von Müller considered answering the message from the steamer, but he feared he might be walking into a trap. He did radio the Squadron in code, but received only a warning against radioing at all. So the *Markomannia* had to be forgotten; if she had fallen into the enemy's hands it was the fortunes of war. The *Emden* and the *Prinz Eitel Friedrich* pulled up anchor and set out on the night of August 11 for Pagan to join the Squadron. They arrived the next day, to be greeted by the *Titania*, which came out flags flying to show that the Squadron was on hand and that all was safe. The *Emden* steamed into the harbor, followed by the auxiliary cruiser, to the cheers of the assembled men who had heard by rumor that spread through the ships that *Emden* had been sunk several days earlier by the Russian heavy cruiser *Askold*.

All the Germans were very pleased. For many days they had been listening to exaggerated news broadcasts that were almost all rumor. They had been told that the German ships *Breslau* and *Goeben* had been sunk in the Mediterranean. (Later they were to learn of the escape of these two ships to safety in Turkish waters, one of the great odysseys of the war.) They had been told that several other German ships had been sunk, and although they referred to Reuters, the English news agency, as a "lie factory," morale had been hurt by the broad-

81

casts. Now to see the *Emden,* so flatly stated by the English to have been sunk, made it possible for the officers to convince the men of the Squadron that all else they heard was lies. And morale, which had been sagging, was raised to a new high.

5

CONFUSING THE ENEMY

FROM THE VANTAGE POINT OF ADMIRAL VON Spee, morale was all-important, especially on August 12, when it was confirmed to the Squadron by Tsingtao radio that the Japanese were launching an attack against Kiaochow colony. Japan would not declare war on Germany until she actually began her attack on August 23, but no one in Kiaochow was fooled: they could now see clearly that Japan had done the same in 1904 when she went to war with Russia.

Admiral von Spee's position was most difficult. He could not take action against Japanese vessels and he could not adopt a strategy that hinged on Japan's activity in the war, and yet he must consider Japan to be an enemy. He must act, one way or another. Already he had heard messages in the clear, and the radio station at Yap had transmitted others, which indicated that the British were beginning to come close to his whereabouts by the process of elimination. It was too dangerous to remain in Pagan long. A plan must be decided upon and acted upon without delay.

The overall task of the admiral and the East Asia Squadron was to wage cruiser war—*Kreuzerkrieg*. The words represented a strategy decided upon by the German Admiralty many years earlier, when the Cruiser Squadron had been established. It was based on the principle that the most effective use of the German navy in a war against England would be to deprive England of the fruits of her colonies and other possessions. The cruisers, then, were to prey upon shipping. They were to avoid open battle with any but forces of their own size or smaller. They were to move about, remaining a constant threat to England. By so doing they followed the old naval theory of "the fleet in being," which meant simply that by its very existence a fleet in a known area tied up at least an equivalent force of the enemy's, and if the enemy wished to be aggressive and try to destroy the fleet in being, it would tie up six, seven, or more times as many ships as the fleet totaled.

This concept aside, the "cruiser war" could never be forgotten. Within a few months the concept of *Kreuzerkrieg* would be transferred to another type of vessel—the submarine—but the concept was sound enough, and effective enough in operation, that it survived two world wars.

Admiral von Spee was an intelligent commander as well as a strong one, and he did not sit in his cabin and hand down dicta to his staff without first ascertaining as many facts as possible, and seeking the opinions of his chief of staff, his captains, and his other officers. Unlike some high commanders, Admiral von Spee liked to consider as many points of view as possible before arriving at a decision. The decision he was called upon to make this first summer of the war was an exceedingly difficult one, and he wanted all the help he could get.

84

At least seven courses of action were open to the admiral, in theory if nothing else. Small wonder, then, that the lights of his cabin had burned late since the end of July, when it became apparent that the Serbian problem would not be resolved by a series of diplomatic encounters.

He could return to Tsingtao and attempt there to organize a defense of the colony. But if it was true, as he had every reason to believe now, that Japan would launch an attack on Tsingtao, then he was doing nothing but playing the role of Wagnerian hero. The Cruiser Squadron would undoubtedly fall before the big guns of Japanese and British battleships and heavy cruisers. He chalked off the return to Tsingtao, then, without further ado.

He could travel to the west coast of Africa and harry British naval stations and trade in that area. He would also be able to protect various German colonies from invasion by sea. But the great disadvantage to this move was that it put him very close to Britain's Mediterranean fleet and not too far from elements of her home fleet which might be detached to swoop down on him. Britain and France had many colonies to be attacked, to be sure, but he would be far from home or friendly waters, and his sources of supply would be limited.

He could travel to South Africa, attack the weak British squadron off the Cape and probably destroy it, then harry the British in this important sector of the Empire. He might even arouse an uprising among the Boers and others of German descent in the south. The problem here was again the same—the problem of logistics and supply and the amount of damage that he might do to the British. He was, after all, a sailor and not a politician, and the fomentation of revolutions was not really in his line.

He could make his way home to Germany, by going around Africa and up through the Atlantic. But once home, what would he do? His job was to harry shipping, and the

85

High Seas Fleet in northern Germany was entrusted with defense of the homeland and the operations against English shipping around the isles. It was not the East Asia Squadron's responsibility to seek its own safety; it was his job to do the greatest damage to his country's enemies without regard to the danger to himself.

He could move into the North Atlantic and harry British and French shipping there, with particular emphasis on the ships going to and from Canada and the United States. Here again he would face the problem of supply, and he would be forced to live off the sea—from the coal and material captured from others.

He might go into the Indian Ocean and disrupt the British trade with India and Burma. This would be most helpful because Britain relied on these colonies for many items. The danger was that the combined forces of the British Navy in the entire Asian region would eventually be turned against him, and he would again have no place to find coal and supplies, save in the Dutch East Indies, where he knew the twenty-four-hour-stay rule would be invoked against his ships. One could coal in twenty-four hours but one could never hope to undertake any major repairs. In a sense, having entered the Indian Ocean, he would have entered a huge trap which might be sprung on him at any time. Barring Japan, he counted two battleships, eleven heavy cruisers, sixteen light cruisers, fifty destroyers, thirteen submarines, and countless small craft and auxiliary craft which could be thrown against the Squadron from Far Eastern and Australian waters.

Or, Admiral von Spee might make his way to the coast of South America. Here he could harry the important British and French trade with the neutral countries of that continent, from Argentina to Panama. There were countless uncharted bays and harbors into which he could creep for refuge if the case so warranted, he could coal and find assistance in many

86

areas among the neutrals, and there existed many German settlements that would be of huge importance to him in matters of supply and intelligence.

On the morning of August 13 Admiral von Spee called the commanders of his warships into his quarters for a meeting. He had his own mind fairly well made up, but he wanted to hear the points of view of his various officers before handing down final orders.

Each of the captains stepped into his gig and was taken to the *Scharnhorst*, piped aboard, and escorted to the admiral's suite, where the admiral was seated in the middle of one side of a long conference table *Kapitän* Fielitz on one side of him, and his lesser staff members straggling down the other. The captains sat in chairs on the other side of the table. The admiral wanted to look into their faces as he talked with them.

The discussion began. Admiral von Spee and Chief of Staff Fielitz outlined the various plans that had been under consideration, and indicated their various difficulties and deficiencies. Of all the captains, *Fregattenkapitän* von Müller was heard most closely, because he had already gone to war and had already captured a prize. He favored the struggle in the Indian Ocean because there was so much British shipping to be found there. True, said the admiral, but the Indian Ocean was also a box, and the Squadron could not take the chance of being caught in a box. And where would the ships coal?

Always, in every plan, it came back to this primary consideration. For example, *Scharnhorst* carried 2000 tons of coal. At 10 knots she would use 93 tons of coal a day, or 38.7 tons for every 100 sea miles. That meant she could steam for 21 days or 5168 miles. Coaling every three weeks? Who was to complain about that? No one, but the key to that analysis was the ten knots an hour. In action, speeding to action, or taking an evasive course, the *Scharnhorst* would be much more likely to be traveling at about twenty knots rather than ten. And at twenty knots the picture was very different. In a day of such steaming she would use 432 tons of coal, or 90 tons for every 100 sea miles. In other words, she must coal then every 4.5 days and she could make only 2222 miles on one coaling. The story was basically the same for every ship in the Squadron. *Leipzig* had the smallest coal capacity, carrying 822 tons, and must coal every 4 days at 20 knots average. *Nürnberg* had the most efficient plant, and could string it out to a bit over five days between coalings. But the facts were very clear. It was not possible for the Squadron, no matter if it took every freighter at Pagan that day, to maintain itself without frequent visits to coaling stations or without phenomenally good luck in capturing enemy colliers. Admiral von Spee could not risk his ships to stand on the vagaries of fortune.

What about a single ship to be detached into the Indian Ocean to carry on cruiser warfare against enemy shipping? asked Captain von Müller. Yes, that was possible, the admiral said. Von Müller pressed the point, and before the day was out he had won permission from his chief to take the *Emden* into the Indian Ocean to wreak what havoc he might among the rich succession of targets all knew would be found there.

As for the rest of the Squadron, it was decided that *Leipzig* should stay where she was, carrying out her mission as cruiser and cargo destroyer on the west coast of the United States. Admiral von Spee would lead the Cruiser Squadron to the west coast of South America, having first done what he could to create confusion in the South Seas. He would remain in this area as long as seemed practicable, and would then travel east, where he had the best chance of solving the coaling problem.

Following the long meeting between captains and the admiral and his staff, preparations were continued for a quick move to sea. The *Emden* coaled simultaneously from two of the freighters. She took on two young lieutenants from the *Gneisenau* and gave in trade *Kapitänleutnant* Herman Mezenthin, an experienced merchant captain who had joined the *Emden* at Tsingtao on hearing of the outbreak of war. Mezenthin would be valuable to the *Gneisenau* as a prize officer, to take charge of merchant ships captured by the Squadron, whereas *Emden* had *Oberleutnant* Lauterbach, who occupied that position with great aplomb and skill.

On the 13th the *Titania* prowled back and forth across the harbor entrance, on guard for friend and foe. She came rushing in at midmorning, leading the *Markomannia*, the freighter bearing 5000 tons of coal, or nearly a month's supply for a light cruiser like *Emden*. *Markomannia* had missed the rendezvous and waited in the wrong place.

Following the meeting of captains there was much to be done. Admiral von Spee had not immediately acquiesced to Captain von Müller's request to be detached. It was a matter he must consider, for the admiral was being asked to relinquish his newest and finest light cruiser with the full knowledge that no matter what happened to her she would not again be available to him. Before the day ended he had sorted out his thoughts, and agreed to two plans: von Müller's request and the idea of Captain Schultz that the Squadron stage a massive attack on some enemy port in eastern waters, to force a concentration of enemy warships in an area where the Squadron had no intention of remaining.

The admiral made one other reluctant decision: all the Chinese in the Squadron would have to be debarked here at Pagan. They were noncombatants and it was not fair to take them into war, whether they wanted to go or not. Some did and some did not wish to return to China. The most serious loss was that of the Chinese crew of *Titania*, which must be replaced by reserve corps sailors from the other merchant ships. This replacement was done on August 13; all the laundrymen

89

and other workers aboard the warships were sent aboard a coastal steamer with two bags of rice, to be transshipped at a neutral port. That is—all, but not quite all, of the Chinese were debarked. The fourteen laundrymen aboard the *Gneisenau* were unloaded, and an equal number aboard the *Scharnhorst* left, and the light cruisers had to follow suit, much as the officers hated to lose the men who kept their clothing clean. But on *Emden* the Captain and Lieutenant Lauterbach conspired and decided that what the admiral did not know could not hurt him, and so the *Emden's* three laundrymen were persuaded to stay with their ship.

That afternoon pigs and cattle were slaughtered again, and the ships made ready for sea. At 1730 the ships weighed anchor and divided into two columns, the *Scharnhorst* leading the warships in the port line, and the *Emden* bringing up the rear so that when she dropped out to turn west she would not upset the formation. The starboard column consisted of auxiliary cruisers and merchantmen, led by the *Prinz Eitel Friedrich*.

The weather was foul, the ships had never been designed as a unit—warships and mail liners and tramp steamers—and during the night the starboard column disintegrated completely, leaving ships wallowing here and there along a distance of several miles. In the morning, as dawn broke, the admiral saw what had happened, and the warships went back to round up stragglers and reform the columns. At eight o'clock in the morning this was done and the Squadron began steaming east, toward the Marshall Islands. At this point the *Scharnhorst* made a signal:

"*Emden* detached. Good luck."

And the little light cruiser turned away to take the exact opposite direction, followed by the *Markomannia*, her coaler, into the Indian Ocean.

The Squadron then moved east, through an especially

filthy day's weather, toward the Marshalls. Had the warships been traveling alone they would have gone along at a steady ten knots, their most efficient speed. But not all their freighters could make ten knots, and few of them could gear their spead to any kind of linear movement, and so it was a ragged procession that straggled across the sea, enough to turn an admiral's hair white. The little *Longmoon,* smallest of the coastal freighters, had to be brought to twice during the day to prevent the excessive rolling from capsizing her, and this stopped the whole squadron. It was a tribute to the tenacity and patience of the admiral, then, that he had the courage to order a battle drill at 1330, and to carry it out.

Precisely at 1445 bugles blew and drums rattled on the decks of the warships, beating the signal that sent the men to action stations. The warships moved their guns into action, practiced reloading, and the other parties carried out their tasks.

All that afternoon was given over to battle practice, the warships taking turns playing enemy for one another, and after each drill the crews and officers assembling on the quarter-deck to hear their captains' critiques. Whatever the crews knew, they must learn more and learn it rapidly, for all were sure it would not be long before the call to action stations would mean action against an enemy.

Admiral von Spee was justly concerned about his enemies, because there were so many of them in the area. They were grouping themselves into two major forces, one under Admiral Sir Thomas Jerram, which had as its nucleus the old British China Squadron, but was to be augmented by French, Russian, and Japanese vessels; another under Rear Admiral Sir George Patey, which was built around the battleship *Australia* and the Australian and New Zealand naval forces.

So far Admiral von Spee had succeeded in one of his primary purposes: he had kept his enemies off balance because

91

they did not know where he was. Until they could find out his location they must search for him in force, and they must be careful lest he cut their communications.

British intelligence was very much confused about the whereabouts and disposition of the ships of the East Asia Squadron. Some reports had the *Scharnhorst* and the *Gneisenau* in company. Some did not. None of the British commanders knew that four of the five ships of the East Asia Squadron had met at Pagan on August 12. Admiral Patey believed von Spee to be somewhere around New Guinea, and he was searching these waters with a strong force led by *Australia*, the 18,000-ton ship that von Spee wished heartily to avoid. Admiral Patey tried, in fact, to persuade Admiral Jerram to come south with his force and seek out the Germans in these waters, so confident was he that they would be found in Friedrich Wilhelm harbor in German New Guinea, or at Simpson harbor in the adjacent island of Neu Pommern.

Admiral Jerram was too busy to respond to such a request. He had decided that the Germans were to be found somewhere around Yap Island in the Palau group. By an almost superhuman effort he had managed to get the cruiser *Triumph* ready for sea. In order to do so the British at Hong Kong had stripped several old gunboats of their crews, and had enlisted more than one hundred *soldiers* from the Duke of Cornwall's Light Infantry regiment. Admiral Jerram wanted to get to Yap in a hurry, fully expecting to find his old acquaintance, Admiral von Spee, sitting there. He sent *Triumph*, the cruiser *Yarmouth*, and the French cruiser *Dupleix* with five destroyers up to watch Tsingtao. He took his cruisers *Minotaur, Hampshire,* and *Newcastle* to Yap. On August 11 he captured the German steamer *Elsbeth*, which had been destined for Admiral von Spee's fleet. She was carrying mail for the crews of *Scharnhorst* and *Gneisenau*.

On August 12, as he stood outside Yap Island, Admiral

Jerram was only 700 miles from Admiral von Spee at Pagan, but he did not know it, and he contented himself with destroying the German radio station at Yap by gunfire from offshore. Had Admiral von Spee intended to remain in the South Pacific indefinitely this action would have been very hurtful to him. Jerram's second shot set fire to the buildings, just after 0930, and a quarter of an hour later the 200-foot radio mast was down and the buildings were burning. The German Squadron had been listening with pleasure to Yap radio's daily news broadcasts which gave them news of the fall of Liége in Belgium to General von Emmich's troops, and the advance against Brussels. When suddenly, on August 12, Yap ceased to broadcast, the Squadron sensed that some disaster had befallen the station, and it had simply reinformed the admiral's decision to be gone from Pagan as quickly as he might—thus the great haste with which the ships had left the islands on the evening of August 13.

For the next few days the Squadron steamed steadily toward the Marshall Islands, nearly 1100 miles away. The drills continued. They were hardest on the stokers, who worked below in three watches, shoveling coal to feed the fiery furnaces. Off duty the stokers still had to participate in the drills, because the services of every man were used on a warship when she was going into battle. The stokers were used as ammunition passers and in the damage-control teams, tasks they were willing enough to perform, but whose practice under the hot sun wearied them excessively before they went below to the even hotter bowels of their ships.

At night the officers gathered on the quarter-decks to wait for sunset, to stroll for exercise, and to gossip, until night fell and they were forced under cover by the lowering of the chain railing across the stern, so as to give the after turret a free field of fire in case of a running night fight. Then the officers adjourned to their wardrooms, painted during the voyage in order to conceal the places where the woodwork had stood. The blinds were pulled for blackout and the junior officers disported themselves with pianos and guitars. On the *Scharnhorst* there was more formality, as it was the flagship, but on the *Gneisenau* even Captain Maerker made it a point to get away from his bridge during the evening and come to listen smiling to a song or two.

The greatest occupation off duty for the officers was to speculate about the length of the war. Uncle Hermann Mezenthin, a doughty sailor and man of affairs in his own right as a civilian, said stoutly that the war would be over in eight weeks. "No nation could stand it longer," he declared, shaking his jowls.

The officers would have liked to have believed him, but somehow they could not, particularly when there were so many enemies around them, and they were steaming directly away from the war, it seemed. They envied little *Emden*, down to the last stoker aboard the two big cruisers, and on the *Gneisenau* morale became so low that Chaplain Rost asked the captain's permission to give a series of talks on great German heroes such as Field Marshal Gneisenau, in order to bring the men's spirits back to fighting pitch.

Meanwhile, as the Squadron steamed for Eniwetok which would be their landfall, on the west coast of the United States the old Canadian cruiser *Rainbow* was looking for *Leipzig* without success, while *Leipzig* on August 14 approached the Farallones, and that night sighted the light. Just before nine o'clock *Leipzig* approached the Golden Gate lightship, and as she came up in dense fog, suddenly the fog cleared enough for them to see the sternworks of a large gray ship. The men of the *Leipzig* were very much on the lookout for two ships, one enemy and one potential enemy. The enemy was the Canadian cruiser *Rainbow*, and Captain Haun thought this

94

gray stern might very well belong to her. It was dark and visibility was bad.

The other possibility was that the ship might be *Idzumo*, the heavy Japanese cruiser which so obviously outgunned *Leipzig* and could blow her out of the water with ease. If they did encounter *Idzumo*, how would the Japanese react?

To the listening ears of the crew came the cry *Klarschiff zum Gefecht* and the men sprang to. In a moment it became apparent that the silhouette was not that of a Canadian, a Japanese, or an English cruiser. For a fleeting moment the wild hope arose in the breasts of several of the officers that this might be a German heavy cruiser—*Scharnhorst* or *Gneisenau*. Then the fog parted again and they saw they were approaching two American cruisers, *South Dakota* and *Pittsburgh*, which were just leaving the Golden Gate.

They exchanged greetings and the cruisers passed on. Not long afterward *Leipzig* was hailed by the lightship, which informed Captain Haun that the German consul had been out in a small cabin cruiser searching the area in the fog for some sight of the *Leipzig*. A pilot came aboard and confirmed the information. Also, the pilot informed the captain that on August 12 and 13 *Rainbow* had actually been anchored in San Francisco Bay and that they had missed her by scarcely more than a day. Captain Haun breathed a sigh of relief when he learned that she had been sighted 120 miles north of the Golden Gate not many hours earlier.

Eventually the cabin cruiser of the consulate found the *Leipzig*, for she anchored to wait, rather than running in to port. At three o'clock in the morning a tired and dispirited Vice Consul van Schack and the *Leipzig*'s old friend Dr. Reimer climbed up the Jacob's ladder. With them came three newspaper reporters from San Francisco. The reporters were soon all over the ship, interviewing anyone—officers and men— and storing up a great deal of misinformation, some of it gained from the mouths of the Germans and some of it from their own observations. They overestimated the size of the cruiser, the size of her guns, and other capacities. They lost some idiom in translation and learned that *Leipzig*, single-handedly, intended to blockade the Pacific Coast against all comers. They lost a little more in idiom and learned that the *Leipzig* crew were simply waiting for the *Idzumo* to come up, so they could blow the bigger ship to smithereens.

As these verbal shenanigans were being performed on deck and in the wardroom, Captain Haun was doing his best to entertain Vice Consul von Schack and Dr. Reimer in his quarters. They had brought bad news. It was fortunate that they had intercepted him, they said, because it would not be wise for him to go inside the harbor until he was ready with a plan that could be put into effect twenty-four hours later. The Americans were taking a very strict view of their obligations under the neutrality laws. Captain Haun would remember the 2000 tons of coal that had been ordered, would he not? said the disconsolate Dr. Reimer. Captain Haun remembered very well. The American government had just confiscated the coal, consul and supply officer said in unison. Why? Because they maintained that it was a war material and they refused to supply any war material to the belligerents.

Coal a war material? If this was the interpretation of the Americans how would the *Leipzig* even get out of harbor, once she got in?

These were matters that had not been ascertained with the Americans, the two officials said, and they would have to be worked out. But the signs were not very promising. The government was taking a definite leaning toward the English, said Vice Consul von Schack. It was apparent in a dozen ways.

Consul von Schack also reported that the *Idzumo* had asked for an anchorage and supplies for August 18, which meant it would be wise for the *Leipzig* to be in and out of

San Francisco Bay before that time. The Japanese had prepared an ultimatum to Germany, ordering her to evacuate Tsingtao and Kiaochow colony by August 23 or face war. To be sure, the ultimatum would not expire for five days after the *Idzumo*'s visit to San Francisco, but who could be sure that the *Idzumo* would not attack a small German cruiser before the declaration of war, if she had a good chance?

Captain Haun made arrangements with the consul to schedule a dock for coal and supplies on August 16; then the consul and Dr. Reimer went back to their cabin cruiser and ashore, taking with them for safekeeping several suitcases filled with belongings of the officers of the *Leipzig*.

The little cruiser then stood out to sea and began to follow the coastal shipping lane north, hoping to come across some British ship or cargo bound for Vancouver. They heard radio transmissions from the Canadian *Rainbow* and gathered that she was far enough away to be no bother.

On August 15 the *Leipzig* sighted Cape Mendocino at 1800. Two hours later, twenty miles north of the cape, she turned inshore and began running back toward San Francisco. Early in the morning, while on watch, Lieutenant Schiwig called several of the young officers on deck to see the "Rocky Mountains" standing snow-capped a few miles in the interior, and although Schiwig's geography was awry, they did have a good view of the more coastal Sierras.

The next day *Leipzig* cruised again to the Farallones and waited the day out. Under the Hague Convention rules of neutrality, they could have their twenty-four hours in American waters more or less as they wanted them, so they chose to run into the Golden Gate at midnight. That way they could be at the coaling dock just as early as they could be taken, could get their work finished during daylight hours, and then steam out at night and make their escape in the darkness in case some enemy warships learned of their presence and

97

lurked outside the Golden Gate for them. Under the circumstances, with the press reports of the *Leipzig's* size and prowess, it would have been remarkable if the enemy had not heard some news broadcasts taken from the newspapers which indicated the presence in these waters of the *Leipzig*. The presence of the reporters, of course, was one reason that Captain Haun had delayed his entrance for a day and a half on the first visit to the Farallones.

No sooner were they anchored off Pacific Heights than Dr. Reimer came aboard with *Leutnant zur See* Jensen, a reserve officer who was second officer of the German steamer *Serapis*. They wanted to warn Captain Haun of trouble ahead. Reimer and Consul von Schack had quite naturally sought out the German steamer when they wanted help in locating the *Leipzig*, and it had been the *Serapis'* motor launch that had brought consul and purchasing officer out to the Farallones for the meeting. All this was common knowledge because the reporters had scented the story and pushed their way aboard. Now the American customs officers were furious, and were declaring that the *Leipzig* had committed a purposeful violation of neutrality. What had been in those suitcases? What messages, what secret documents, what fruits of espionage had been interchanged in that meeting outside the Golden Gate? These were the questions that were being asked ashore in very unpleasant tones.

There was little sleep for the men of the *Leipzig* that night. Shortly after their German friends left the ship, word came from the harbor command that they were to change their anchorage. The captain took the conn, along with the pilot, and they moved to the lower end of Market Street, near the Oakland ferry slip. At eight o'clock in the morning the coal barges came alongside, the provisioning of the ship began, and from that moment on during all the rest of the daylight hours it was hard work for the crew.

The captain and his officers who were not directly concerned with the coaling and loading of food went off to do the honors demanded by navy protocol. They went to the USS *Raleigh*; they went to the cruiser USS *St. Louis*; whereever they went they were followed by five motorboats filled with reporters and photographers, all of them crying loudly for interviews and poses.

During the morning's travels they passed the German steamer *Alexandria*, which had been interned because she was carrying a cargo of war material—or so Captain Haun understood. She was anchored in the bay near Sausalito, and as they passed Captain Haun's face fell as he considered the 1000 tons of good coal aboard her that he could not have.

In the morning the coaling suddenly stopped, and the captain could not understand why. A customs official came aboard and began berating him for violation of neutrality. Captain Haun grew uneasy and worried, for the customs men were most unpleasant.

Where was Consul von Schack?

What had happened to the coal supply?

At around 1100 von Schack showed up, red-faced and breathless. He had been spending the morning borrowing money from Germans in San Francisco. The consul general was at home on leave, and as a mere vice consul, von Schack was not given much attention by the authorities. But he knew why the coaling had stopped—the American supply firm had refused to deliver it without cash payment. Germany's credit was no longer good in San Francisco. The money was paid over and the lighters began moving again.

Captain Haun and the vice consul went ashore then to visit the station admiral in his headquarters on Goat Island. How much coal were they to have? That was the problem to be resolved. The admiral's responsibility as a neutral was to supply them with enough coal to get them back to a German base. The nearest of these was Apia in Samoa, which they could not possibly reach with the 500 tons they were taking on at San Francisco. So it was decided that they could call at Honolulu and would be given another five hundred tons there.

Aboard ship, the crew of the *Leipzig* was joined by *Leutnant* Jensen, the reserve officer, who brought with him six seamen who were also reservists and wished to get into action. The four Chinese laundrymen were disembarked after a long and bitter argument with the customs men. One Chinese, the second cook, decided to stay when Captain Haun raised his pay from $25 to $75 a month. But the others went ashore in an immigration boat, to be shipped back to China on the first available steamer.

There was another quarrel with the immigration and customs men—this one about the *Leipzig*'s mascot, their small bear. The bear is the symbol of the city from which the cruiser had its name, and that is why they kept so unusual a mascot. Now, with war facing them, the problem of caring for the bear became overwhelming, and they wanted him delivered to the Fleischacker Zoo, at least for the duration. The immigrations men replied snappishly that they were not animal trainers, and began searching through their manuals for regulations governing the importation of bears. Captain Haun and his officers muttered unkind words about the state of "freedom" in a country that was completely—as far as they could see—in the hands of a particularly unpleasant breed of bureaucrats.

At eight o'clock (2000 hours) the work and the arguments were finished and it was time for *Leipzig* to prepare for sea. The crew prepared to raise anchor, and the captain ordered all to action stations, because he did not know what he might find as they cleared the Golden Gate. They moved swiftly through the darkness—when suddenly there was trouble.

Crack!

It came as a loud and unexpected noise on the starboard side just forward of the bridge. The officer of the deck, Lieutenant Schiwig, was sure they had been hit by a torpedo. But how could this be, in a neutral harbor? He consoled himself with the thought that the Americans were scarcely acting as neutrals anyhow.

But it was not a torpedo, this sudden noise. It was the result of a collision.

When the pilot had come aboard the *Leipzig* late in the afternoon, he had made for the officers' mess, and there had managed to get himself thoroughly drunk. Now, in the darkness, he had taken the ship toward the narrows. Not far from the old San Francisco World's Fair grounds was anchored a small English sailing ship, with her anchor lights showing. The drunken pilot had mistaken these for the lights of a light buoy, and had run into the anchor chain of the sailing ship. The crack had been caused by the breaking off of the sailer's jib boom, which had become entangled with something on board the *Leipzig*—in the confusion no one knew quite what.

Captain Haun was on deck in a moment, taking over from the drunken pilot (who was sent below). They backed off from the Englishman, without a word, and went on their way, while a damage-control party went to see what had happened to the ship.

The first officer reported that the sailer's jib boom had torn loose the armor plating of the Number-5 gun and had caused some other damage to the installation. The gun itself was not hurt, but it had been partly torn loose from its mounting post. That was what had caused the tremendous crash; as it was torn loose, the gun had come down heavily on the deck. The sailing ship had suffered far worse damage, because the gun had torn her shrouds to ribbons and had broken a backstay.

The officers suggested that at least the drunken pilot had

helped them in their war against the damned English, but Captain Haun did not think the joke a very funny one. He put the pilot over the side as soon as he could do so, with instructions that he was to report to the authorities that it had been an accident. No one really believed he would do so.

The damage-control party was put to work repairing the pilot's night's efforts. With torches and welding it was soon put right, and the *Leipzig*, her guns again ready for action, steamed out past the Golden Gate to seek action against her country's enemies.

6

INTO ACTION

CAPTAIN HAUN OF THE LEIPZIG WAS SORELY DIS-
appointed by what he had learned in San Francisco of the
American attitude toward coal and captures. He had checked
with the American port and naval authorities to see what their
behavior would be if he came in bringing prizes. For example,
if he captured a collier outside American waters and brought
her in, could he not claim her as a prize of war under the
Treaty of 1828 between Prussia and the United States?

He could bring in prizes, the Americans said, but the ships
would be interned if they remained in the harbor longer than
twenty-four hours, and he could not unload them in harbor
and transship war materials aboard his own warship.

So, Captain Haun learned that he could not use San
Francisco or any American base as a station for coaling or
for prize-keeping. What he had hoped to do was to send any
colliers he might capture into the Golden Gate, and then call

103

for them to come out when he needed coal. The Americans had said flatly that this would not be permitted.

It was with growing doubts about his mission that Captain Haun headed southward, to see if he could not work out some sensible arrangements on the coast of Mexico.

Before he actually turned south, Captain Haun took the ship ostentatiously past the gossips of the lightship, heading due west in the direction of Hawaii, and he continued on that course for seventeen miles, until he was sure he was over the horizon. Then he turned south. When the *Idzumo* arrived in San Francisco she would be told that *Leipzig* had left heading toward Hawaii and Samoa. For the next five days *Leipzig* cruised up and down the sea lanes, seeking, without any success at all, some enemy freighters to attack. Traveling at ten knots—her best speed for low coal consumption—she could last for twenty days without coal, but of course no captain could afford to operate without knowing where his ship's next supply was coming from, so Captain Haun put his mind to a solution of his major problem.

On August 23 he was just outside Mexican waters, for he had been edging southward all the time as he searched for steamers. A good collier would have solved his problems—it would not have been too difficult to put a prize crew aboard her and conceal her in the empty fastnesses of the coast of Lower California. But while the officers of the watch manned the crow's nest dutifully, not a steamer was sighted. It was as if the five boatloads of reporters and photographers who surrounded the *Leipzig* in San Francisco harbor had been birds of ill omen. Perhaps the publicity, perhaps just plain bad luck, caused the steamers to stay strictly away from the area in which the *Leipzig* was operating.

On August 23, north of Magdalena Bight and Ballena Bight, just off the Mexican coast, the *Leipzig* came to anchor. Here, without the knowledge of the nosy American authorities, they were to meet the Mexican flag liner *Mazatlán,* owned by the San Francisco firm of Jebsen and Company. Jebsen was a good German who had agreed to help the *Leipzig;* the *Mazatlán* would carry the 500 tons of coal for the cruiser. Jebsen himself was in the east at the moment, but Dr. Reimer had made the arrangements and had telegraphed Jebsen to come back immediately because the *Leipzig's* need was so urgent. Jebsen and the *Mazatlán* arrived at midday on August 26, but they had with them an official of the Mexican government who had joined the ship at San Francisco. The Americans had not been gulled by Dr. Reimer's seemingly innocent workings. They had only allowed the *Mazatlán* to sail after Jebsen had made an affidavit and guaranteed that he would not unload the coal except at Guaymas, where it was intended to go. The official was there to be sure that the *Leipzig* did not take it off in international waters.

What a problem! It seemed that *Leipzig* would never be able to get into action simply because of her dreadful need for coal.

While Captain Haun was struggling with this dilemma, his commander was proceeding purposefully on the major mission of the Squadron: to confuse the enemy and then make a strike where it would least be expected. On August 19 the Squadron made a landfall at Eniwetok in the Marshall group, coming in through the south channel and anchoring in the inner harbor. They had moved along majestically, holding very close formation, considering everything, but they had not managed anything like the ten knots' cruising speed the admiral would have liked. It had been more like eight knots, which meant wasted coal.

Nürnberg moved first into the channel and into this most northwesterly of the Marshall Islands, checking for shoal water. She pulled proudly up to anchor quite close to a little coral island, showing the other ships that the water was deep even here in this most shallow part of the harbor. There was no time to waste, so as each warship anchored, a pair of cargo ships came alongside and the coaling began.

Coaling in wartime was an entirely different matter from coaling in peacetime. The ship was virtually defenseless when it was engaged in coaling. The gun muzzles were covered and they were pointed upward to be out of the way. Tarpaulins were strung everywhere over decks to soak up the coal dust as much as possible, and they were put all over the men's quarters to eliminate unnecessary cleaning. The small boats were either hoisted out of the way or were let down into the water, and the crew was divided into four divisions, each given a special task. In peacetime, coaling could easily be done at night, but not during war, for no light could be allowed to show. Perhaps the worst job of coaling was the trimming up of the bunkers, which was done by the stokers, working with goggles for their eyes and sponges thrust into their mouths so they could breathe without choking on the dust. The coal slid down the coal chutes into the bunkers and piled up; the stokers distributed it into corners and leveled it off. In this way, one stoker in each bunker was on guard to see that his fellows did not find themselves buried under the shifting black mountain. The coaling began at dawn, and lasted until the sun was high in the sky, the men refreshing themselves with cold tea and cold coffee. Then, when the sun was directly above, came a two-hour break. Men were given buckets of fresh water with which to wash, and they had a hot meal. Then they went back to coaling again.

The ships of the Squadron took turns coaling, one cruiser always standing aloof and on guard, its crew ready for action.

So passed the night of August 19 and the day and night of August 20, in coaling, animal slaughtering, cleaning boilers, testing pumps, and renewing fittings.

A little after midnight on the second day in port, the

weather suffered a sharp change. There had been nearly no warning. Oh, the swell had grown a bit heavier in the evening, and the two cargo ships on the sides of the *Gneisenau* seemed to be riding high and uneasily, but that was to be expected: *Longmoon* was a shifty craft at best, and the crew of the *Gneisenau* had just finished the unpleasant task of "emptying" the *Prinz Waldemar*—taking every bit of coal out of every nook and cranny, as a seaman always wanted his successor to do.

Suddenly a freak storm struck the little fleet, not a storm that is presaged by predictable warnings, but a huge gust of wind immediately followed by a downpour of rain.

Scharnhorst and *Nürnberg* were battened down for the night and suffered no damage. The remainder of the fleet of steamers and the *Titania* bobbed up and down for a bit like corks, but suffered no damage other than some broken crockery. *Gneisenau*, however, was most vulnerable; she was just cleaning up after coaling, and she was not ready for an emergency.

When the gust of wind came along to shock *Gneisenau*, *Longmoon* chose to slip her bow anchor. The wind caught her and slapped her around in a 180-degree arc, her bow facing up to the *Gneisenau*'s stern on the starboard side. Heavy seas broke between the two ships—fortunately the stern anchor held and kept *Longmoon* from crashing into the warship—and the seas caused the two steam pinnaces to snap their mooring cables. At this moment stokers had gone into the two pinnaces to light their fires and make them ready for the next day's work.

Aboard one pinnace, the stoker had just come up from below, and he grabbed the iron ladder and hauled himself back into the *Gneisenau*. On the other pinnace the stoker was not quite so fortunate: he managed to leap into one of the rowing pinnaces as he felt himself being carried past and away from his ship. Unluckily, the *Gneisenau* pitched, the rowing pinnace's mooring lines broke like string, and off the stoker went into the tideway between the ships, riding his cockleshell of a boat.

Aboard the *Gneisenau*, the officer of the watch manned the larboard cutter and sent it after the fugitive boats. *Korvettenkapitän* Pochhammer, first officer of the *Gneisenau*, was sound asleep in his bunk when the blow began, and he sensed that something was wrong. Half-dressed, he swung to the quarter-deck, to be caught in a downpour of rain so fierce that in a moment he was soaked through. Later he wrote:

> The wind howled, the rain came down in torrents, and it was pitch dark. As we could not use the searchlight, which we would have done in peacetime, there was no alternative but to await the results of the cutter's search and to take shelter, as it had become extremely cold. The rain ceased when the wind dropped, and we listened intently for the sound of the cutter's oars.

Pochhammer's anxious musings were interrupted when one of the watch noted that the jollyboat, moored at the front of the line of pinnaces, had also disappeared. Unfortunately it sunk, carrying with it a precious cargo of soap which Pochhammer had begged from one of the steamers that very afternoon.

Pochhammer went to the bridge to ponder how he would explain this night's activities to the captain, and above all to the admiral, who simply would not understand how a warship could lose its boats. His problems were not becoming any the less complicated as he considered them. Then came a new crisis.

"Man overboard," was the cry.

A seaman had fallen over the other side of the *Gneisenau*, between the cruiser and the *Prinz Waldemar*. Quickly a buoy was tossed to the unfortunate in the water, but in the darkness and the rain he could not see it. A young officer of the *Gneisenau* watched the man in the water, and saw that he was in danger of being swept past the ship into the tide beyond. In this darkness the young officer knew that, if this happened, the man would never be found, nor could they break the blackout. He grasped a second life ring, handed the end of the line to a seaman, and leaped into the water to save the swimmer. It was a gallant rescue in water filled with sharks.

No sooner had the two dripping swimmers been brought back aboard the *Gneisenau*, when Pochhammer heard the unmistakable splash of the oars of a cutter.

"Have you found the boats?" he shouted.

"What boats?" came the answer.

"*Gneisenau*'s boats," came his more hesitant voice.

"Oh. No. This is the cutter from the *Nürnberg*."

"What do you want?" asked Pochhammer with some suspicion.

"To save the man who fell overboard here."

"Thanks, we have already saved him."

At least that much disgrace was avoided—to have the *Gneisenau*'s man saved by the boat of another ship while her own boats were out joyriding in the harbor.

In half an hour the *Gneisenau*'s own cutter did arrive, carrying the lost stoker, who had much to say about his wild ride. The Number 2 steam pinnace had been safely moored to ride out the storm, and the rowing pinnace into which the stoker had leaped had been moored alongside it. But the Number 1 steam pinnace had quite disappeared.

With a feeling akin to despair for what would happen on the morrow, First Officer Pochhammer shivered a little in the cold rain and thanked his stars that it was no worse. At least they had the stoker back and two of the boats. The other steam pinnace would undoubtedly be found the next day, wrecked on the island or on the reef.

But when morning dawned bright and clear, and the angry seas of the night before had gone and the calm Pacific lapped at the sides of the *Gneisenau* in a manner befitting her name, through a glass *Korvettenkapitän* Pochhammer saw his Number 1 steam pinnace bobbing up and down, saucy as could be, on *the other side* of the reef. Unerringly she had made her way during the night through the entrance and was now going out to sea, up on the crest of a wave at one moment and down in the trough the next—for outside the reef the Pacific was up to her old tricks.

There was hell to pay on the *Gneisenau* that morning, for at breakfast came a rocket from the admiral: What kind of games was the *Gneisenau* playing in the middle of the night? The occasion for this complaint was the simple request of *Gneisenau* for the loan of one of *Scharnhorst*'s steam pinnaces to rescue her own boats. Captain Maerker caught the blast, and he passed it along to his officers.

But after the admiral had calmed down, *Scharnhorst* did lend her Number 1 steam pinnace to *Gneisenau; Kapitän-leutnant* Born, the first navigator, set out and picked up the *Gneisenau*'s boats, and life returned to normal. First Officer Pochhammer, who had been chewed out by Capitan Maerker, passed the unpleasantness along to the officer of the watch, who blamed his boatswain, who had some words to say to the stokers and the man who had fallen overboard. They looked over the side and spat, and the broad Pacific carried the incident away.

On Saturday, August 22, Admiral von Spee dispatched the *Nürnberg* to Honolulu on a secret mission. She was to carry some papers for transshipment to Germany. She was to carry messages which could be coded and sent from Honolulu to the Reichsmarineamt. Under normal conditions this could have been managed from Eniwetok, the admiral sending his coded war messages to Yap radio station, where they would be transmitted, station by station, to Berlin. But by wrecking the Yap wireless station, the British had made this simple means of communication impossible. And the admiral must tell Berlin what he had on his mind, for he had developed a detailed war plan.

He was going to take the Squadron off the west coast of the United States and Latin America for operations against the British and their allies. He informed the Admiralty that Yap had fallen on August 12, which seriously impaired his communications. But he had learned of the Japanese ultimatum, which of course meant war, and had made the decision to take his command eastward in the best interests of Germany.

He had dispatched *Emden* with 5000 tons of coal to carry out the *Kreuzerkrieg* in the Indian Ocean. He intended to send the *Prinz Eitel Friedrich* and the *Kormoran* (the old *Rjasan*) to carry out cruiser war in Australian waters, or as much of this kind of war as auxiliaries could manage without running afoul of the Australian fleet.

The admiral added that he intended to take the Squadron to the coast of Chile with 16,000 tons of coal, leaving the Marshalls about August 23, and that they would arrive at the Juan Fernandez Islands about October 15. He hoped to have an additional 35,000 tons of coal from San Francisco and Valparaiso. Captain von Schönberg was to try to make such arrangements with German authorities in those places by cable when the *Nürnberg* arrived in Honolulu. Here is the way the admiral wanted it laid out:

San Francisco should send 5000 tons of coal to the Juan Fernandez Islands, to arrive about October 15. The colliers were to anchor twenty miles west of the islands.

A supply of 10,000 tons of coal and provisions for a thousand men for three months were to be sent to Port Low at the same time, and fourteen days later, 10,000 tons of coal were to be sent from Valparaiso. The shipments were to be made (preferably) in German bottoms, and the wireless stations of the ships were to be dismantled. Also, another 10,000 tons of coal ought to be sent to Chilean ports, to arrive around October 20.

In order to help *Emden*, and also the auxiliary cruisers that he was leaving behind, the admiral had written a letter to the German authorities at Manila, asking them to supply 6000 tons of coal, to be sent out by steamer to a point off Timor, where these ships might find it.

So there was the long-range plan. It was the best plan the admiral and his advisers could devise, given the serious difficulties under which they worked. As to the fates of the auxiliary cruisers and *Emden*, sailing in waters so heavily traveled by the British, the admiral could have had no illusions; thus the minor provisions for their future. They would have to make their own difficult ways in the world of war.

Nürnberg set out for Honolulu at six o'clock on the morning of August 22. The Squadron and its supply train steamed away from Eniwetok, too, bound for Majuro Atoll, also in the Marshalls. The *Staatssekretar Kraetke* and the *Gouverneur Jaschke* had been emptied of supplies, so they were detached from the train and directed to travel to Honolulu for safety.

Leaving the security of Eniwetok's lagoon, the *Scharnhorst* suddenly slowed and left the line. A few moments later the men aboard the other ships saw her launch a boat. And fifteen minutes after that launching came a signal to the *Gneisenau: I have picked up one of your buoys.*

That was all. No chiding. No complaint.

None was needed.

Capitan Maerker sought out *Korvettenkapitän* Pochhammer for a little talk. The first officer had left one of the buoys, and Admiral von Spee had spotted this calling card for the British and had picked it up. For the rest of the day the *Gneisenau* was not a happy ship.

During August 23 and 24 the admiral occupied himself with gunnery practice for his two big cruisers. He was merely killing time, waiting for *Nürnberg* to get to Honolulu, do her job, and start back for the rendezvous. August 25 and 26 were the same, except for two incidents.

The first of these was of a piece with the carelessness of *Gneisenau's* crew, which had threatened the Squadron's well-being twice at Eniwetok. During gunnery practice the *Titania* was deputed to tow targets for the two armored cruisers. In the process she passed astern of the *Gneisenau* and came much too close at one point.

A heavy sea caused *Titania* to lurch and her bow anchor caught in one of the cruiser's portholes, ripping off a long piece of the quarter-deck. The anchor broke, and the fluke and a piece of the shaft hung down from the bigger ship's side, all this under the astonished eyes of the admiral. He consoled himself, as best he could, with the reminder that the crews were not used to making emergency repairs at sea, which they might have to do for months, and here was good practice for them.

The second incident was one that did not bother the admiral one whit. On the night of August 25 the alarm bell was suddenly sounded aboard the *Gneisenau,* and every man in the ship sprang to his action station. The officer of the watch saw five shapes on the horizon, shapes moving toward them from the port side. Captain Maerker came on deck from his cot in the chartroom where he was catching forty winks. First Officer Pochhammer rushed to the bridge with his field glasses, and began to search the horizon. From the crow's nest the junior officer of the watch shouted down excitedly

113

that he could see them now—"two cruisers and three torpedo boats"—coming in from the northwest. That would mean, in all likelihood, that the ships were Japanese—enemies as the ultimatum expired. And then, as the officers watched anxiously, the shapes changed and drifted away—as was often the case with low-lying clouds.

While the alert was on, the captain checked and found that every man was actually *at* his action station, that all was ready in case there had to be a fight, and that the ship was not only ready but eager for battle. He was not displeased.

Had it been peacetime, the Squadron would have put in at Jaluit, the seat of government of the Marshalls since the Germans had taken over the islands in 1885. But Admiral von Spee had no idea how long it might be until a British squadron took the islands—certainly *he* could not hold them and there was no one else to do so—and he wanted as little notice or publicity about his visit as he could manage. Instead of seeking out Jaluit, he put in at Majuro, a much more deserted place, on the afternoon of August 27. *Titania* went in first, for with her shallower draft she could sound out the channel and warn the cruisers of any difficulties. There were none. *Titania* anchored at one point where the channel moved around in a broad curve, acting as a huge buoy, but otherwise the passage was completely usual. The *Scharnhorst* and *Gneisenau* moved in under the lee shelter of the land in fifty fathoms of water, so they might coal in as much quiet as could be managed.

On the morning of August 28 *Kormoran* came into the harbor; this was her rendezvous point with the Squadron. She was cheered lustily by all the men of all the ships—for here was their first tangible sign of the war, a Russian ship that had been captured and converted to serve His Majesty's navy. Her captain, *Korvettenkapitän* Zuckschwerdt, was an old friend of the officers of the East Asia Squadron. He was one of

114

them, and his men, too, came from the old gunboat *Kormoran* which had been dismantled and would be sunk in Tsingtao's harbor defense.

Kormoran brought the last news from Tsingtao and a bit of mail. She also brought two welcome cargo steamers, the *O. D. J. Ahlers,* and the *Göttingen.*

Two more days were spent in exchanging news and provisions, and then on August 30 at dawn the admiral ordered the Squadron out to sea. *Titania* took the lead as guide and watchdog. *Kormoran* and *Prinz Eitel Friedrich* were detached, along with the steamer *Mark,* and turned south toward enemy waters. Admiral von Spee headed the Squadron due east.

7

THE SQUADRON STRIKES

CIRCUMSTANCE AND STRATEGY HAD GIVEN AD-
miral von Spee one great advantage over his vastly superior
enemies, and at the end of August the admiral was playing this
advantage for all it was worth.

The entrance of Japan into the war on August 23 had
relieved the British navy of the responsibility for guarding
the waters north of Hong Kong. Admiral Jerram had sloughed
off the old *Triumph* to the Japanese force assaulting Tsingtao,
and had taken in exchange the heavy cruiser *Ibuki* and the
light cruiser *Chikuma*. Besides this, the Japanese took over the
search-and-seizure operations for the Ladrone, Caroline, and
Marshall Islands, a huge chunk of the Pacific. They established First and Second South Seas Squadrons, and built these
with fast cruisers and destroyers.

In spite of the building of so strong a force to chase two
heavy cruisers and one light cruiser in the Pacific, one light
cruiser in the Indian Ocean, and a handful of auxiliary

116

cruisers, the British and their allies were operating at one grave disadvantage. They had no idea where Admiral von Spee was, or what he was planning to do.

On August 30 he was steaming toward Christmas Island, planning to rendezvous there with the *Nürnberg* when she had finished her mission. The British simply did not know where the Germans were, and their ignorance was very costly to them.

British naval commanders as far east as the coastal waters of the Americas and as far west as the coast of Africa were afraid that the admiral might show up at any time. Consequently whatever actions they planned must include enough heavy ships to fight the German East Asia Squadron. Admiral von Spee, for the moment, was enjoying the benefits of the British "fleet in being" theory with a vengeance. New Zealand and Australia were mounting expeditionary forces to seize the German South Seas colonies. Admiral Patey was forced to use his entire fleet to protect these invasion groups, and could not hunt out enemy ships.

As he set out on the night of August 12 to supervise the occupation of German Samoa, that British admiral suggested that the Germans would head for the coast of South America as the logical area of operation, but no one could be sure. Consequently, for many weeks Admiral Patey and Admiral Jerram disposed their forces to be ready to fight Admiral von Spee, while that admiral was far away and going farther.

On September 1 the East Asia Squadron crossed the 180th meridian and celebrated two Tuesdays that week. On September 3, the admiral was in radio contact with the *Nürnberg*.

Nürnberg had much to report.

Captain von Schönberg had steamed steadily northeast from the Marshalls to Hawaii, his major concern to avoid any large capital ships of the enemy, such as the battleship *Australia* or the Japanese heavy cruiser *Kongo*, which were known to be operating off the west coast of the United States. His voyage was without incident until August 27, when his radio men caught signals that they identified as those of the *Kongo*. The captain doubled the watch, but otherwise steamed ahead at ten knots and waited the coming of events. He took the precaution of timing his Hawaiian arrival for nightfall, when he could come quickly into the neutral zone without being seen from afar. On September 1 he entered Hawaiian waters, quickly steamed into Pearl Harbor, secured a pilot, and hoisted the signal asking for coal.

There was an argument about coal. A belligerent warship was supposed to coal not more often than once in three months in a neutral harbor, and it had not been three months since *Nürnberg* was last in Honolulu on her way to join the Squadron. Rear Admiral Moore, the commandant at Pearl Harbor, pointed this out to the German consul who came to argue in behalf of Captain von Schönberg. The consul responded that Germany had not been a belligerent when *Nürnberg* was last in port.

Captain von Schönberg entered the argument. He demanded 750 tons of coal, which, he said, was enough to take him to his home port of Tsingtao. Admiral Moore said he might take 550 tons. The loading was begun at the coaling pier. Later the admiral consented to give the *Nürnberg* another 150 tons of coal.

Then von Schönberg and his men got down to business. The ship began embarking reserve officers and sailors, forty-eight of them from the colony and nine men from the North German Lloyd steamer *Pommern* which was in the harbor. The provisioning and coaling was accomplished quickly, the messages were turned over to German Consul Rodik for disposition, and Captain von Schönberg made ready for sea. He wanted to be out of port during the night, so as to make his escape from the

118

Kongo, which was now reported to be only fifty miles off the Hawaiian coast.

Under cover of darkness the *Nürnberg* steamed away, and it was not until forty-eight hours later that the *Kongo* learned of the call and decided to give chase. *Nürnberg* was much too heavily engaged in the Kaiser's business to worry about *Kongo* at that time.

On September 6 the *Nürnberg* arrived at the rendezvous point and met the Squadron. They had been in constant wireless contact, and hour by hour *Nürnberg* had given *Scharnhorst* all the tidbits of information she picked up from the newspapers and from the radio broadcasts she heard from Honolulu. The admiral had thus learned of the seige of Tsingtao; the sinking of the *S-90,* his old gunboat; the escape of the *Goeben* and the *Breslau* into Turkish waters; and the bogging down of the German drive on the western front.

Now *Nürnberg* came in sight, just after lunch on this Sunday. The Squadron had been steaming back and forth slowly. To save coal the admiral ordered the ships to stop and drift as *Nürnberg* came up. She came close by the *Scharnhorst,* and Captain von Schönberg quickly went over the side into his gig and was rowed to the flagship to report. In a few moments the *Scharnhorst* signaled the other ships that they might send boats to the *Nürnberg* to pick up newspapers, fresh vegetables, and fruits that the cruiser had brought back from Hawaii for the Squadron.

There were laughs in the newspapers. One story said, straight-faced: "*Scharnhorst* and *Gneisenau* have been towed into Hong Kong suffering serious injury," and when the men of the Squadron read that article they wondered what they might believe, if anything.

There were also items in the newspapers that brought worried frowns. "*Rainbow* and *Idzumo* hunt down *Leipzig*," was one of them.

119

The Squadron had no way of knowing, at this moment, what was happening to *Leipzig*. The last they really knew of her had come from Consul von Schack in San Francisco, who had reported on her visit and her troubles there. After she left San Francisco and traveled out—apparently bound for Honolulu—there was silence.

In the heat of the Gulf of California, Captain Haun of the *Leipzig* was struggling with logistical problems that caused him every bit as much pain as Admiral von Spee's caused that more experienced gentleman. The steamer *Mazatlán*, with coal aboard, was committed to deliver that at Guaymas, so there was no alternative but for *Leipzig* to show herself at that port if she wanted coal. Captain Haun squirmed and struggled in the net. Half his margin of safety in these waters was secrecy about his whereabouts. Every time he was exposed it meant he must take new evasive action, or indeed the *Rainbow* and *Idzumo* might well hunt him down.

On August 27 *Leipzig* began to cruise and on September 1 she reached Cape St. Lucas at the southern tip of the peninsula of Lower California. The water and the air were very warm. At first the men of the *Leipzig* appreciated the heat, because in all their cruise through northern and central California waters they had felt the damp and cold intensely. From the time that they reached the Farallones until the day they left, they had enjoyed only one sunny day. Here in the Gulf of California they were repaid a hundredfold, and soon they felt the heat as much as they had earlier felt the cold.

The coal situation threatened to become desperate. The *Leipzig* could not conduct *Kreuzerkrieg* by running from one neutral port to another, for every time she appeared in a neutral port the English consuls warned the world that she was there, and the hunt began. Equally important, all the cargo ships she might seek as prey would give the entire area a wide berth until she had disappeared. If *Leipzig* was to carry out her war mission on the coast of the Americas this infernal coal shortage must be resolved.

Herr Jebsen, the German who owned ships that plied between the United States and Mexico, had done his very best to evade the neutrality laws of both nations. He had sent *Mazatlán* loaded with coal for them, but they could not now use that coal in the way they had hoped. He had also sent another coal-laden steamer, the *Marie*, and this, too was lying in Mazatlán port. Now, off the southern coast of Lower California, *Leipzig* was discovered by still another Jebsen ship, a small auxiliary sailer, which might be able to carry some coal for them. The sailing ship found them on September 7, and the Jebsen agent outlined a plan: they must steam into Guaymas and fill their bunkers from coal owned by the Germans in that city. The line had been restored to use and coal could be brought in. *Leipzig* was down to 150 tons in her bunkers and Captain Haun was concerned. She could fill up at Guaymas, then *Marie* would follow her out of Guaymas and become her collier. It would be most unwise to transship coal from the *Mazatlán* to *Marie*, but coal could be shipped in the auxiliary sailer without arousing the suspicions of the English or Americans. Captain Haun agreed readily to the plan; it was put into effect, and he began steaming toward Guaymas that day.

Meanwhile, *Nürnberg* was hard at work again. Following his report to the admiral, Captain von Schönberg had been detached on special duty the very day that he had met the Squadron. On his trip to rejoin the Squadron after the successful Honolulu mission, Captain von Schönberg had heard a number of signals from the British radio and cable station at Fanning Island, northwest of Christmas Island. He had discussed these with Admiral von Spee and had been detached to make a quick raid and destroy the cable and wireless facilities of the British at Fanning. *Nürnberg* was accompanied by *Titania*, which was equipped with cable cutting equipment.

Nürnberg arrived off Fanning Island at five o'clock on the morning of September 7. The men on night watch at the signal station had seen a large steamer come up on the horizon at dawn, and had left their work to come down to the beach and watch her, supposing that she was a friendly ship. At six o'clock she was close enough so that they could distinguish her three funnels (which might have given some indication that she was German, since most British cruisers in the area carried four funnels). In any event, the men of Fanning had little time to consider the nature of their visitor; she glided in close to shore, and in the gathering light put over the side a boat filled with armed sailors, when she was still several hundred yards offshore. The men also had a machine gun.

The boat came in, the men leaped ashore and carried their machine gun off, the landing officer strode up to the Englishmen and told them to raise their hands, they were his prisoners. The English did so, quickly if not eagerly.

The landing party proved courteous and correct, to the relief of the English, but also very efficient. The Germans made their way to the wireless station and broke down the wireless mast. They destroyed the telegraph station. They set fire to the cable station and blew it up with hand grenades. They broke the glass jars that contained the batteries. They set two charges at the point where the Australia-Canada cable came ashore, and in a few moments up rose two huge towers of water, sand, fish, and debris ninety feet in the air. Soon, even as the wireless station was still smoking, up came the *Titania* with her cable-cutting equipment. Her crew found the cable, traced it back, and cut it in several places.

At eight o'clock the men of the *Nürnberg* were ready to leave. They took all the papers they could find, some 20 rifles and 13,000 cartridges, and a number of gold bars, valued by

122

the Germans at 14,690 marks. The small boat was hoisted back aboard the *Nürnberg*, and she and *Titania* steamed off quickly, bound west.

The next day *Nürnberg* and *Titania* rejoined the little fleet.

The Squadron, meanwhile, had again been engaged in the tiresome process of coaling. To escape the dirt, a number of the officers made a visit to Christmas Island, a British possession. They got out of the dust, and they brought back coconuts and a few tropical birds which were more interesting for their color than for their food value. When they returned to their ships, they were greeted by the news from the admiral that he was planning a raid on Samoa, which had been occupied by the British landing forces under Admiral Patey's protection. So on the morning of September 9 the *Scharnhorst* and the *Gneisenau* left to make their raid, while the *Nürnberg* remained to escort the supply train to the next rendezvous point, which would be in the Marquesas Islands.

The excitement aboard the two big cruisers was intense. After all, *Nürnberg* had been in action; *Titania* had been in action; *Emden* was off on the most glorious adventure possible, and every man in the Squadron envied her. (They did not know it, but *Emden* was just that day going into her round of captures of enemy freighters. That night she would capture the Greek freighter *Pontoporos* on the East-West steamer route from Colombo through the Indian Ocean.)

The promise of action came to the men of the crews when they were asked to deliver their pinnaces and other big boats to the steamers *Yorck* and *Ahlers*. The boats could only be in the way in case of battle. The deckloads of coal were moved swiftly into the bunkers, so they would not become extra fire hazards in time of battle. On September 10 the two cruisers crossed the equator, and war or no war, the Pollywogs were initiated into the mystic rites of Neptune, king of the sea, and all became loyal Shellbacks.

Such games and the unending cleaning of the ship after coaling kept the men busy enough. They steamed ahead south and west, back toward the international date line, but they would not go so far; their destination lay at approximately 171 degrees west, 3 degrees south. Sunday came, and with it divine services held under the blazing sun on the quarter-decks. As they approached Samoan waters the two ships took care to begin burning Tsingtao coal, for they prized this fuel, which was as nearly smokeless as they had ever enjoyed.

In the wardrooms, the officers endlessly discussed the possibilities. The purveyors of gloom argued that the enemy would have left by the time they arrived and they would be wasting their time. The optimists said there ought to be two light cruisers there, escorts for the troops, and that they could eat those up before breakfast.

Just before dawn of September 14, *Scharnhorst* and *Gneisenau* parted company. The flagship moved in to take a position northwest of Apia; the *Gneisenau* would come in from the northeast. Thus they lessened chances of being suprised and overcome if they encountered a superior force.

It was a beautiful, quiet night, dark as pitch along the horizon, but with the skies brightly lit by a full display of the southern stars and a crescent moon. That night some of the precious fresh water of the ships was sacrificed for baths, and the men all changed their linen and put on clean outer clothes. In case of battle all was being done to reduce injury and infection. Each man wore his "pince-nez," a small wire-and-cloth device that he would use to pinch his nostrils together in case of a gas or smoke attack. Then he might breathe through his mouth, filtering the foreign substances by sponge or rag. Each man wore an identification disc attached to a red silk ribbon, in case of the dreadful necessity of identifying a torn and mangled or even lifeless body.

As the ships approached Apia harbor, they saw lights which were either shore lights or those of ships in the harbor. In the darkness the admiral could not determine which they were, so he reduced speed and waited for dawn to come over the horizon. The plan called for each ship to reach a specific position, then swing around so that each bow faced into shore, presenting the smallest possible silhouette. When morning came they could see their enemy, they would know whether to charge in for a torpedo attack headlong, or to swing back around for a broadside.

At dawn, *Gneisenau* found herself out of position; the current had carried her past the spot indicated by the admiral. To get back into position took some maneuvering, which did not please the admiral overmuch, but it could be explained away, because that day the southwest monsoon was blowing thunderously, stiffening the seas so that as the two warships plunged ahead the spray broke across the bridges in bursts.

Closely following the dawn the great red ball of the sun burst from the ocean, and by its light the men of the two cruisers could see the detail of the land. First came the dark blue mass, with lights still twinkling in some secret rendition of the Morse code that they could recognize but not understand. Was it ship-to-shore signaling? Had they been seen? Would *Australia* suddenly open up on one ship or the other with her twelve-inch guns?

As the light of day broadened, the blue-gray mass of land suddenly developed special characteristics. They could see the thin white line of coral rocks and sand, and behind it the Mulinu Peninsula, and the town of Apia. Behind the town rose Vaea Mountain, and the long volcanic range that towered almost 4000 feet above the sea.

Soon they could see into Apia's harbor. There was nothing

there; the pessimists had been right. An American three-masted schooner lay at anchor inside, and an even smaller sailing vessel was closer in—but otherwise there was nothing.

The admiral had been an optimist, and now he took *Scharnhorst* in close, searching for something that was not there. All that could be seen of their enemies was the Union Jack flying from the German flag mast above Apia.

There was, of course, the radio station. The admiral said he did not destroy it because he did not wish to destroy German property. The English sneered that the station was 100,000 meters away and the range was impossible. No shots were fired, and to keep the station from informing the enemy about the coming of the German ships, the wireless operators of both cruisers began jamming the frequency. The men were released from battle stations by the "All Clear" signal, and the senior navigating officer of the *Scharnhorst* was ordered to take a course along the north coast to Upolu.

At nine o'clock in the morning, approaching the strait of Apolima at the west end of Upolu Island, they saw the black, white, and red flag of the Empire hoisted and a white launch left the shore to speed toward them. In a few minutes two men came aboard and announced themselves as German planters. They told the story of the occupation of Samoa. A British and French fleet had appeared off Apia on August 30, led by the *Australia*, which was flying Admiral Patey's flag. The French heavy cruiser *Montcalm* was also in the fleet, flying the flag of Vice Admiral Huguet, commander of the French East Asia Squadron. The colony was forced to surrender or be bombarded by a large fleet of cruisers. Some fifteen hundred New Zealand troops were landed, and then the next day the naval force departed.

The planters suggested to the admiral that he land a party of men from the two ships. They promised him that he would have no trouble in raising an army of Samoans, and that within a few days they could launch an attack on the New Zealanders and take back the colony. Tempting as the idea seemed, it was outside the competence of Admiral von Spee. He had no right to jeopardize his ships, or to lose the life of a single man in a land venture unless it involved his ultimate aim, which was to fight the enemy at sea. He could not hope to hold Samoa against the forces that could be directed there— so much was obvious. No, the recapture of South Seas colonies was not within Admiral von Spee's list of alternatives.

The Squadron traveled along the coast of Upolu all afternoon, which meant in a northwesterly direction, knowing that they would be observed by the enemy. At dark they were still traveling northwest, and the admiral was immensely cheered to learn the nature of the messages sent in the clear by Radio Apia:

"The enemy ships are disappearing in a northwesterly direction."

As soon as darkness fell, Admiral von Spee turned directly east, to meet his collier *Ahlers* at the prearranged point of Suvarov Island. The admiral had not stopped there before, and was under the mistaken impression that Suvarov could claim a proper bay for coaling. Such was not the case; *Scharnhorst* tried to bring the *Ahlers* up for coaling and soon saw that the heavy swell would make it impossible, unless the admiral wanted to risk both broken gear and broken heads. So the decision was made to transfer the point of attack to Tahiti. The French had invited it, had they not, in sending the *Montcalm* to help the English occupy Apia?

8

CONVERGING

ADMIRAL VON SPEE'S DESTINATION WAS NOW THE
Society Islands, a chain inhabited by Polynesians, an outpost
in the middle of the Pacific Ocean, off the major steamer lines,
7000 kilometers from Sydney and 9000 from Valparaiso. Specifically his destination was to be Papeete on the northwest
coast of Tahiti Island, between Point Fare-Ute and Point Nuu
Tere, on a long deep beach bordered on the outside by a
mighty coral reef, with a passage into the harbor of about
900 yards in breadth—dangerous but passible.

On September 18, Admiral von Spee sent a message from
the *Scharnhorst* to the *Gneisenau* to inform Captain Maerker
of the new plan.

"I intend to attack the enemy warships that we may find
in Tahiti," he said, "to seize coal that is there and supplies."

He added that the ships would stand outside and send in
a small boat under a flag of truce. If the port surrendered,
well and good. If not, the ships would go in and begin shoot-

ing. The *Gneisenau* was to be ready to sweep for mines, to have her armed landing parties and boats ready, and above all to be ready to shoot at any fortifications, ammunition dumps, or public buildings that presented good targets.

On September 21 the two ships and their collier reached the island of Bora Bora in the Tahiti group. They went in without flags, hoping that the people of Bora Bora would not recognize them, or perhaps would not know of the coming of war to the peaceful islands of the South Pacific.

As the big cruisers anchored, out from shore swung a large canoe, bearing a dozen native paddlers and two Europeans. They came alongside *Scharnhorst* and then the two Europeans stood up to salute. One was a brigadier of gendarmerie and the other was a civilian. Soon they were aboard the ship, in the presence of the officer of the deck and the admiral, in his gold braid. The military man stepped forward.

"I am the representative of the French government at Bora Bora and I now put myself at the disposal of the admiral."

Admiral von Spee repressed a smile. He could not have asked for anything more. Obviously the French of Bora Bora did not know about the war, or who he was. He decided to keep them in ignorance.

An officer opened the conversation, in French.

"What news of the war?"

"None," said the brigadier. "We have learned from another British ship that you have declared war on Germany, but I do not know if France is in the struggle."

It was really quite reasonable that the French here had not heard of the war, for Bora Bora, while in the French group, is one of the Petites Iles Sous-le-Vent, and it is located some 120 miles to the northwest of Tahiti. The admiral was ready to take advantage of this situation.

"France marches at our side against Germany," he said.

"But I fear that the German fleet has captured Tahiti, otherwise we would go there to coal. Have you heard anything?"

"My goodness, no," said the brigadier. Then, ruefully, "But if they attacked Tahiti it wouldn't be long before they had it."

"Why? The island has its defenses . . ."

"Because it is impossible," said the French officer. "For batteries she has only the guns of the *Zelee* [a French gunboat] which had been moved to land. The *Zelee* is moored in the harbor. For garrison she has only twenty-five soldiers and a lieutenant. To be sure you might add the twenty gendarmes and their adjutant, but what does that add up to. Nothing."

The civilian then entered the conversation. He was a business man at Bora Bora, and quickly he offered to supply the ships and completed the information the admiral wanted. Before being disarmed, he said, the *Zelee* had captured a German collier with 3000 tons of coal aboard. The Germans of Tahiti had been interned.

So in five minutes the admiral had learned all that he needed to know—or all that these Frenchmen knew, at any rate.

Champagne was broken out, and after a glass or two the brigadier and the French civilian went swiftly ashore, all the more quickly to meet the needs of their allies. Soon, alongside the two gray ships came canoes filled with fruits, fish, pigs, and other foods, including cattle, which were immediately slaughtered by the ships' butchers. Then the ships began to coal. *Scharnhorst* moved to the forward end of the *Ahlers* and *Gneisenau* moved to the after end; thus the warships could coal simultaneously from the collier. Several officers went ashore to supervise purchasing, and they were presented with a huge bouquet of flowers for the admiral.

Mid-afternoon saw the coaling completed. With British gold from Fanning Island the admiral paid for all his purchases, and at four o'clock the two warships put to sea again. As they reached the cape which marked the entrance to the harbor, a great French flag was broken out on the land and dipped to salute them. At this gesture of politesse, Admiral von Spee could hardly refrain from raising and dipping the red, white, and black naval ensign of the German Empire, could he?

He could not.

Admiral von Spee set his course now for Tahiti, planning to arrive at dawn. The night was warm and wet, for the rains fell on the two ships briskly and for many hours. At dawn the captains discovered that the current had pushed them too far west, but in an hour this error in navigation was rectified and they stood off Tahiti. The trouble with the delay, however, was that in the hour they had been sighted and the people of Tahiti had time to avoid surprise. They would have been reported anyhow, because they were first seen by sentinels on the island of Moorea, a few miles northwest of Tahiti, and just before dawn lights flashed to the shore of Tahiti warned of the presence of two shapes off the coast.

Lieutenant de Vaisseau Destremau, commander of the *Zelee* and now of the Tahitian defenses, alerted his men throughout the island, for whatever good that would do. He used semaphore and telephone to reach as many posts as possible. The telephone was in constant use, and then the old bronze cannon used for signaling in the harbor was fired three times to show the coming of emergency.

At 6:30 in the morning, the two ships suddenly became visible offshore. After one glance Destremau recognized them: the two equal masts, the four similar funnels, the ramming cut-water bow; all these signs indicated the ships he feared most, *Scharnhorst* and *Gneisenau*.

The French lieutenant acted with great presence of mind. There was nothing he could do at the moment to prevent the

131

entry of the ships into harbor, but he could make it unprofitable for them. He ordered his second in command to destroy the buoys that marked the harbor entrance. He ordered his men at the coaling depot to set fire to the coal that lay ashore. He also ordered the fires lit in the disarmed gunboat, and told an officer and ten men to be ready to take her out and sink her in the channel. He spoke to his gunnery officer, Ensign Charron.

"Open fire in slow salvos on the head cruiser," he said. "Cease fire when he shows his colors. Wait. They are too far out now to do any good, and there is no use in showing the placement of our guns. But, if they try to come into the channel, then begin firing."

From the shore the cruisers could be seen bearing down toward the entrance to Papeete harbor, traveling along the coast 2000 yards off the reef.

As they came within range, the cruisers could see the shore as well as they could be seen. Aboard *Scharnhorst* the admiral and his officers looked through their glasses. The first unusual sight was dismaying: a tall plume of black smoke going up from the edge of the harbor. They guessed correctly that it was the coal they had hoped to find. They could also see much excitement among the people along the quay, and they knew that they had been recognized as the enemy.

Suddenly puffs of white smoke broke out from the hills beyond the town, much to the surprise of the admiral, who had not expected to be attacked by a peashooter. Three salvos were fired by the guns, falling to the right and left of *Scharnhorst*, scoring no hits.

"What impudence!" said one of the German officers.

Admiral von Spee had hoped to enter the port, take what he wanted, and then make the decisions about the destruction of facilities and weapons. Now the French had changed his plans. He held his fire and turned his ships full-line ahead to about 8000 yards from the town, then ordered his ships to open fire against those telltale spots of smoke they had seen earlier. Soon the coastal batteries—such as they were—had been silenced. And as the German guns opened up, the people of Papeete fled their town, running back to the hills for cover. Houses were deserted, doors left open, lights still on, but there were no people in Papeete.

Admiral von Spee ordered his cruisers to move across the neck of the harbor entrance, and to give the harbor a broadside. They also opened fire on *Zelee* and on the captured German steamer *Walküre* which flew a huge *tricolore,* much to the disgust of the Germans.

The ships moved back and forth, firing. At eight o'clock they crossed the neck of the bottle for the third time, firing on the ships and on the harbor installations beyond. *Zelee* received several direct hits and began to sink; her bow submerged, and she capsized. *Walküre* had received several hits.

At 8:30, for the fourth time the German cruisers made their turn and came back across the harbor mouth, firing. Finally, after using some ninety rounds they ceased fire and the admiral gave serious consideration to entering the port. But now he had doubts. If the French had been so ready for him, perhaps they had sowed mines in the entrance to the harbor. Perhaps they had time to radio the outside world that he was there. He had spent three hours outside that harbor already, and he had the feeling that it was time to be gone. So in midmorning *Scharnhorst* and *Gneisenau* turned away from Papeete, and after setting a false course for the shore-watchers until they were out of sight of land, they turned north and then east, bound for the Marquesas and their rendezvous with *Nürnberg* and the supply train.

Admiral von Spee was playing an important game. He had written home from the Marshalls on August 29 that, since Japan was in the war, "it is totally purposeless to remain in

East Asian waters and so I shall go from these." He had written from Samoa on September 14 that he had not attacked the New Zealanders ashore because that, too, would have been purposeless. But he knew as well as anyone else in the world that his appearances off Apia and Papeete were far from purposeless. They brought serious fear to his enemies.

The British naval commands in the Pacific received two bad pieces of news on the same day, September 14. First they learned of the appearance of the *Emden* in the Bay of Bengal on the Colombo-Calcutta steamer route. This news shocked Admiral Jerram immensely because it was exactly what he had spread a wide net to prevent, and he was positive that no German ship could slip between his pickets that guarded the eastern entrances to the Indian Ocean.

Second, the British learned of the appearance of Admiral von Spee and the two large cruisers off Apia on that same day. This news brought worries to Admiral Patey. The entire defense system of the Far East was suddenly thrown into confusion. The British Admiralty had taken the position that von Spee was making his way toward the coast of South America, his Squadron intact.

Suddenly, in a week's time, *Leipzig* was reported by the English consulate of Guaymas to be in Mexican waters, and apparently with no intention of trying to join the Squadron. *Nürnberg* had been seen at Fanning Island—alone save for a coal ship. *Emden* was in the Bay of Bengal. And now up turned the two most powerful units of the fleet, first off Apia and then off Papeete. To make matters worse, the German cruiser *Königsberg* had appeared off Zanzibar on September 20 and destroyed an old British cruiser, HMS *Pegasus*.

The result of this cruiser warfare was all that Admiral von Spee could have asked. Australian and New Zealand convoys were suddenly canceled. Expeditionary forces against German New Guinea and other points were suddenly delayed.

The army forces did not want to put to sea without sufficient protection, and this meant in every case a flotilla that could outgun the two heavy cruisers. Also other cruiser forces must be spread out across the Pacific and the Indian Oceans, to catch the German light cruisers which were causing such havoc in the seaways.

The British Admiralty had begun to believe that Admiral von Spee was going to South America, and they had taken certain measures to strengthen the fleet that was guarding the west coast of that continent, a squadron of cruisers under Rear Admiral Sir Christopher Cradock. The Admiralty had issued orders for the British heavy cruiser *Defence* to leave her station at the Dardanelles and proceed to South America to reinforce the Cradock Squadron and make it a proper fighting force to defeat von Spee when he was found. Suddenly, with the von Spee appearance off Apia, the Admiralty panicked. *Defence* was stopped at Malta, and new instructions were issued to Admirals Patey and Jerram, telling them to cover much larger areas of sea.

Above all, they were to find and destroy the German East Asia Squadron, either as a squadron (which the Admiralty hoped) or as individual raiders (which the Admiralty now feared).

The pace of the search was increased and increased again, except on the west coast of North America where *Leipzig* had been having so many difficulties that she had failed to carry out effective cruiser war.

Leipzig hoped on September 8 to resolve these difficulties with the assistance of German civilians in Mexico. Captain Haun brought her into Guaymas for coaling, with the understanding that she would obey the Hague Convention rule about twenty-four hours in port. He anchored near the USS *Albany*, which was protecting American interests in the harbor. Herr Jebsen had done all he said he would, and coal in quantity was waiting for them on the quay. To save time they decided to try to take the ship into the mole, rather than bringing boats and lighters out to the anchorage, and having first tested the depths with the cutter, they made the change-over safely. The harbor was just deep enough for them.

At the end of twenty-four hours they were still in port, enjoying the hospitality of Consul Moeller and others. The French and English consuls were furious and made official protests. (Also, of course, they had warned their various naval units of the appearance of the *Leipzig*, but Captain Haun was quite sure that none of his enemies were near enough to bother him just then. Haun was not lazy or foolhardy. He was taking on coal, and at coaling's end he had taken 930 tons of bunker and deck load.)

In the meantime, arrangements had been made that *Marie* would follow *Leipzig* out and would become her servant. Herr Jebsen, having sacrificed so much for his country, went blithely back to San Francisco by rail.

No longer did the *Leipzig* feel trapped. She had nearly 1000 tons of coal herself, and *Marie* had another 600 for her. So now, on September 9, she went out for the first time prepared to wage *Kreuzerkrieg*.

Captain Haun was careful as he went out of the Gulf of California and rounded Cape St. Lucas. He sent the *Marie* ahead, ablaze with lights, and lurked in near the shore, in case his enemies had ganged up on him. There was no sign of any of his enemies. So he set out to cruise the area between Cape St. Lucas and Panama, seeking enemy shipping.

The night of September 9 was quiet. So was September 10. On the night of September 11, the restless roving of the *Leipzig* brought her within sight of a steamer. Captain Haun hailed her and ordered her to stop. The steamer paid no attention, so he ordered a shot fired across her bow. Immediately she slowed, and stopped. *Oberleutnant* Johnke and

136

Leutnant Jensen were dispatched with a prize crew to board her, for this ship was the British tanker *Elsinore*, a vessel of 7000 tons, just six months old. She had carried a cargo of fuel oil from Central America to San Francisco and was traveling under ballast. The captain came aboard the *Leipzig* with his papers, and said he would have stopped but his helmsman had misunderstood orders. He reproached Captain Haun for having shot at him.

Captain Haun had little time to listen to reproaches. He ordered the crew of the *Elsinore* moved to the *Marie*. Then he sent several of his officers, deck and engineering, to see what might be useful to the warship aboard the tanker. The engineers took a ventilator but that was about all that could be found except some extra food and tools, and a number of valuable charts. Captain Haun would have liked to have kept the *Elsinore* as a prize, but how could he? He was far from waters where the ship could be useful to Germany, and he certainly did not want it to be useful again to his enemies. So she was made the object of a little artillery practice, and at 5:30 in the afternoon she sank, stern first.

The *Leipzig* then headed for the Galápagos Islands, off the coast of Ecuador. In Guaymas they had learned that the German collier they had requested so long ago had been dispatched with their 3000 tons of coal and was expected to arrive and lie in Freshwater Bay from September 15 for several days. *Leipzig* was delayed because the news had been a long time in coming. She had received it by way of Chile, San Francisco, and Guaymas, and now it was impossible to steam to the Galápagos Islands so quickly. The question was whether or not the steamer would still be there when the cruiser arrived.

By daylight on September 18 the *Leipzig* had reached the Galápagos Islands. On the west side of Albermarle Island lies a little bay, Tagus Cove, which is much like a Norwegian fjord. Here *Marie* anchored, and here *Leipzig* took on coal and then moved out to deeper waters. Then began the search for the ship that was supposed to be bringing 3000 tons of coal from the Peruvian port of Callao for the use of the light cruiser. Captain Haun took *Leipzig* to Indefatigable Island, the center of the group. There on the northeast side, lies Freshwater Bay, and there, just after church services on Sunday, the *Leipzig* found a small European sailboat. Signals were exchanged and it was quickly discovered that this was a boat of the steamer for which they were searching. More quickly the boat was hoisted aboard the cruiser. The men of the steamer had begun to wonder if the cruiser was ever going to arrive.

The steamer was the Kosmos liner *Amasis*, an 8000-ton freighter which was carrying 3000 tons of clean-burning Cardiff coal, potatoes, meat, and other supplies. But then, doubting if the *Leipzig* was truly coming, the crew had salted down some of the fresh meat for safekeeping.

The next two days were spent refreshing the *Leipzig's* stores and water. The officers of the two ships went ashore. They found a large ranch and bought some cattle for shipment to the *Leipzig*. They transferred stores from the *Amasis* all day long. They also learned that it would be possible to put ashore their English prisoners from the *Elsinore*, and that, by putting them off in the Galápagos Islands, they might delay discovery of the fate of the *Elsinore* for a considerable time, thus adding to the confusion of the English. But to do so they must go back to the *Marie* because she did not carry a wireless station.

So the *Marie* was reached and the Englishmen were unloaded to await rescue at some future date. (They *were* rescued.)

On September 22, the *Leipzig* and her freighters set out

138

for Cape Santa Elena, north of the Bay of Guayaquil, a point they reached the next evening. The two steamers were kept at good distance, one on either side, and they searched an area twenty-five miles out from the coast.

On the morning of September 25 *Oberleutnant* Schiwig had the watch. He saw smoke on the horizon and sent a signalman up to the crow's nest. The man reported a black funnel on the skyline, and Lieutenant Schiwig reported immediately to the captain. At first the captain thought it might be the *Amasis*, which had strayed away from its position, but as they overhauled the ship they could see that she was a stranger. She was the English steamer *Bankfields*, carrying 5000 tons of sugarcane from Peru, and headed for the Panama Canal. Schiwig and an engineering officer went aboard the Englishman to discover what they might use before they sank her. The engineer disappeared into the bowels of the ship and began opening sea cocks, after the crew had been taken aboard the *Marie*. Lieutenant Schiwig and an enlisted man discovered a treasure-trove of hens, and began loading them into a sack. The ship's steward, who was a German, led them to a pen filled with young Yorkshire pigs, and they loaded those into their boat as well, much to the disgust of the seamen who had to handle them. Then it was back to the *Leipzig*, and waiting for the *Bankfields* to sink.

They cruised south, eating like kings from the stores brought to them and captured. On Sunday, Schiwig was particularly pleased with himself and proud because all 310 men aboard the *Leipzig* had a marvelous dinner of roast pork—for which he took smiling credit.

It was coaling again on September 27—or the problem of finding a safe place to carry out the enterprise. They decided on a guano island, Lobos de Tierra, not far off the western coast below Puenta Parina, and here they pulled into a tiny anchorage. So that the English prisoners of war would not see anything more than they should, the *Marie* was sent around to the other side of the island, while *Leipzig* coaled from *Amasis*. Until now the *Leipzig* had been burning the dirty American coal and the Japanese coal that had been aboard *Marie*, but now they took on their first Cardiff coal, and both officers and men swore that even in the coaling process it was much superior to anything they had been using. As for burning, they could expect it to make half the smoke.

In the harbor lay an English four-masted barque which was loading with guano, and on the morning of September 28 a suspicious pair of characters came from that ship to the *Leipzig*. One of them was a Peruvian official. The other said he was an American. They protested that the Germans must not hurt their boat because it belonged to an American firm. Captain Haun said that because of the friendship of Germany for Peru they would leave the tub alone, quite sure in his own mind that the second man was no more an American than Haun was. The important matter at this juncture was to avoid trouble with a Peruvian government that could be most useful to the Germans in the weeks to come.

They were to pay for their leniency: two days later, while they were traveling south, Radio Callao broadcast a report that the *Leipzig* and two "auxiliary cruisers" were raiding up and down the west coast of Peru. The report could have come from no one but their friends of the guano pier.

On September 30 the *Leipzig* came into the Pescadores Islands and cruised about Callao. Here there were messages for the ship, one telling Captain Haun of the presence on the west coast of South America of a British fleet strong enough to be a threat to the cruiser. It was the squadron of Admiral Cradock, consisting of the heavy cruiser *Good Hope*, heavy cruiser *Monmouth*, the light cruiser *Glasgow*, and the auxiliary cruiser *Otranto*. The second message informed the *Leipzig* that the German light cruiser *Dresden* was working along the Chilean coast, and instructed Captain Haun to begin working with the *Dresden*.

9

DRESDEN

IN THE SPRING OF 1914 THE LIGHT CRUISER DRESDEN
had been placed on the East American station, replacing
the old cruiser *Bremen* on the Atlantic side of the Americas.
Dresden was a modern ship, sister ship to the *Emden*. She
was 6 years old; she could make 24 knots; she carried 10
4.1-inch guns and the usual pair of slim masts with searchlight platforms; she displaced 3544 tons; and she had an
850-ton coal capacity. She was a good fighting weapon for her
day and for the job she was supposed to do: to represent the
might of Germany in any difficulties in which the rights of
German citizens of Latin-American countries were threatened.
She did her job well. Captain Erich Kohler was very popular
among the Europeans and Americans of the various navies
who kept ships in Mexican waters, and the Germans were
popular with the Mexican government of President Huerta,
too. Unlike service on the west coast of Mexico, service on the

east coast was pleasant and desirable, with good food and good harbors.

Long before the Reichsmarineamt had any indication that war might come to Europe in 1914, it had been planned that *Dresden* would be brought back to Germany for a complete refit late in the summer of 1914. She had been continuously in service in the water longer than any German ship afloat, and after several months on the American station without the services of a German naval dockyard she needed a good deal of work. Of course, the most important parts of a ship are not metal or vegetable or mineral at all, but are the people who man her and the man who commands her. In this *Dresden* was most fortunate; *Fregattenkapitän* Kohler was as good an officer as had been trained in the service of His Imperial Majesty, so good that he was to be given command of the much newer and much larger cruiser *Karlsruhe*, and another captain was to take *Dresden* back to dock for her refit. Chosen for this task was *Fregattenkapitän* Fritz Emil von Lüdecke, a West Prussian by birth who was forty-one years old that year. He had served two years as chief artillery officer of the First Squadron of the famous German *Hochseeflotte* (High Seas Fleet) and three years as a leading staff officer to the admiral of the division. He was, in other words, a professional staff officer, and the task of taking *Karlsruhe* out to the South Atlantic and bringing *Dresden* back for a refit was as much of a lark and an honor as a mere *Fregattenkapitän* was likely to enjoy in the service of His Majesty. Captain von Lüdecke was a serious thoughtful officer, much more akin to Captain Karl von Müller of the *Emden* in appearance and temperament than any of the more swashbuckling captains of the other cruisers in the Squadron. As will be seen, however, Captain von Lüdecke had none of the aggressiveness or audacity that made von Müller become in a few months one of the legendary commanders of German naval history.

143

During the month of July, Captain Kohler had been working very closely with the British ships HMS *Essex* and HMS *Berwick* for the protection of foreigners during these testy days of revolution when President Huerta was losing his office and his very life was threatened. On July 13 *Dresden* left Vera Cruz and most of the international fleet behind and steamed to Puerta Mexico, along with the British light cruiser *Bristol*. Then, on July 20 she embarked President Huerta, War Minister Blanquet, and their families, who would be taken to safety in Kingston, Jamaica. *Dresden* was on the high seas, just off the coast of Jamaica, on July 24, when she learned of the Austrian ultimatum to Serbia. She had just disembarked her important passengers and was going back to duty, the very pleasant duty of steaming to Port-au-Prince, Haiti, to meet *Karlsruhe* and then carry her crew back to the fatherland.

Two days later *Dresden* was in port, and Captain Kohler took leave of his shipmates, sad to break the association in a way, but proud to have the command of the shining new *Karlsruhe*, with her 4800 tons, 27-knot capacity, and 12 guns. Captain von Lüdecke took the bridge of the *Dresden* and made ready for a routine cruise home, after which he would undoubtedly be reassigned to staff duty while the ship was put up for major overhaul.

On July 28, suddenly Captain von Lüdecke's staff job seemed far, far away, for on that day the Admiralty warned him of the worsening diplomatic situation. The next day he left Port-au-Prince and moved to St. Thomas in the Danish West Indies, an important port for the Hamburg-Amerika Line, which had excellent dock and communications facilities. Captain von Lüdecke coaled there, taking on 828 tons, and left nervously that same day for Germany. He was out of port only three hours when the Admiralty warned him that war was imminent.

"War threatens with Great Britain, France, Russia," said the terse Admiralty message. "Allies Austria-Hungary, probably Italy. Do not come home. Be ready to carry out *Kreuzerkrieg* on mobilization order."

So Captain von Lüdecke's lark was over almost before it began, and now he found himself given responsibility for cruiser warfare along the entire east coast of the Americas, with a tired ship and a crew of 360 men entirely new to him. It was a difficult position for a staff officer.

At least the Admiralty appreciated his newness and his position. Soon he had a new order.

"Go to Zone III," said the wireless message from San Juan station.

That message meant he was to head into the South Atlantic, where he could prey on the important shipping that ran between the Latin countries and England.

For the next few days, as war came, Captain von Lüdecke and his officers were deluged with information about the war, from the Admiralty, from the wireless stations, and from messages they intercepted that were exchanged by the British heavy cruisers *Suffolk* and *Berwick* and the light cruiser *Bristol*. Although many of the messages were in code, they were instructive. The frantic spate of them very much concerned *Dresden*. The British wanted to know where she was; so much was apparent.

In late July, after *Dresden* had taken the Mexican President to Jamaica, Admiral Cradock had been in touch with Rear Admiral Paul von Hintze, German ambassador to Mexico, under whose orders *Dresden* had made the trip, the British admiral congratulating the German for his fine act of mercy. In his reply, Admiral von Hintze had said something vague about the *Dresden* being on special duty at the moment. Then, on July 27 the British received intelligence reports about

145

the *Dresden*'s appearance at Port-au-Prince. It was learned that she left there. And then there was nothing.

During the first few days of the war, the *Dresden*'s disappearance proved a most effective weapon for the Germans. Scores of ships in North American and Central American waters were afraid to move, suspecting that the *Dresden* might be lurking off the shore of New York or Boston—or anywhere. The British wireless station in Newfoundland reported both *Dresden* and *Karlsruhe* in those waters, and ships in the St. Lawrence were thrown into panic. The British Admiralty added to the fright by ordering ships in North American ports to remain in port until Admiral Cradock arrived from the Caribbean with a number of cruisers to protect merchant shipping.

The British received their "war telegram" on August 4, and the search for the *Dresden* became frantic. She was moving south steadily, and was at that point off the South American coast in the Guianas region. Admiral Cradock had definite intelligence that day placing *Dresden* off New York harbor.

Admiral Cradock was becoming vexed and worried. He wanted to sink those cruisers, but he *must* find out where they were. Shipping was flatly paralyzed. The Canadian Navy Department at Ottawa indicated a fear that the Germans were attempting to establish a naval base in the St. Pierre and Miquelon Islands. All Canadian ports were closed to local shipping, and there were no sailings.

Now, for nearly ten days Admiral Cradock worried, millions of dollars worth of goods were delayed, thousands of precious minutes were lost, and *Dresden* had done absolutely nothing except steam along as peaceably as she had done a month before.

She was stripped for action, of course. This had been done the unhappy and expensive way, at sea, and she was on a war footing after the night of August 2. But she was not in action yet.

On August 6 *Dresden* was cruising in the Amazon River region, back and forth along the sea lane, hoping to discover a British or French steamer—it being unlikely that a Russian ship would be found in these waters. At 1330 that day the crow's-nest watch reported smoke on the horizon, and by increasing steam Captain von Lüdecke quickly overhauled the British steamer *Drumcliffe*, 4072 tons, traveling in ballast from Buenos Aires to New York. There was no trouble about stopping the *Drumcliffe*. The captain did not know there was a war on, although he carried a wireless outfit.

The boarding party from *Dresden* climbed into one of the ship's boats and lowered her over the side in the calm sea. They rowed swiftly to the merchantman, the officer in charge carrying sword and pistol, and the men with rifles by their sides as they rowed, some with Lugers at their belts as well. Up the Jacob's ladder they went and then to inform the English captain that he was their prisoner. It took a bit of time for the shock to penetrate, but then the captain was amenable. The German sailors had a shock of their own: the English captain had his wife aboard with him, and a small child. What would the *Dresden* do with them?

Captain von Lüdecke now made an important decision: he wanted no part of women and children, the *Drumcliffe* contained nothing of value, and she was badly in need of coal. He let her go. First, of course, the wireless equipment was taken off the ship and moved over to the *Dresden* for future use. Captain and crew were forced to sign a statement that they would not engage in war against Germany. Then the English freighter was released to go on her way.

An hour after the release of the *Drumcliffe*, another ship was stopped. She was the *Lynton Grange*, another 4000-ton British freighter, traveling from La Plata to Newport News.

And she was no sooner stopped than along came *Hostilius*, a 3000-ton freighter traveling from La Plata to Cuba. Neither ship carried wireless, and neither had anything *Dresden* wanted, so these ships, too, were allowed to go on their way unmolested, unsunk. On August 11, the *Hostilius* arrived at Barbados and the location of the *Dresden* was public knowledge. Next day the *Drumcliffe* also reported in and Admiral Cradock was notified. Immediately, the shipping lanes were clogged with freighters making their way east. (*Karlsruhe* had also been located in the south.)

For a ship with such opportunities as *Dresden* enjoyed to strike heavy blows at British merchant shipping, she showed little verve. Captain von Lüdecke knew the principle of *Kreuzerkrieg*: to stay out of the way of British warships and to harry the Englishman where it hurt most, in his belly and in his line of supply. But Captain von Lüdecke did not agree that ships should be destroyed just because there was war, unless those ships carried something of value for the British and were going to Britain. His theory was not new; it was old and tested and gentlemanly. If an enemy ship were carrying cargo for a neutral it might be spared. If a neutral was carrying cargo for an enemy, it might be spared. If an enemy was carrying cargo destined only for civilian use, it might be spared. Captain von Lüdecke saw no purpose in destroying valuable equipment without a specific relation to the British war effort. He was a very gentle man, as was indicated by one incident during the boarding of the *Hostilius*. There, when confronted by Germans pointing guns at them, the crew and captain became hostile, and flatly refused to sign the declaration of personal neutrality in the war. What was to be done with them? Some officers aboard the *Dresden* were for taking them prisoner and sinking their ship, but von Lüdecke saw nothing to be gained thus, and the angry British seamen were

148

released and sent on their way by the embarrassed German warship.

That night, after releasing her captives, *Dresden* moved south and east toward Rocas Reef, 130 miles off Cape San Roque, and just off the juncture of the sea lanes. A few miles away the traffic separated, with those ships going up the east coast of the Americas bearing northwest, and those going to Europe heading northeast toward the Canary Islands. This point to which *Dresden* was heading would become the great rendezvous point for the German raiders as the war progressed.

Dresden cruised for a few days without incident. Then came the inevitable need for coal. But *Dresden*'s case was unique among the cruisers of the Squadron. She had no shortage of coal, for there were plenty of German colliers about the east coast of the Americas to be called upon. Waiting for her at the end of the first week of war was the collier SS *Corrientes*, of the Hamburg-South American service, which was waiting in the little port of San Luis de Maranhao. *Dresden* called her on the wireless and set a meeting place: Jericoacoara, a little inlet on the Brazilian coast, just west of the 40th meridian. *Corrientes* reached the rendezvous on the afternoon of August 8, and *Dresden* was already there. Coaling was done in a very leisurely fashion during the next two days, and then the cruiser and her supply ship again began to patrol.

In this period Captain von Lüdecke seemed most reluctant to strike when ships came in sight. *Dresden* was sighted by the British steamer *Dunstan*, and close enough were the two that the British recognized the German for what she was—yet von Lüdecke did not attack. The Brazilian steamer *Bahia* also sighted the *Dresden*, and since she had a wireless, she gave the world an accurate fix on the warship.

149

As if one collier was not enough at a time, on August 7 the steamer *Baden* arrived at Pernambuco, carrying 12,000 tons of good English coal. After several fruitless days of cruising off Cape San Roque, *Dresden* called up the *Baden*, by way of the Olinda wireless station near Pernambuco, and ordered her to rendezvous at the Rocas Islands, 240 miles north-northeast. On August 12 they met there, and on seeing the *Baden* Captain von Lüdecke decided he had discovered his permanent supply ship. She was clean and relatively new and she could make twelve knots. Besides this, the *Baden* had a wireless rig and its operators knew how to use it. He would keep *Baden* with him.

In spite of the heavy Atlantic swell on August 13 and 14 an attempt was made to coal from *Baden*, but the water was so rough *Dresden* could take aboard only 254 tons. While the coaling was attempted, the Brazilian lighthouse-keeper became curious about these ships and asked their names. Captain von Lüdecke evaded some questions and gave untruthful answers to others. His was the Swedish warship *Fylgia*, he said, carrying out some repairs to defective engines in the shadow of the rocks. Since Sweden was neutral and Brazil was neutral, there could be no complaint about the *Fylgia*.

But concerned about such curiosity, Captain von Lüdecke sent *Corrientes* into Pernambuco. Then out came the *Prussia*, another German supply ship. Unlike all the other cruisers, *Dresden* suffered from an oversupply of coal and other necessities, and there was a reason for it: at the outbreak of war, fifty-four German and Austrian ships lay in North Atlantic ports and these were made available to the German navy.

On August 14 the *Dresden* went to sea again, having turned over five sick crewmen to the steamer *Persia*, for landing at Cabedello. She sailed at nine o'clock that night, for the waters off Trinidad. Coming up from the south was the British freighter *Hyades*, carrying a cargo of corn. The freighter had

150

been stopped by HMS *Glasgow* farther south, and warned in a friendly way that the area around Pernambuco was dangerous. Even if it meant heading out to sea and adding many miles to the journey it would be a good idea to avoid the area of German cruiser operations. The warning was given on August 8, but the captain of the freighter did not heed it. He went into Pernambuco, and there he was again warned by the British consul. He came out. He reached a point at latitude 6 degrees south; longitude, 32 degrees 46 minutes west, and there he encountered the *Dresden*. Captain von Lüdecke decided to sink this enemy ship, and did so after transferring the crew to the *Prussia*. The next day *Dresden* stopped the British merchantman *Siamese Prince*, carrying merchandise from London to La Plata. Captain von Lüdecke took the position that this was neutral cargo, even if the bottom was enemy—and so *Siamese Prince* was allowed to pass on.

By this time British confidence in England's ability to ship goods across the seas was thoroughly restored. *Dresden* had quite lost a good chance to become a scourge of the Atlantic.

The *Prussia* was detached to take the British crew of *Hyades* into Rio de Janeiro—again showing Captain von Lüdecke's unfamiliarity with proper procedure for his own safety. He might have forced the *Siamese Prince* to take on the crew, thus giving far less information about his whereabouts. When the men of *Hyades* arrived in Rio de Janeiro, they, of course, went immediately to British authorities and told them everything they could remember about the German warship and their encounter. At least Captain von Lüdecke took the proper precaution of disguising his true course as he parted from *Prussia*.

Now came an incident which indicates the really remarkable resources available to *Dresden* in these early days of the war. Captain von Lüdecke steamed for the barren Brazilian island of Trinidada (not to be confused with Trinidad) which

151

lies some 580 miles east by south of Abrolhos Rocks. *Dresden* arrived at Trinidada on August 19, accompanied by *Baden*. Within three days a little fleet had assembled off the barren rocks. The freighter *Steiermark* from South Africa had come west. She was to meet the old gunboat *Eber* at the islands. Then too, up from Buenos Aires, pretending to be on her way to Togoland, came the German merchantman *Santa Isabel*, carrying forty bullocks, oil, coal bags, and other supplies. Also up came the liner *Sevilla*.

From among this squadron *Dresden* found most of the immediate needs of a warship, and after two days of loading she was ready to move out again to begin harrying the trade route that came up from the River Plate. Before he left the deserted islands, Captain von Lüdecke gave orders to the remainder of his fleet to strip the old-fashioned *Eber* of her armament and create in the fast passenger liner *Cap Trafalgar* an auxiliary cruiser or raider. *Cap Trafalgar* was then on her way north from the River Plate. Then von Lüdecke steamed off to the southwest looking for enemy merchant ships.

On August 26 the officer on watch in the crow's nest of the foremast reported smoke, and soon the *Dresden* had overhauled the British steamer *Holmwood*, bound from Newport to Bahia Blanca with a cargo of Welsh coal. Such a find would have delighted any of the other German cruisers at large in the world, but *Dresden* was so well supplied with coal that Captain von Lüdecke simply removed the crew, sent his boarding crew into the holds where they opened the sea cocks, and finally set time bombs in the holds. That same day *Dresden* sighted and stopped the steamer *Katherine Park*, another English ship, but one carrying a cargo for New York from Buenos Aires. Again, this was business involving neutrals, and Captain von Lüdecke contented himself with exacting promises about nonintervention and putting the British crew of *Holmwood* aboard this freighter.

The *Dresden* continued what was becoming a most un-distinguished cruise, particularly in view of her unique situation as best-supplied of all the German cruisers. On August 31 she reached Gill Bay (also known as the Gulf of St. George) about 800 miles down the slender tip of South America from the River Plate. Captain von Lüdecke was in cold waters now, so he sent the *Santa Isabel* through the Straits of Magellan to make arrangements for warm clothing for the crew and machinery to replace some of the worn-out parts of the *Dresden*.

What a difference this was from the situation in which *Leipzig* and other cruisers of the German East Asia Squadron found themselves!

The volunteers who had joined *Nürnberg* at Honolulu had a most difficult time finding uniforms, and had put them together out of the seconds and leftovers of the others of the crew. The officers and men of *Gneisenau* and *Scharnhorst* were very much concerned about their shortage of leather and cobbler's tools. Tools had been sent to them, but they had been mislaid at Ponape. All the time that the big cruisers were in the warm Pacific waters the men went barefoot, saving their shoes for the day when they would be needed. Among cruisers, *Dresden* lived the life of the "haves," most certainly.

Operating in these neutral waters, *Dresden* was able to make most effective use of her supply ships. The rules of war still held that a warship could enter one port of a given neutral nation only once in three months, and that then she could stay only twenty-four hours. No such rules governed the conduct of apparently innocent merchantmen, so Captain von Lüdecke was able to make very effective use of his supply ships. On September 4, when *Santa Isabel* arrived at Punta Arenas, she was able to make arrangements for the supplies *Dresden* wanted, and to communicate with the German Admiralty in Berlin. From that office came a wire ordering *Dresden* to get

153

together with the *Leipzig* and begin joint cruiser operations. It would be more than three weeks before the same message would be given to *Leipzig;* that time lag was one of the difficulties of the *Kreuzerkrieg* in these days of limited reception by ships' radios. *Dresden* knew at this point, however, that *Leipzig* was off the Mexican coast and that the next scene of operations would be the Pacific side of South America.

So *Dresden* rounded the southern tip of South America, and put into Orange Bay, off snow-covered Hoste Island, on the Pacific side of Cape Horn. So few ships braved the cold and windy seas of this region after the completion of the Panama Canal that it became the custom for seafarers to leave their calling cards at such places as Orange Bay, and when the men of *Dresden* were given shore liberty on this forsaken island, some of them found boards and rocks that had been decorated by previous sailors. They added their names and the name of their ship and the date, September 11, 1914, to the information of the others. But the "X was here" of the previous sailing men had all been put down in peacetime, and when the men got back to ship and the Captain discovered what they had done he was furious. He sent a work party back to shore to find the evidence and destroy it, and the party did the best it could to undo the dangerous work of their thoughtless companions. *Dresden* then sailed on for new adventures.

On September 12 the *Santa Isabel* returned to the side of the cruiser, with supplies and the messages from Berlin that would direct her future course. During the next four days *Dresden* remained in the cold, windswept, but landlocked harbor of Orange Bay, transshipping supplies and coal, and clothing men and ship for an ever harsher war.

On September 16 she left her anchorage, accompanied by the collier *Baden.* Two days later she sighted the British steamer *Ortega,* bound for England from Valparaiso. Captain von Lüdecke began to chase the fourteen-knot ship, confident of his ability to catch her, but the British captain had no desire to be caught and he undertook a desperate strategem. He headed for the coast and ran into Nelson's Strait below Hanover Island. This was uncharted water, dangerous for any oceangoing ship, and Captain von Lüdecke did not see any advantage in pursuing a single merchant ship into such danger. Captain D. R. Kinneir of the *Ortega* made his way safely into Smyth's Channel, and then to the Atlantic Ocean.

Dresden continued to move north. She coaled in the Gulf of Peñas, then steamed north and west to the island of Mas-a-Fuera without further action. There, on October 3, she was in touch with the Cruiser Squadron, and she learned of the plans of Admiral von Spee.

10

SEARCH AND DESTROY

FOR THE BRITISH ADMIRALTY, THE MONTH OF September was a month of worry, and the main objects of concern were those gadflies of war, the German cruisers.

Early in the month there had been some very thorough analyses made either at Whitehall or in the intelligence offices of the Admiralty, for as early as September 14 Admiral Cradock in the Americas had been warned that the *Scharnhorst* and *Gneisenau* would be coming to the Straits of Magellan or around the Cape. Since *Dresden* and *Karlsruhe* were known to be working on the east coast of the Americas, Admiral Cradock was instructed to leave a sufficient force there to deal with the two German cruisers, and then to concentrate his squadron in the south, using the Falkland Islands as his base. He was to have the old battleship *Canopus*, as well as the *Defence*. Until they came, he was to keep one cruiser with his flagship, for protection. After the reinforcements arrived, he was to begin searching the Straits of Magellan for the enemy.

"As soon as you have superior force," said the order, "search the Magellan Straits with squadron, being ready to return and cover the River Plate, or, according to information, search north as far as Valparaiso, break up the German trade, and destroy the German cruisers."

Simple and clear. Find and destroy the enemy.

Unfortunately, the very day that the above order was given to Admiral Cradock, the Admiralty learned of Admiral von Spee's appearance at Samoa, and of *Emden's* destructive foray into the Bay of Bengal (*Emden* had then taken six prizes). Nobody told Admiral Cradock directly, but the movement of *Defence* was stopped, and he would have to be content with *Canopus*, which (the Admiralty admitted) could only make seventeen knots as against a half dozen more for von Spee's slowest warship.

On September 16 a thoroughly rattled Admiralty wirelessed Admiral Cradock, saying that the appearance at Samoa had changed everything. The cruisers *Hampshire* and *Yarmouth* would work down the west coast of South America. Two cruisers and an auxiliary should be enough to search the Magellan Straits, because it was quite apparent that Admiral von Spee was not there.

Admiral Cradock was delayed until September 22 by bad weather. Then he sent *Glasgow* and *Monmouth* to search the straits, and disposed of the rest of his squadron at various points around the coastal areas.

That very day the admiral learned the whereabouts of *Dresden*, when Captain Kinneir reported his narrow escape through the uncharted Nelson Straits. Admiral Cradock then began a sweep south with his flagship *Good Hope*, the cruiser *Monmouth*, the light cruiser *Glasgow*, and the *Otranto*. It was established what had happened: the ever-courteous Captain

157

von Lüdecke had fired two rounds of blank at the *Ortega*, and then had ceased the chase, as was quite proper under international law, when the British ship reached the three-mile limit and entered Chilean waters.

Admiral Cradock learned that he would not have *Defence*, but there was nothing he could do about that. He began to believe that if the German East Asia Squadron was not on the west coast, it was certainly coming that way, and he laid his plans accordingly. *Good Hope* entered Orange Bay after rounding Cape Horn, and there an investigating party discovered one of the boards on which the seamen of *Dresden* had written their names and the date. To the British it seemed quite likely that *Dresden* was poking around, attempting to establish an island base for the Cruiser Squadron.

Admiral Cradock also became aware of much of the German freighter activity on the west coast of South America. From London the Admiralty misread this business of the supply ships and jumped to the conclusion that the Germans were developing a sudden brisk trade with Chile.

At Punta Arenas on September 28, Admiral Cradock called on the British consul, and learned that the Germans had sent *Santa Isabel* into that port from Orange Bay. British intelligence reports indicated that several German seamen had been talking, and had let it slip that the German major base was to be at Orange Bay. This information tied in very neatly with the careless "calling card" left by the *Dresden* there. The consul told how one big German merchant ship had sailed recently with a cargo of livestock and fresh provisions and had returned a few days later, empty. Admiral Cradock's staff could see visions of Admiral von Spee sitting down to roast beef dinners.

But where? Admiral von Spee had disappeared again after the Tahiti raid.

Orange Bay, of course, said all the intelligence reports.

On the night of September 28, Admiral Cradock made it a point to inform the Chilean admiral at Punta Arenas that he was heading for Valparaiso. Then, after midnight, he brought the squadron out of harbor running without lights, and turned in the exact opposite direction, headed for Cockburn Channel, uncharted since 1820, trading the risk of a lost ship for the advantage of surprise. They traveled through heavy weather, through snow storms, in waters filled with sharp rocks and tricky currents. They planned their voyage so as to arrive at daybreak on September 30 off Orange Bay. Admiral Cradock did not really believe the German flagship and *Gneisenau* would be here, but he did think it quite likely that he would trap *Dresden, Leipzig, Nürnberg*, and perhaps a double handful of supply ships.

Admiral Cradock's plan was very simple, but very effective. He disposed his ships so they covered every entrance to Orange Bay, and, then, at a signal, they rushed in. There was only one missing element in their surprise attack: the enemy.

The bay was empty.

11

TWO SQUADRONS PREPARE

WHEN HE LEFT TAHITIAN WATERS, ADMIRAL VON
Spee felt the need for a respite from constant cruising. Ships
and men needed attention and he wanted time to assess his
situation and consider the future. Course was set for the
French-owned Marquesas Islands where *Nürnberg* had led
the supply train to safety, while the big cruisers made their
raid.

Scharnhorst and *Gneisenau* arrived on September 26 and
headed for Controleur Bay on the south side of Nuku Hiva
Island. Their first task was the nastiest—the replacement of
the coal in their emptying bunkers. Nuku Hiva was not the
most satisfactory of coaling stations, for the long ocean swell
caught them and bothered them all during the operation. But
soon enough it was done, and more pleasant work could be
enjoyed. On the night that Admiral Cradock and his staff
officers were shivering in the chartroom of *Good Hope* amid
the glaciers of Cockburn Channel's tiny islands, Admiral von

Spee and his staff sat down to a groaning table, loaded with Dutch cheeses, sausages, fresh meat, yams, and fresh fruits. The coaling was finished for the moment. The admiral had announced the need to give the men of the ships shore leave and a rest from routine. It was, in other words, the beginning of a holiday for the Squadron. As far as the admiral was concerned, it was as pleasant a day as he had enjoyed since the beginning of the war. Both his naval sons were with him at dinner—Otto and Heinrich—Otto visiting from the *Nürnberg* and Heinrich from the *Gneisenau*.

Early the next morning, the admiral sat down at his desk to write a letter home to his wife. Otto would be with him again at lunch that day, he said comfortingly. Heinrich could not be there. The admiral had just sent the *Gneisenau* on a special mission, to seize the government establishment at Hiwaoa, and take the French money her officers found there. *Nürnberg* had turned over the money taken from Fanning Island, but that had been used to buy provisions at Bora Bora, and the admiral wanted to make more purchases. The way to get the money was to seize it from his enemy—the French government. In that way he could pay in cash to the French and other citizens whose provisions he preempted, and it could never be said that the German Squadron consisted of corsairs.

While *Gneisenau* traveled to Hiwaoa, the officers and men of *Scharnhorst* began some resupply work on a very leisurely basis, with the war watches released. In the Marquesas were two branches of the trading house of Scharf and Kayser, an old Hamburg South Seas firm. Their warehouses had been locked up by the French at the beginning of the war and the German managers and their families had been taken to Tahiti for internment. The *Scharnhorst*'s men unlocked the doors of the warehouse at Anne-Marie Port, and began reprovisioning themselves from the stores. *Gneisenau* would take what she

161

wanted at the other branch, on Hiwaoa. All of the smaller ships were in better state than the two big cruisers, which had been longest at sea without refitting.

Three months away from supply bases had taken their toll of the niceties of naval life. Aside from the shortage of shoes, there were shortages of nearly all other basic materials of civilized life. After so much coaling, and so many scrubbings of the decks, the pails and brushes were quite worn out. Brushes were improvised from rags. Pails were made from oil barrels cut in two and zinc boxes in which butter had been stored. They ran quite out of soap, and used sand and soda for personal scrubbing. The linoleum covers tore off the deck with the coaling, and they walked on steel plates. They ran out of matches, and an engineer invented an electric cigar lighter which was hung in the wardroom.

Now all these needs were met again from the stores of the German traders. They also secured wine, condensed milk, sugar, tobacco, tinned sardines, tinned vegetables, needles, cloth, and even a sewing machine. They did not get some purely naval supplies: fenders to replace those that had quite worn out in the coaling. But by this time the ships did not really need fenders, for the seamen in necessity had invented new fenders that worked much better than the old and lasted much longer. These were made of old hawsers, unstrung and wound into balls, then suspended from chains. Of course not every problem could be solved so neatly, but the Squadron was in as good shape as might be expected for ships long overdue at drydock.

While the *Scharnhorst* gobbled up supplies that suddenly seemed luxurious, the *Gneisenau* was off on her special duty. After the admiral's dinner on the night of September 30, *Gneisenau* sailed in the gathering darkness. The next day she was rounding the southern point of Hiwaoa, decks cleared for action, coming in deliberately like a soldier entering a seemingly deserted street in an embattled village.

The honor of leading the boarding party belonged to *Korvettenkapitän* Pochhammer, *Gneisenau's* first officer. He dressed in a clean suit of summer whites—epaulets on the shoulders—armed himself with pistol and cutlass, and entered the cutter. Captain Maerker supervised the conning of the ship into the bay that led to a stairway hewn in rock. Above was lined the town along the slopes of the volcanic island.

First Officer Pochhammer ordered the men into their boats, and the captain ordered them launched before anchoring. They swept in to shore, Pochhammer's armed cutter first.

It seemed an easy landing, and yet when they came up to the hand-hewn steps, in the swell, the cutter danced up and down, never quite making it to the point where Pochhammer thought he could jump onto the slippery rock without falling back into the sea. Up and down they slid, back and forth they worked. A large crowd of civilians gathered at the top of the stairs and giggled. Then a French gendarme saw the plight of the landing party and rushed down the stairs to give First Officer Pochhammer a hand, and to assist him onto the dry land of the Marquesas.

Pochhammer suddenly realized that he was fraternizing with the enemy, and he stiffened. The gendarme was immediately surrounded by stern-faced German troops with fixed bayonets, and he was ordered to take *Korvettenkapitän* Pochhammer to his leader.

A little puzzled at the strange turn of events, the gendarme led them across a short cut, crossing a small tongue of land that took them into the second of two bays (they had landed in the wrong bay). They passed the police station and stopped to put a guard on the safe there, so the French could not hide the money.

The column moved on to the house of the governor of

the island, a medical doctor by profession. First Officer Poch-hammer led his men up the road, past the tall hedge that surrounded the governor's house, up the stairs, across the wide veranda, and toward the front door. As he walked across the veranda, the governor appeared, obviously having just struggled into his official uniform, complete with boots and spurs.

In his direct German way *Korvettenkapitän* Pochhammer warned the governor that resistance would be useless. He intended to seize everything of value that belonged to the government, and then to use those assets to pay private citizens for the supplies the *Gneisenau* needed.

They all returned to the police station and found the assistant paymaster of the *Gneisenau* suspiciously counting the money. It was an interesting collection. Among the silver were some coins of the République Française, some of the days when Napoleon was first consul, and some from Napoleon's Imperial period. There was also money left over from the days of the Kingdom. Altogether there was 10,000 francs plus a number of postage stamps and postal money orders, all of which were seized.

The governor was then invited—not to say, urged but forcibly invited—to pay a call on Captain Maerker on the *Gneisenau*. Trembling, sure that he was going to be butchered by the deadly Boche, the governor went up the rope ladder onto the quarter-deck, and was immensely pleased to be given a drink in the captain's cabin instead of roasted alive.

The afternoon was given over to the stripping of the Scharf and Kayser warehouse. The provisions were much the same as those found on the other island. More interesting to the officers of the *Gneisenau* was the offer of the governor, once his fears had been allayed by a few glasses, to stage a pig hunt for them. These were not wild pigs but domestic pigs which were allowed to run loose until needed for the table. So the afternoon was spent searching out pigs and loading them into sties in the impromptu barnyard that was being constructed on deck. Pigs, pigs, pigs. Large pigs and small pigs. Huge pigs and baby black pigs. Fat pigs and lean pigs. Snorting pigs and thoughtful pigs. All of them came, dozens of them, and they soon filled the sties, oinking and squealing and trying to root under the boards into the hardness of the steel deck.

The pigs joined hens that clucked and skittered and pigeons that clattered and fluttered, but the pigs had it all when it came to making noise. Some of them even leaped up on the sides of their sty and tried to drown themselves in the Pacific.

In the end, much of the pig hunt had actually been carried out by the torpedo room personnel and the engineers, although the actual carrying of pigs slung on poles and the loading into the cargo nets was done by the natives with naval supervision. The next day the governor suggested a cattle roundup. The cattle belonged to the Scharf and Kayser manager who lived on the outskirts of the town. The trader was in jail, but his native wife was there on the premises, and she supervised the roundup in a fenced park. The roundup, from the military point of view, was supervised by the deck division of the ship, and several young officers were involved. The officer in charge decided that he would lead the animals away, and when the gate was opened, with a mighty lunge the lead animal broke loose, which brought on an eight-cow stampede. Finally the cattle were recaptured and a squad of men was assigned to each animal to get it back to the *Gneisenau*. The entire party was accompanied by armed guards, because the island teacher had taken to the bush with natives and was reputedly armed to the teeth, seeking an opportunity to avenge the French nation's honor.

Even with all this armament and hardware and personnel,

one brave cow did escape and made her way into the bush. She was a fortunate beast indeed, because on arrival at the landing stage, the butchers were waiting with their long knives, and the other seven were slaughtered and their corpses taken for hanging in the *Gneisenau's* refrigeration chambers.

On October 2 the *Gneisenau* made ready; in the evening she left the harbor, beginning her return to *Scharnhorst.*

The *Holsatia* and the *Ahlers,* having been emptied of coal, were sent to Honolulu to seek their own fates, either to become interned for the duration of the war or to work their way to some German port. They carried the mail from the Squadron, including letters from the admiral to his wife, in which his major personal complaint concerned the loss of the Chinese cooks and laundrymen. She ought to be there, said the admiral, to watch them chasing chickens and wild livestock across the decks. . . .

On October 2 the Squadron had not waited for *Gneisenau,* but had steamed away from the Marquesas, with orders to the big cruiser to intersect their course a few miles to the east. The *Titania* had been sent ahead to Easter Island, their next destination, in order to scout. She was an ideal vessel for the purpose because she had very much the appearance of an ordinary freighter, and yet she was fast enough to outrun many of the warships in these seas. Following her, then, came the main squadron, consisting of the flagship, the *Nürnberg,* and the freighters *Yorck* and *Göttingen.* It was not a large train, but the admiral had sent messages to Berlin to send coalers to him later: he planned to be at Easter Island until October 25. He would go then to the Juan Fernández rendezvous and would remain there until November 5. The wireless messages crackled across the world, and the provisioning arrangements were gotten under way almost as soon as the ships were.

Leipzig and *Dresden* were still moving about on the

Pacific side of South America. *Leipzig* was having her troubles. On October 2 she left her haven in the Galápagos and headed southward. She coaled, and then the bunkers of *Amasis,* her tender, had to be filled from those of *Abyssinia.* In the process a coaling net broke and a load of coal fell thirty feet onto a torpedoman, breaking both his legs. Such accidents were not uncommon. First officer Pochhammer of the *Gneisenau* was incapacitated for several days after he tripped and fell into a coal bunker during the filthy process of refueling.

On the night of October 3, *Scharnhorst* managed to make radio contact with *Dresden* at the remarkable distance of 3500 miles, and immediately Admiral von Spee made arrangements to call his light cruisers to him. *Dresden* was in touch with *Leipzig,* and the orders to move to Easter Island and join the Squadron were transmitted. On October 4 *Scharnhorst* sent a coded message to *Dresden,* giving some details of the plan, and noting that the objective of the East Asia Squadron was now the west coast of South America.

This message was intercepted by Admiral Cradock's wireless operators on the *Good Hope* and was passed to the British Admiralty in London for possible decoding. The German naval code was broken, it was decoded, and the British had a good idea of what they ought to expect.

German intelligence was equally as effective, although the Germans had not broken the British code. *Dresden* reported the presence of Admiral Cradock's squadron and its strength—but Admiral von Spee had little reason to fear that squadron since he outgunned it, and he reasoned shrewdly that the British would head up the west coast of South America to try to break off the supply line.

Having been in what seemed to be personal contact with the *Dresden* through that unfortunate signboard left by the crew, Admiral Cradock felt very much the German presence in the area, and although the British squadron routed a nonappearing enemy at the first battle of Orange Bay and then dispersed for coaling, the admiral kept Orange Bay on his mind.

Glasgow was sent to the Falklands to coal, and arrived at Port Edgar at 9:30 in the morning. Here Intelligence Officer Lloyd Hirst was sent on a mission that gave some indication of the difficulties of carrying on a sea campaign in the gusty cold waters of southern South America. He was ordered casually to find his way to Fox Bay settlement and try to get into communication with the governor of the islands, to see if he could secure intelligence about the movement of the Germans. He was also to secure fresh mutton for the fleet.

Hirst dressed as warmly as he could for the occasion— short jacket and macintosh, puttees and shooting boots, gauntlet gloves and a heavy jersey—but this was scarcely Arctic clothing and the land to which he was heading was very nearly the Antarctic.

First he crossed over to *Monmouth*, hoping that the larger ship's steam launch would take him into shore. The launch had broken down so he was an hour and a half waiting for its repair. Then, when the launch approached shore just before eleven o'clock in the morning, the water was too shallow, so Intelligence Officer Hirst had to wade. (The cadet in charge of the boat had forgotten to unship his rudder in the shallow water and she ran aground.)

At 1100 hours, thoroughly soaked, Hirst set out on land, the wind behind him, fortunately, and a little sun showing through the lightly falling snow.

The ground was cold and boggy, so Hirst struck off along the hillside to his left, keeping his bearings by use of a pocket compass.

"Splendid keen air for walking," he had said in the beginning.

But soon the snow increased and he had had to put his head down and follow a sheep trail.

At 12:30, when the snow cleared, he found himself above Fox Bay. He lit a brush fire to warn the inhabitants that he was coming and sat down and drank a little from a flask and ate sandwiches. Behind him he could see *Monmouth*'s masts above the barren ground. The hillside was entirely covered with snow, but a handful of sheep were wandering about on the low ground.

He made his way to the settlement, a cluster of red-roofed houses on the shore of Fox Bay. There he frightened a shepherd's family with his uniform, but he managed to find the manager of the place, a Mr. Robson.

There was no way of getting in touch with the governor. There was no telephone. A wireless-telegraph installation had been scheduled by the Admiralty to be installed in this harbor, but it had not gone beyond the planning boards.

The next problem was to get sheep to the squadron. Since all the able-bodied men had enlisted and gone to Port Stanley, this was to be quite a chore, but the manager said he could find men from other settlements, and Hirst took a cutter run by an outboard motor across the mile of the inlet to the other settlement, while horses were rounded up for his return journey to his ship.

As they crossed the inlet it was sleeting and the wind was acting up. On the other side they found a local landowner who was recovering from a broken leg, and whose house had just burned down. The settlers were out collecting penguin eggs, he said, so their journey was useless. On the return trip the outboard motor broke down, and the officer and his guide had to row back in the face of the wind, pelted by sleet. One mile it was, but it seemed much farther.

It was 1630 hours, and Intelligence Officer Hirst had been told to return by dark, which meant not later than 1830 even in this beginning of spring in October. Now they must round up the sheep on horseback, with dogs, which they did in an hour, collecting forty-five animals.

Intelligence Officer Hirst then rode ahead to find a fenced-in corral for the sheep, and when he did find one on the bank of the hill, he lit a large brush fire and made Morse signals asking for two working boats and lashings for the sheep, which would have to be shipped alive, seeing the time of day.

It had been snowing steadily, but the snow stopped as night fell and the cold moon came out to light the bleak shore. The boats did not know the way, so he must ride down to the shore and pilot them, while his shepherd from the other bay came along to herd the sheep with his dogs. The creek was sandy, and the steersman remembered to pull up his rudder in time, but the steam cutter had to be left fifty yards out in the harbor, so only one boat could come in, a cutter under the charge of a fifteen-year-old naval cadet.

By this time it was pitch dark. The forty-five sheep were penned inside the kitchen garden of an old hut. Three large brush fires were lighted so the men could see what they were doing. Intelligence Officer Hirst and two Falkland Islanders wrestled the sheep, the young cadet hogtied them, and the sailors stood around the fence yelling like banshees to keep the sheep from breaking out through the rotten stakes. One old ram made a determined charge, leaped over the fence, bowled over a bluejacket, and escaped into the night to save his fleece. But the other forty-four sheep were safe in hand by eleven o'clock that night. Then they must be carried to the boats and delivered to the ships. The whaleboat grounded with the weight and the men had to get out and wade waist-deep in the frigid water, to the point where the boat would float again—just where the steam pinnace was located. The sheep averaged about 120 pounds each, but in twenty minutes

170

in this cold water they were all aboard the boats, and at 11:45 they had been delivered to the *Monmouth*. Intelligence Officer Hirst drank a hot toddy, changed his socks, and reported on his walk of twelve miles, ride of fifteen miles, row of one mile, and fourteen hours spent wet to the waist.

On the following day the young officers of the *Monmouth* were landed to shoot geese. The men proved to be abominably lazy; they stayed down on the shore, where they shot only inedible kelp geese instead of climbing a mile or two where they could have shot the tender upland geese. Both ships were awaiting the return of *Good Hope* from her venture around Orange Bay.

When the ships left the Falklands on October 3, the weather was so rotten that they made no headway for an hour. They were ordered to patrol between Punta Arenas and Valparaiso—just as Admiral von Spee suspected, because, as the officers of the *Glasgow* said, "some fool has told the Admiralty" that the German trade was reviving. They saw nothing and were very pleased that they did not see *Scharnhorst* and *Gneisenau*, because the Germans would have made short work of the lighter ships.

On October 5 Admiral Cradock again suspected that the Germans were in Orange Bay, so he organized another foray there. Through a westerly gale the ships headed for the harbor, the weather so severe that they could not have manned their guns even if they had found the Germans. Two days later they reached Orange Bay. Nothing stirred.

The chase of the Germans became a very serious matter to the British admiral and his ships, for the decoding of the German message had shown that the Germans were lurking somewhere nearby, making ready to strike.

In the seven-day search that followed the "Second Battle of Orange Bay," they hunted in Tierra del Fuego, among the Chilean islands, where they established a secret coaling base,

171

and then went to Coronel, up the coast, all but *Good Hope,* which stayed at Falklands. *Monmouth* chased a French ship for a few hours on October 13, and they guarded Coronel harbor so that two German auxiliaries could not escape at least for a few days.

The British were very much annoyed by the attitude of the Chileans, for far too many of them were pro-German. On the night of October 14 the Chilean wireless stations had told the world (quite against neutrality rules) that the British were coming in. The British squadron complained to the Chilean admiral, who replied that he could not trust his operators with ciphers because they always sold them, so he sent almost all messages in the clear.

So the hunt for the German East Asia Squadron stepped up.

As the search activity increased, Admiral von Spee and his ships were heading at ten knots, or as close as they could keep to that economical speed, across the 2000 miles that separate the Marquesas and Easter Island, where they would meet the *Dresden* and the *Leipzig.* They crossed the Tropic of Capricorn on October 9, at longitude 118 degrees west, and almost immediately began to feel the cold to which they were so unaccustomed after two and a half months in the Tropics.

Now a new problem beset the fleet, apparently a result of the liberty given the men in the Marquesas: dysentery. Immediately the surgeons went to work to alleviate the epedemic, dosing the men, isolating the sickest, and enforcing strict sanitary rules.

The German fleet arrived at Easter Island on October 12, the *Dresden* coming in first to take a look around and see that all was well before the admiral would take the chance of bringing in his other ships. All *was* well, and the train anchored.

The island chosen by Admiral von Spee for this as-

172

sembling of his forces was a deserted spot a thousand miles from the Chilean coast, although belonging to that country. It was, in other words, another piece of neutral territory, and according to the neutrality rules Admiral von Spee should have stayed there for only twenty-four hours. He had no intention of abiding by those rules, however.

This island had been discovered by the Dutch Admiral Roggeveen on Easter Sunday, 1722, and that it how it got its name. It is best known to the Western world for its strange idols, some of them thirty feet high, which dot the island. There is neither timber nor brushwood on the land, so the idols stick out even more visibly than they might otherwise.

For Admiral von Spee's purposes the island was ideal. It was shaped like a triangle, thirteen miles long at the base, rising suddenly out of the depths of the Pacific. There was no regular traffic with South America, except for an occasional official visit by Chilean authorities. In 1914 the only connection was by a sailing schooner that called occasionally at the island. The schooner belonged to a Merlet company, which leased part of the island and operated a ranch there. When the German East Asia Squadron arrived in October 1914, the total population of the island consisted of a Mr. Edmunds, the English ranch manager; a German tobacco planter; a Mrs. Routledge, who had come to the island for scientific study of the idols, and her assistant; and 250 Polynesian natives. First in came *Titania*, then *Scharnhorst, Gneisenau, Nürnberg,* and the two steamers with *Dresden.* Two days later in came *Leipzig* and more steamers. Altogether in the harbor there were six steamers and six ships of the German navy—quite a handful for an island whose last visiting ship had been the schooner *El Dorado,* a lumber ship bound between Oregon's Columbia River and Chile which had suddenly sprung a leak. That visit had occurred in June 1913.

The Easter Islanders knew nothing about the war, and

173

Admiral von Spee did not enlighten them. The Squadron was obviously a squadron, and what could be more normal than that it might be cruising from the China Station to Valparaiso on a friendship mission? That tale was the admiral's contribution to friendship. There was no disbelief. Mrs. Routledge, an Englishwoman, had no hesitation about handing the Germans letters to post for her in Valparaiso (and all but one eventually reached their destinations). Mr. Edmunds, the rancher, was quite willing to sell meat and supplies to the Germans, and to take their check.

Where the men had enjoyed their stay at the Marquesas, however, the stay at Easter Island was miserable. All day long the southwesterly swell attacked the ships, making them roll incessantly, and impeding the simple processes of coaling and supply loading until they became dangerous to life and limb. The officers had the chance of moving from ship to ship. First Officer Pochhammer of the *Gneisenau* renewed acquaintance with his young brother-in-law, wireless officer of the *Dresden*, but for the men there was no time for play, nor did the weather lend itself to relaxation. Bumboats came by from the shore, bearing natives who seemed to the seamen to be exceedingly dirty, and in Spanish they inquired if the sailors wanted any eggs for their mess. The sailors did, and they bought eggs and hens from the natives, but except for the few who went ashore on duty this was the extent of the contact.

The *Yorck* and the *Göttingen* had come with the two heavy cruisers as coalers. The *Baden* had been *Dresden*'s faithful companion. *Leipzig* had picked up the freighters *Anubis* and *Karnak* in Chilean waters and *Amasis* had run in and replenished her supply of coal. For the first time since the war began, the ships had no shortage of fuel. It was a good feeling for the admiral.

On the very day of their arrival Admiral von Spee had

some bad news to offset all the good. One of the colliers, *Baden*, tried to come alongside *Nürnberg* to coal, and the captain misjudged his distance in the rough water, smashed into the port side of the cruiser just ahead of the stern, and bent one blade of her port propeller, ruining the torque and making the propeller useless. When the accident was reported to the admiral he ordered repairs to begin at once—which meant *Nürnberg* must be canted over 15 degrees to starboard, and divers from *Scharnhorst* and *Gneisenau* must go below and try to straighten out the bent blade.

On the morning of October 15 a shore party landed on Easter Island. It consisted of the admiral and his son Otto, who were going ashore to indulge their interest in natural history. They wanted to photograph and examine the strange idols and several massive lava buildings made of blocks laid together without mortar.

Others going ashore that day were doing so for more mundane reasons. Every butcher from every ship in the Squadron went ashore, and they were accompanied by the first officers of the ships and by the Squadron paymaster, *Marine-Stabszahlmeister* Braun, who would pay for all the provisions they might secure that day.

It was a miserable day. The rain came down in buckets, and had the admiral not been so enthusiastic a student of the world around him, he would never have gone on his shore junket. The butchers in their oilskins had no recourse, but they were pleased enough, rain or not, to be away from the tossing of the harbor for a few hours.

Now for several days the "mozos" of the ranch rounded up beef and sheep. A miniature slaughterhouse was set up on shore and the boats began moving regularly from shore to the ships, carrying quarters of beef and sides of mutton for hanging in the refrigerators.

In the beginning of their stay there occurred one worrisome incident; it came on the second night of *Gneisenau's* stay. She had coaled and a large heap of coal had been left on deck. The boats were over the side, on their mission of seeking and carrying supplies for the holds. One boat came alongside loaded with sacks of flour, just as darkness fell. The crew was ready to unload, when fires were sighted on the island and a strange wireless set was heard in the radio room. The captain ordered the flour loaded immediately, so they could get under way, and it was picked up as quickly as the donkey engine and the cargo hoists could work it, and flung on deck for later disposition. It was flung, unfortunately, on top of the coal pile, which made a very interesting batch of flour—as the cooks discovered after the boats had been waved away. *Gneisenau* had rushed out to sea with the crew at action stations, and it had been found to be a complete misreading of innocent intentions.

The weather continued foul. On October 15 it was so rough in the harbor that *Gneisenau* moved to the southern coast and anchored behind a sharp tongue of volcanic rock which gave her some protection. At best, however, the rolling was so intense that her lower decks shipped water on two out of three waves and the boats required hoisting and extra security lest they be bashed to pieces.

The bad weather did not help anything below, particularly in the lazarettos and more sumptuous hospital quarters, depending on the ship involved. The sick grew sicker. Among the ships that had visited the Marquesas, where the dystentery outbreak had come, there were several deaths, among them that of Chief Gunner Kraft of the *Gneisenau*, who became the Squadron's first casualty.

The body was removed from the ship's hospital, taking care that the other seriously ill men did not see it and lose heart. The corpse was taken below, sewn up in sailcloth, and weighted with irons at the feet. It was then taken on deck

176

and covered with the German flag. The ship's first division stood at attention (for this had been Chief Gunner Kraft's own division) while the body was carried along the starboard side of the ship to the stern. There stood Captain Maerker and all the officers. The captain read the service for the burial of the dead at sea, and then he saluted the body while the boatswain piped it overboard, into the boat that had been brought alongside the anchored *Gneisenau.*

The Number 1 steam pinnace led the convoy that carried Chief Gunner Kraft to his watery grave, towing the bier in the rowing boat. In command of the funeral boat was the ship's gunnery officer, *Kapitänleutnant* Johann Busch, who wanted to pay this homage to the petty officer who was responsible for the important 8.2-inch guns of the forward starboard casemate. The little convoy circled gently around the *Gneisenau* and then headed out for the depths of the sea, while the crew remained on board on the starboard rails, from quarter-deck to stern, and the flags dipped to half-mast and remained there.

Outside the roadstead, the chaplain blessed the body and said the religious services. The men belonging to Kraft's battery fired the last salute by rifle—three sharp volleys—and the body was committed to the sea.

It was a sobering experience for every man on the *Gneisenau.* Suddenly the meaning of war took hold and that night few slept without remembering the death of Chief Gunner Kraft, and hoping or praying that they would not be forced to join him before many nights were over.

The lesson was repeated the next day, when another sailor died, but it had not the same significance. The men did the honors again a little less carefully, a little less sorrowfully. A second death is never so frightening as the first, and on the night after Chief Gunner Kraft's funeral every man on the *Gneisenau* had made some kind of peace with himself.

177

For another reason, too, the death of the second man did not distress the sailors of the *Gneisenau*: they were being kept too busy. The admiral was eager to be about his business, which was to carry out *Kreuzerkrieg* against the enemy, and he wanted to find and destroy the Cradock squadron if he could, before the British sent strong reinforcements to the region.

From the admiral's point of view, the unfortunate fact was that even as he prepared to move onto the western coast of South America, the superior naval strength of the British was being brought slowly to bear against him.

Acting on his intelligence and on the driving hunch that had been born by seeing the *Dresden's* "calling card," Admiral Cradock had suggested that Admiral von Spee's Squadron was assembling at some point off the coast and that it must be the sole objective of the British western Pacific warships. The danger was that Admiral von Spee might get into the Atlantic, where he could wreak far more havoc than in the Pacific. Cradock suggested that if the British squadron was sent up the Chilean coast, as originally ordered, this danger was extremely great.

On October 14, the day that *Leipzig* arrived at Easter Island and the German East Asia Squadron was reunited for the first time in nearly a year, the British Admiralty wirelessed Admiral Cradock that he was to take *Good Hope, Canopus, Monmouth, Glasgow,* and *Otranto* for operations on the American west coast. The message was not very helpful. It would take Cradock some time to assemble his force as a unit. Nor was there any mention as to whether he was to concentrate and search for the Germans or to follow his original orders. He had hoped to be given a larger force, and then to concentrate at the Falklands. But he was told that Rear Admiral Archibald Stoddart was being sent out in the *Carnarvon* to Montevideo, where he was to gather up the *Cornwall* and *Bristol,* the auxiliary cruisers *Macedonia* and *Orama,* and

178

where the *Defence* would be sent, to join Stoddart and not Cradock.

Admiral Cradock faced two difficulties: pulling his far-flung force together in a hurry and the presence in his fighting group of the lame-duck battleship *Canopus*. She really had no business being anything but a guard ship. The Admiralty in London possessed a highly inflated opinion of the value of the old *Canopus* as a ship of war. Her performance, in fact, was indicated by what happened to her in October, after the Admiralty's new orders were issued. She was supposed to arrive in the Falkland Islands on October 15, and for a ship capable of seventeen knots it was no great task for her to arrive there from the River Plate area where she had been left as guard ship by Admiral Cradock. But instead of arriving on October 15, she was slowed to the point of exhaustion by bad weather, and she did not come in until the night of October 18. Then she was in such poor condition that three days were needed for an overhaul before she was ready for sea again. She was not making seventeen knots at all, but more like twelve knots even under the best of conditions, and her poor steaming capability was neither understood nor accepted by the Admiralty in London. This negative attitude was Admiral Cradock's special cross, because the Admiralty took the position that he had a strong asset in *Canopus*, when actually he had a heavy liability. He warned the Admiralty that as long as he had *Canopus* with him his squadron could not be expected to make a speed of more than twelve knots. Then he set out to keep Admiral von Spee from reaching the Atlantic, if it was in his power to do so.

On October 18 the Germans made preparations for sailing. The English cattle rancher was paid off for his animals. The *Nürnberg*'s repairs were completed, and for the first time in nearly a week she could be righted from the crazy angle that made every moment aboard her seem like a trip through

179

an amusement park crazy house. A last few live animals were loaded aboard the warships, the emptied colliers were detached and sent to Chilean ports to fill up their bunkers again, and the Squadron set out in the afternoon for the Juan Fernández Islands, 1500 miles away.

12

THE BATTLE OF CORONEL

ADMIRAL VON SPEE WAS WEARY. IT HAD BEEN A
trying voyage thus far and he had little hope of ultimate victory, for his position, however well he might exploit it, was
ultimately regulated by the great material differences between
the British and German naval forces. In his messages and in
the diaries of his men appears a note of *Gotterdämmerung*.
The officers, particularly, exhibited a resentment against their
English cousins ("perfidious Albion") for joining what could
have been "so nice a little war" against the Russians or even
the Russians and the French.

The British gathered that the admiral was coming to the
west coast of the Americas seeking battle, and he was aware
of the search for his squadron by Admiral Cradock's force.

"It appears an English squadron comes to do battle," he
wrote home to his countess, "so I hope and trust in God for
victory. It will not be easy."

On October 22 the birthday of the Empress was observed

181

at sea by a special dress inspection of the crews, an address by the admiral aboard *Scharnhorst*, addresses by the captains of the other vessels, and wine in the officers' mess and beer for the men, plus fresh meat and puddings for all.

"It was with a feeling of deep respect that our thoughts turned toward the mother of the country, who had herself sent six sons to the battle, and we dwelt on the example which she must be giving, in these terrible times, to German women; consoling them, healing their wounds, and devoting herself entirely to the country's service." So wrote the gloomy Hans Pochhammer, first officer of the *Gneisenau*, in words so serious as to be ludicrous had he not been so sincere.

As the Germans celebrated their Queen Mother's birthday the British squadron of Admiral Cradock was setting out to round the Horn, leaving *Canopus* to make her way through the easier Straits of Magellan. Admiral Cradock was certain that she was fit only to guard colliers and escort convoys. He asked for the *Defence* to be sent to him, as was originally planned, but his message was mutilated in transmission and he never got the ship. The Admiralty believed it knew better than Cradock how to conduct the strategy of the war.

The telegram he received read: DEFENCE IS TO REMAIN ON THE EAST COAST UNDER ORDERS OF STODDART. THIS WILL LEAVE SUFFICIENT FORCE ON EACH SIDE IN CASE THE HOSTILE CRUISERS APPEAR THERE ON THE TRADE ROUTES. . . .

The British squadron jolted through the rough seas around the Horn, as the Germans made the far easier trip eastward to Mas-a-Fuera in the Juan Fernández group, yet the states of mind of the two squadrons were much the same— gloomy as the weather and the seas that leaped upon the decks of their ships and drenched the watches, chilling them to the bone.

The British had more reason at the moment for gloomy mien; their officers on the scene knew what they were facing.

Admiral von Spee did not know what lay ahead, and the Admiralty in London did not seem to understand the situation at all, particularly Winston Churchill, who kept referring to the *Canopus* as if she were a fighting bulldog instead of an elderly brood bitch.

The gloom of the British was based on their knowledge of their own capabilities. *Good Hope* was the largest ship of all, British or German, but the Germans had more ships, and more big guns, and more speed than the Cradock force, and the British on the scene knew it.

On the morning of October 26 the Germans came in sight of Mas-a-Fuera, a rocky island whose western coast was a wall that rose three thousand feet above the sea. The Squadron pulled into the protected harbor beneath the huge wall and coaled. For two days the warships made ready for their cruise down the Chilean coast, for they now expected the action the enlisted men had been hoping for since the outbreak of war.

While the Germans were coaling, the British *Good Hope* joined *Glasgow*, *Monmouth*, and *Otranto* at Vallenar. The consul at Coronel was receiving copies of all Admiralty telegrams, which must be decoded and put in order so they would make sense for the admiral. Paymaster Commander Lloyd Hirst was now the squadron's assistant intelligence officer. He was deputed to remain aboard *Glasgow* with Captain Luce. *Glasgow* was to be sent into Coronel to pick up the telegrams and to advise London that she was proceeding northward with the squadron.

Intelligence Officer Hirst then went aboard *Good Hope* and *Monmouth* and took the mail, which he would post in Coronel. The visits to the two ships were most trying experiences. In *Monmouth* two of the lieutenant commanders took Hirst aside and gave him farewell messages for their wives.

"*Glasgow* has got the speed, so she can get away," they said, "but we are for it."

On the evening of October 27, *Glasgow* left Vallenar for Coronel. Two nights later she picked up the *Leipzig's* wireless, and knew that at least one ship of the German East Asia Squadron was less than 150 miles away from her.

The next day Admiral Cradock called up the *Canopus*, the old ship that seemed more sitting duck than bulldog every day, and told her and her colliers to come north. He was awaiting the intelligence reports from *Glasgow*; then his intention was to run to the Juan Fernández Islands and coal!

That same evening, no earlier, Admiral von Spee's work of coaling and rechecking of provisions and ammunition at Juan Fernández was finished, and in the broad moonlight of night the Squadron left "the rock," as they called their unfriendly haven. By morning they were off Mas-a-Tierra, which came up on the starboard with the dawn, and heading for the Chilean coast. The ships had been augmented by one more fighting ship, the auxiliary *Prinz Eitel Friedrich*, which the admiral had left long before in the South Pacific, but had encountered here in these dangerous if not unfriendly waters. (She was to go off on her own.)

On October 30 the German East Asia Squadron truly reached the coast of South America, for in the sunlight that day the men could see the snow-capped peak of Mount Aconcagua, the highest mountain of the continent, rising far above the others of the Cordillera range, and the night before they had spotted the lights of Valparaiso.

The air hummed with messages day and night, in German and in English. The German intelligence network on Chile was complete and effective: the admiral learned when the British squadron stood in the roads off Vallenar. *Glasgow* had scarcely appeared in Coronel when a German message was intercepted—informing Admiral von Spee of her arrival there. *Glasgow*, meanwhile, was collecting German cipher messages— copies of which would be sent to London for decoding. Captain Luce informed Admiral Cradock of the heavy flow of wireless traffic on the afternoon of October 29, and the admiral sailed at six o'clock on the morning of October 30 for the north, where he expected to find the Germans.

The coaling prospect did not work out as hoped for the British, for as *Canopus* came wheezing up it was learned that her high-pressure piston gland was out of order and would require twenty-four hours' work at dockside. So she was detached for repairs—almost as usual it seemed—and the other ships set out to sea. The admiral informed *Glasgow* that it was their primary mission to find the enemy and not worry so much about the visit to Coronel. *Glasgow* had anchored there at 1830 hours on October 30 and the British consul had immediately come aboard to report on the news of fighting, and the completeness of the German espionage network. The latter could not be questioned: almost immediately came a message to the Germans, in the clear, announcing the arrival of *Glasgow* in the harbor.

Admiral von Spee knew of the whereabouts of the British squadron, and he was confident that his own force was superior. A sudden change now radiated through the Squadron, communicated somehow almost immediately from the wireless room to the admiral, to the captains and ships of his command. The two heavy cruisers and the three light cruisers seemed to bound through the water, bones in their teeth, and the throbbing of their engines was musical and sound. The ships were clean of coal, and washed by the seas mounting their decks, but the men did not mind wet or cold, nor were they the gloomy seamen who had looked up at the 3000 feet of Mas-a-Fuera towering over their little ships and written final words to home just hours earlier. The men of the East Asia Squadron were ready for action and calm in their belief that their forces were superior to their enemy—even if the British proved stronger in actual ships and men, their beloved admiral would somehow find a way to lead them to victory.

The British squadron was strung out, searching for evidence of the Germans. On October 30 and 31 the *Glasgow* cruised westward and northwest of Santa Maria Island. The auxiliary cruiser *Otranto* cruised to Puerto Monte, and found that place so pro-German that she could not get any information at all. At one o'clock on the morning of October 31 she identified the call sign of *Leipzig*, very close—and *Glasgow* was off Coronel.

Given all this information, Admiral Cradock decided that Admiral von Spee was heading for the Galápagos group and the approaches to the Panama Canal. *Glasgow* was ordered back into Coronel to dispatch messages in which the admiral explained that he was going out to find the enemy, even though his forces were inferior.

These messages arrived in the Admiralty just after a major change in command of the British naval forces. So unequal to the task had the Admiralty proved that a new naval board had been installed, and with it a new First Sea Lord, Lord Fisher. When he saw the messages from Admiral Cradock, and examined the situation, he tried to undo what had been done. A message was sent to Cradock, informing him that the *Defence* would be sent to him, and that he would not be expected to act without the use of the *Canopus.*

It was too late.

The message never reached Admiral Cradock. He had grown tired of complaining to an Admiralty that seemed to pay no attention to his pleas. Admiral Cradock had decided, as he said, to try to close with the enemy with the force at his disposal.

He ordered *Glasgow* to meet him fifty miles west of Coronel at noon the next day.

What happened next was a comedy of errors, or it began

that way, at least. From German intelligence, Admiral von Spee understood that the British cruiser *Glasgow* was working in and out of Coronel. He believed, then, that he had a single enemy light cruiser with which to deal, and he moved in eagerly to intercept her. From the constant strong signals he received from *Leipzig*, British Admiral Cradock believed that he had a single German light cruiser with which to deal at the moment, and he moved confidently to find her.

Each admiral realized that the other was in the area, but they did not expect to meet at this moment; each believed the other's force was at the moment scattered, when the fact was exactly the reverse.

At noon on November 1, Admiral Cradock's two heavy cruisers were at the rendezvous, and there they were joined by *Glasgow* and *Otranto*. He formed his squadron into a broad line of search, covering a front of forty-five miles, and with a steep following sea he began a methodical hunt moving northward, hoping to find and take *Leipzig*.

The search had barely begun—*Glasgow* had not gotten into her position, which was nearest the Chilean coast—when her lookout spotted a blur of smoke on the horizon. Captain Luce of the *Glasgow* turned, signaled to *Otranto* and *Monmouth*, and they, too, turned onto a course that would intercept the vessel making the smoke.

On the night of October 31, Admiral von Spee had felt certain that he had *Glasgow* within his grasp, and when he received the news that his steamer train had moved safely into a Chilean port, he increased speed with the intent of bottling up *Glasgow* and destroying her. *Glasgow* was supposedly in Coronel port, and the Germans (who paid no attention to the rules of neutrality themselves) hoped that the Chileans would force her out within twenty-four hours. If they hurried they might catch *Glasgow*, so the Squadron's speed was increased from ten to fourteen knots.

187

On November 1, day broke for the Germans with a blue sky and a fine breeze from the south. It was Sunday, All Saints Day, and the day of the Feast of the Reformation. Chaplain Rost preached a sermon to his warriors, urging them to be strong. The men sang the old hymn of Martin Luther, *Ein feste Burg ist unser Gott*, which to Luther meant that God was his stronghold, but which might also be taken to mean that a strongly fortified castle was as God.

That morning the *Titania*, accompanied by an armed steam pinnace from the *Gneisenau*, captured the Norwegian sailing ship *Helicon*, which was carrying 2000 tons of Cardiff coal destined for the British. *Helicon* was taken in tow by *Titania*, which was ordered to proceed to the Juan Fernández Islands and there meet the ships of the supply train, when they returned filled with useful material.

As the Squadron moved south this morning, a number of ships were sighted and stopped, but they proved to be neutrals. The ship was bustling and noisy, with the particular sounds and briskness of a well-trained team of dedicated men who are going into action at last. On the enemy's track, the men were happy and smiling. At the coffee break after religious services they enjoyed a special treat, a cup of thick hot cocoa and bread thickly spread with margarine.

At 1600 hours, the men of the Squadron began to prepare their ships for the night. The smoking lamp was snuffed out, and the call to all hands went through the ships. The ships must be cleared and swept down, every crust and every drop of liquid must be cleaned from her decks.

Then came the call to battle stations—a routine nightly call. The men went to their weapons. They checked bolts and operating mechanisms. They oiled. They wiped. They scrubbed. They checked the ammunition cases to be sure the ready supply was safe from dampness. They set the night glasses and checked out the night signaling apparatus. The chief engineers toured the engine rooms and stokers' holds. The torpedo officers checked their "tin fish" and their tubes. The deck officers checked the boats and the upper works. The doctors checked their supplies and their dressing stations. The first lieutenants checked the damage control parties and the equipment, and reported to the captains on the readiness of the ships for action.

At 1617 hours the routine check was finished and the men of the Squadron were waiting for the usual order, "to your stations," which would free those off watch to do as they pleased, and put those on watch back on the routine of sea duty.

The order did not come. Instead came an observation, sung out from the foremast crow's nest. *"West zu Sud Rauchwolke!"*

A smoke cloud, off the starboard bow!

A moment later came another shout! *"Zwei Rauchwolken!"*—two smoke clouds.

Admiral von Spee, on the bridge of the *Scharnhorst*, strained through his glasses. There was nothing to be seen. But from the crow's nest came the word: the cloud had separated into *four* distinct smoke clouds. Four ships. It could be, it must be the British.

"Klarschiff zum Gefecht," came the order. ("Clear the ship for action.")

"Klarschiff zum Gefecht. Toppflaggen setzen," came the cries echoing back. The ship was being cleared and the battle flags run up so there could be no mistake in the fleet or with the enemy.

The word spread throughout *Scharnhorst*, and the signalmen gave the word to the Squadron. Drums began to roll on the decks of the ships. The sirens erupted with their unholy shrills.

It was 1620. Nothing could be seen from the decks or

189

even from the bridges of the ships, and then, suddenly, from the bridges, into the view of the straining telescopes came slender masts poking above the horizon: the enemy—if it was the enemy, and not a fleet of Chilean freighters traveling together for safety.

Nürnberg was out of sight, to the northeast of the flagship. *Dresden* was back about twelve miles. *Scharnhorst* and *Gneisenau* and *Leipzig* were together, about forty miles north of the bay of Aranco.

At first, peering hard through his glass, Admiral von Spee could see only two ships. At 1625 a third ship came in sight about fifteen miles away. Soon he was able to recognize two of these ships for warships, *Monmouth* and *Glasgow*. (The third was *Otranto*, the auxiliary cruiser.) They appeared to be traveling on a southerly course.

When he recognized the enemy warships, Admiral von Spee kept his eye glued to his telescope.

"Full speed ahead," he shouted, without taking his eye from the piece.

The signal bells on the *Scharnhorst* began to clang and the telegraph jangled the orders to the engine room. On the radio the operators were calling up the other ships. Some time was to be lost, because two of the boilers of *Gneisenau* were down for cleaning, but there was plenty of time. On the *Gneisenau* the engine room crew hastened to prepare their ship for action. On deck the younger officers were jubilant.

"They will get a drubbing," they said of the English.

The men believed so too, and they sped to their work with good will. They loaded the guns. They hoisted the boats, half-filled with water in case of fire, and fastened them to their cleats. The ammunition passers moved into the magazines.

Below, the stokers began to shovel with more zest, faster and bigger loads at a time. From the *Scharnhorst* came thick

190

puffs of smoke—*dampfbälle*—which indicated the increase in speed to all who would see.

Gneisenau came along to answer the signal to follow the flagship, and *Leipzig* came after her. *Nürnberg* and *Dresden* were alerted and moving as quickly as they could to join the battle.

From the enemy ranks, *Glasgow* had spotted smoke just three minutes after the *Scharnhorst's* lookout, and had altered her course to south 84 degrees east to run toward it. At 1640 *Glasgow* reported to her flagship the presence of *Scharnhorst*, *Gneisenau*, and one German light cruiser.

Admiral von Spee turned toward *Glasgow* and began steering a course between southeast and south, in order to keep himself between land and the British ships, and to close with them. When *Glasgow* was about 4 degrees to starboard, she turned suddenly and moved back to join her flagship, whose presence Admiral von Spee had not yet ascertained.

The wind was now kicking up the seas in strength, blowing at Force 6 from the south, and where the German Squadron was steaming both ground swell and sea swell had grown very strong. Admiral von Spee's problem of seamanship here, he quickly saw, was to be sure that he was not forced into a windward position in the battle to come.

Actually, von Spee had two objects in selecting his course. One object was to keep the British ships away from the shores of the Chilean coast—from neutral waters where they could run in and save themselves. His second object was to seek the lee position, that is, to be sure that the wind would be blowing the funnel smoke of his ships clear of the ships from the engaged side, and that the light was behind him, and not in his eyes. As the sun sank and the day grew shorter, this latter point grew in importance.

After 1630, action speeded up on all the ships. The air began to crackle with messages: *Glasgow* to *Good Hope*, *Good*

Hope to *Canopus*, asking her to come quickly. (The wallowing *Canopus* was 250 miles astern and could not possibly arrive in less than a day.) Admiral von Spee ordered his wireless men to jam as many of the enemy messages as possible, and so the airwaves buzzed with noise.

Even the *Scharnhorst's* boilers were not all operative at the moment of sighting, for Admiral von Spee had no reason to expect a call for more than fourteen knots that day, but they were cleared and *Scharnhorst's* propellers began to turn ever faster, until soon she was making twenty knots.

The British, at this point, had the sun setting behind them. At 1700 hours *Glasgow* came into sight of *Good Hope*. Ten minutes later Admiral Cradock signaled for all his ships to raise full steam. Admiral von Spee still did not know of the existence of the *Good Hope* in the area, and would not learn of it for half an hour.

Admiral von Spee's course now was to steer south, stay between the enemy and the shore, and wait for the sun to go down. As long as the sun stood in the sky, it was behind the English squadron, and would work to the admiral's disadvantage. But once the sun set, the tables would turn. Then the German ships would not be easily visible against the blackening Cordillera Mountains, while the British ships would stand out clearly against the last light of day along the horizon.

So the two squadrons moved south, each commander drawing his ships around him, and each hoping for the advantage.

At 1747 *Good Hope* began to lead the line of battle of the British, *Monmouth* behind her, and *Glasgow*, then *Otranto*. Admiral Cradock cut onto a southeasterly course, and made an attempt to wrest the lee position from Admiral von Spee. But it was not possible. The seas were too heavy; his cruisers rolled and plunged into them, and the wind was in his teeth. The worst problem was the performance of the towering merchant cruiser *Otranto*, which simply could not maintain the speed necessary to take this advantage. In spite of message after message from Admiral Cradock, *Otranto* could not manage more than sixteen knots.

After a little time Admiral Cradock saw that he could not take the lee position, and he turned to parallel the Germans, traveling south-southeast. At six o'clock (1800 hours) he turned south.

As Admiral von Spee steered southwest and then south, he slackened speed to let *Nürnberg* and *Dresden* catch up. At 1807 *Dresden* was still astern about a mile, and *Nürnberg* was still too far away to be of value. That was all right with Admiral von Spee because he wanted to wait until sunset, when the light advantage reversed to his favor.

The two squadrons were steaming south on converging courses. At 1818 Admiral Cradock ordered speed increased to seventeen knots and ran up his battle flags, which meant "Follow me."

"Die Engländer setzen auch Toppflaggen," muttered Admiral von Spee, eye still glued to his glass.

Admiral von Spee also saw that the *Good Hope* was moving in toward him, for in fact she had altered course one point to port. Then the Germans heard the British ship calling up *Canopus*.

Admiral Cradock gave his position: latitude 37 degrees 30 minutes south, longitude 74 degrees west.

Then came the answer from the old battleship: "My position 41.10 south, 76.20 west. Course north 10 west."

Canopus was now *more than* 250 miles away.

Admiral von Spee was not so bemused with the radio signals that he failed to understand what Admiral Cradock was trying to do. The British admiral saw that his position was very nearly desperate, and he was trying frantically to close, even with *Otranto* dragging him back, so he could take

193

advantage of the only superior factor he possessed—the waning light.

Only superior factor?

What about the ships themselves?

The two flagships would oppose one another in a fight. *Good Hope* was 14,100 tons in displacement, by far the heaviest ship of either fleet, outweighing *Scharnhorst*'s 11,420 tons by nearly 3000 tons. An advantage? Perhaps, if all other factors had been equal. But *Good Hope* had been built in 1902 and *Scharnhorst* in 1908. In those six years one of the major developments in naval engineering had been the improvement of naval guns, a result of observations during the Russo-Japanese War as much as anything else. *Good Hope* carried a pair of 9.2-inch guns and sixteen 6-inch guns, to *Scharnhorst*'s eight 8.2-inch guns, six 5.9-inch guns and twenty 3.4-inch guns.

Except in the matter of individual escape, the speed of the individual ships was not nearly so important a matter as the effective speed of a squadron as a whole, and in this matter the British were far outdone. They could make a speed of only 18 knots under the best of conditions, while the Germans could make 22.5 knots.

As for comparisons between the *Gneisenau* and the *Monmouth*, the former at 11,400 tons outweighed the British ship by 1600 tons, which really put her into quite a different class. Their speeds were almost the same—perhaps effectively at this point *Monmouth* had a slight advantage with her 23.3 knots, for although *Gneisenau* was listed by Brasseys Naval Annual at 23.8 she was not making anywhere nearly that much after four months away from base. *Monmouth* carried fourteen 6-inch guns. Like *Scharnhorst*, *Gneisenau* was armed with eight 8.2-inch guns, six 5.9-inch guns, and twenty 3.4-inch guns. Obviously, in the respect *Monmouth* was hopelessly outclassed.

At 4800 tons, *Glasgow* would seem to have been more than a match for any of the German light cruisers, the largest of which, *Dresden*, displaced only 3544 tons. *Glasgow* mounted two 6-inch guns and ten 4-inch guns, too, as against the twelve 4.1-inch guns and four 2.1-inch guns of the Germans'. Yet the range of the more modern German 4.1-inch guns was *nearly equal* to that of the British 6-inch guns, because of the sensational development of naval artillery in a few years. *Glasgow* was built in 1910; she was the newest British ship, yet she could not hope to be a match for three German light cruisers. As for *Otranto*, the auxiliary, with her 12,000-ton bulk rising high out of the water, she was more target than anything else in this situation, in spite of her eight 4.7-inch guns. She was quite a valuable ship, and could hold her own against a destroyer, and perhaps even against a single light cruiser of the less modern variety, but not in these waters or on this day. Added up, the Germans had five fighting ships, the British, the equivalent of three and a half ships.

Equipment was not the only area of German superiority on this day. At the outbreak of war, three months earlier, the only ship of the British squadron that had been in commission was the *Glasgow*. *Good Hope* and *Monmouth* were in the mothball fleet, and *Otranto* was running as a liner. Consequently the crews of three of the British ships had been together, and in fact the ships had been in operation, only for a very short time. Neither their gunnery nor their seamanship had been tested seriously. On the other side, the German East Asia Squadron had a long tradition, half the officers and men were old hands at their job, and the ships had all been in commission for two years.

It was apparent to Admiral von Spee, then, that Admiral Cradock would try to close quickly.

"*Feind wendet,*" shouted Admiral von Spee, wiping from

195

his face the spray that had blown back from the plunging bow of *Scharnhorst.*

The weather seemed to be thickening, if anything. So the enemy was changing course, moving toward him. He ordered his captains to give way. The sun had not yet set. *Dresden* had not yet come up close enough. He was not ready for action, and he was in control. The range was still almost 18,000 yards, but would close rapidly, because Admiral Cradock had just turned four points to port toward the East Asia Squadron. Admiral von Spee turned away four points.

So they proceeded, Admiral Cradock trying to close; Admiral von Spee waiting for the best advantage. Now his squadron was nearly assembled: *Scharnhorst, Gneisenau, Leipzig, Dresden.* It was too much to hope that *Nürnberg* would arrive in time to begin the action.

Every minute, it seemed, the sea was increasing in that Force 6 wind. The ships plunged into the green water and came up shaking off the spray. The small cruisers were affected most—the heavy seas interfered seriously with the gun training and aiming. Even on the *Scharnhorst* and *Gneisenau* the seas plunged through the forward turret, soaking the men there and in the magazine below.

Admiral von Spee was very careful. He had time and he was using it to best advantage.

"Does my smoke disturb you?" he inquired of the *Gneisenau.*

When *Gneisenau* gave a positive reply, the admiral changed course and position, until there was no problem for certain.

Finally, at 1847, Admiral von Spee was nearly ready. The sun was sinking low on the horizon, and would no longer disturb the calculations of his gunners. The British ships were outlined sharply against the blaze of the setting sun. Behind the German squadron, from the British point of view, the lofty mountains of the Chilean coastline stood sere and blackening, with a heavy cloud cover above them.

Admiral von Spee ordered Captain Schultz to move a point (11¼ degrees) toward the enemy. Admiral Cradock saw the move and slowed, in order to cover the *Otranto*, which was still laboring along in the heavy seas. *Otranto* then moved out to starboard of the *Glasgow*, out of range and out of the battle, for she was of no use in a fight against warships and could only be destroyed.

Just as the sun began to set, the admiral maneuvered to a point about 12,000 yards from the British squadron.

"I had maneuvered so that the sun in the west could not disturb me," he said. "The moon in the east was not yet full, but promised good light during the night, and there were rain squalls in various directions."

Just after 1900 hours, when the sun was sinking and the ships were 11,400 yards apart, the admiral gave the order.

"*Feuer eröffnen*," he cried.

"*Jot Dora*," shouted Captain Schultz. The signal for opening fire was picked up by the *Scharnhorst*'s gunnery officer, by the signal officer, and by the signalmen on the other ships, and the German squadron began to shoot.

From the purist's point of view, Admiral von Spee was premature in opening the battle: his line was not formed in accordance with the best naval tradition. The British ships were in fine formation, two cable lengths apart, but there were five cables between *Gneisenau* and *Leipzig*, and seven between *Leipzig* and *Dresden*. Admiral von Spee was not interested in such niceties at that moment. He wanted to join the battle, and to finish it before night fell and created new difficulties.

All the ships were rolling heavily, and this movement added considerably to the disadvantage of the British fighting men. Under the best of conditions the British squadron was in for trouble; the German ships fired a total broadside of 4752 pounds as opposed to the British squadron's 2085 pounds —*Scharnhorst* firing 2190 pounds against *Good Hope*'s 1160, *Gneisenau* 2190 pounds against *Monmouth*'s 600, *Leipzig* and *Dresden* throwing 186 pounds each against *Glasgow*'s 325.

Almost as great as this disparity was the problem posed by the heavy seas. *Good Hope* and *Monmouth* would have great difficulty in getting away any shots from their lower casements. *Scharnhorst* and *Gneisenau* were far better designed in this respect; their low guns were higher above the water level.

Yet *Scharnhorst* and *Gneisenau* in particular enjoyed still another advantage, a very human one. Both ships had excellent reputations for gunnery. *Gneisenau* had won the Kaiser Prize in 1913, in competition with the entire German fleet.

When fire was opened, *Scharnhorst*'s first salvo burst on the water 500 yards short of *Good Hope*. Her second salvo was over the British ship. Her third salvo struck the forward turret of *Good Hope*. At least one shell hit the 9.2-inch gun. A sheet of flame arose from the forward 6-inch casement, and the big gun was not fired throughout the remainder of the battle.

The weather was felt on both sides. Admiral von Spee noted from his bridge that the observation and range finding of his gunners suffered considerably from the weather. The seas rushed over the forecastle and the command post of the forward guns. Those on the middle deck were splashed and washed and nearly capsized by the high-running ground swell.

But the Germans shot very well.

The *Gneisenau* chose the *Monmouth* as her target; on the admiral's order, she began firing. Three minutes after the action began, *Monmouth*, too, was on fire in the forecastle, even though she had been stripped of paint and woodwork.

198

They were firing from the left, as the admiral had ordered. The *Gneisenau's* range finders were in constant action, talking and shouting. The yellow shells ranged in line behind the guns bore messages chalked on by the crew for their cousins across the water.

Salvo followed salvo, on the big cruisers the 8.2-inch guns opening up on the British first, the 6-inch guns coming in later.

Leipzig opened fire on *Glasgow*, but the range was too great for her smaller guns and she could not reach the larger cruiser. Soon all the British ships were firing, too, but with the light gone, with the Germans lost against the dark mountains, they could not see the shell splashes, and could not learn how far they were overshooting or undershooting the enemy. In fact, the *Scharnhorst* was being regularly overshot, and by so great a distance that her baptism of fire seemed almost unreal.

Otranto began a daring move, zigzagging and trying to confuse the German gunners about the course and speed of the British ships. But *Gneisenau* ended that attempt, by putting one salvo fifty yards off *Otranto's* starboard bow, and another a few yards astern. Captain Edwards then took *Otranto* out of an action in which he did not belong, and moved astarboard to watch.

At 1910, *Leipzig* was close enough to begin straddling the *Glasgow* with her shots. *Dresden* was also firing at *Glasgow*.

On their part, the British were having exceedingly great difficulties. The heavy seas bothered both sides, but they bothered the untrained British gunners more. Bursts of spray smashed into the faces of the gunners, and their telescopes were obscured. Then the problem of the spotters in the tops continued: they could not see the fall of the shot.

The smoke of the German ships drove down the line, not bothering the Germans, but sometimes completely obscuring the *Leipzig* from view of her enemies.

199

Leipzig was firing well, too. At 1919 she put a shell against the conning tower support in the captain's fore cabin, but fortunately for the commander of *Glasgow*, the shell did not explode.

When fire broke out aboard *Good Hope*, the men of *Scharnhorst* and *Gneisenau* broke into cheering, so loud that some officers below decks feared some disaster had overtaken their own ship. But no, it was the British day for disaster. Soon *Gneisenau* laid a shell into *Monmouth*'s fore turret, and a tongue of flame shot up.

Monmouth sheered off to starboard, and never did come back into position. She had been firing, although not hitting well, when suddenly aboard her enemy *Gneisenau* there was a thump, a sound quite unlike those that any man had heard before.

"Enemy shell rib eighty-nine. Over armored deck"—came the word from damage control. First Officer Pochhammer called the stoker at that point through his speaking tube. There was no answer. He called again. No answer.

In a moment the chief of the fore-section control reported water coming in through the safety hatch of Compartment XI. An enemy shell had come through the starboard side just above the armor plating, into the wardrobe. It had burst there, damaging the substructure of the 8.2-inch turret, then spending itself in the master storeroom. The damage was not severe. The ship was not taking water from the sea at water line, but because of the heavy weather water was coming on deck. Carpenters rushed to the scene, in water up to their necks, and stopped the holes with wooden billets and wool covers. Planks were laid over, braced, and the whole was calked. In a few moments the damage was repaired as well as it need be for the moment.

"Fire in the after battery" came the anguished cry on *Gneisenau*, as *Monmouth* again found her mark.

Up went the damage control party, *Korvettenkapitän* Pochhammer on the double, leading them, for this was a matter so serious that he could waste no time. In a moment, perhaps even before they could get there, the fire would reach the cordite, and then one explosion would follow another. There would be little chance for any man trapped in that inferno, and the gun would be out of action.

The men tugged at their fire masks as they ran, lugging hoses. Then came the matter of tracing the origin through the thick smoke. It was found in the substructure of the eight-inch after turret, luckily. The smoke had come up through the turret, and had frightened the men inside into their anguished call. The enemy shell had hit the after turret, smashing against the armor plating. But instead of penetrating the armor, it destroyed the protective sheet iron that enclosed the revolving tower and the barbette that was built into the upper deck, then had gone below, starting thick smoky fires in several life-belts.

But the shell had done some damage. The after turret jammed, when the sheeting had bent crazily. The officer in charge of the gun leaped out of the turret, grasped a fire axe, and began chopping away the offending iron. In a few moments the turret was back in swing.

By 1920 the British ships were in severe trouble. The Germans were nearly invisible, and the only targets for the British gunners were the flashes of the German guns which brought so much disaster to *Good Hope* and *Monmouth*. The Germans were firing very well, at the rate of three salvos a minute. *Monmouth* had fires fore and aft. Her damage control men managed to put out the fire foreward, and then there came another direct hit and the fire started over again.

Glasgow quite lost track of *Leipzig* and *Dresden* and began firing with her forward turret on *Scharnhorst* and her after turret on *Gneisenau*. She claimed to be making hits on

201

both ships, and six-inch shells were landing on both, but without doing much damage.

At 1935 *Good Hope* was in desperate straits. The battle had closed until only 5500 yards separated the British and German flagships. Aboard *Scharnhorst* it was believed that some thirty shells had hit *Good Hope* already (another five or six would be claimed). The British flagship was on fire and had been almost constantly since the beginning of the battle.

At 1935 she could be seen altering course, apparently trying to make a torpedo run on the *Scharnhorst*. At 1940 another fire broke out in the vicinity of the forward 9.2-inch gun. The *Good Hope* was *in extremis*. The *Monmouth* was not much better off. Since almost the beginning of the engagement the forward ends of both ships had been ringed with a glow that indicated constant fires.

Of all the British warships only *Glasgow* was in condition to carry the fight against the Germans, and she had to be very wary; she was outnumbered, and her guns were scarcely large enough to do much damage to the two big German cruisers, except when she made a lucky hit that slipped underneath the armor.

As the moon rose, occasionally *Glasgow* caught sight of one of the German light cruisers, and whenever she could see, she fired. Suddenly the Germans retaliated with a vengeance, and a 4.1-inch high explosive shell burst on her water line below the seamen's mess deck, just above the port outer screw of the *Glasgow*. The explosion stove in the side of the *Glasgow* and made an irregular hole which destroyed about six square feet of surface.

The British flagship *Good Hope* was losing ground fast. At 1945 she began to lose way, and dropped from a point eight cables on the *Glasgow's* port bow to a point midway between the *Glasgow* and the Germans.

It was dark. The moon was obscured by clouds and rain

squalls. Suddenly the gloom was split by the light of a tremendous explosion, where the *Good Hope* could be seen dimly, burning, a second before. The explosion came amidships, lighting up the sky and water for many miles. Wreckage and sparks rose 200 feet in the air from her after funnels. Then she seemed to settle. Her guns were all silent, and the *Scharnhorst* stopped firing on her. For a few moments the dim light of the fires in her after part could be seen—and then *Good Hope* quite disappeared from the sight of Germans and British.

A shot had obviously penetrated one of her magazines and sent the whole up. She was never seen again, and undoubtedly went down within a very few moments after the explosion.

For a few minutes the German ships stopped shooting. Admiral von Spee took this respite to check on his squadron.

"Batteries cease fire," came the order. "Transport the wounded."

Wounded? Who were the wounded? There were two slightly wounded men aboard the *Gneisenau*, but there was not another man in the German Squadron who claimed to have been hurt.

Aboard the ships, the doctors waited in their white gowns, expecting to see maimed men brought in at any moment. None came. The stillness was eerie.

On *Gneisenau* the two injured men were the stoker who had been at station when the six-inch shell hit forward, and a helmsman, who was stationed on the upper bridge. He had been struck by a shell fragment which had hit the foretop. The fragment had opened a gash on the back of his hand, causing profuse bleeding. He came down briefly to the emergency station and demanded that his hand be tied up so he could get back to his post.

"Man the searchlights," came the orders from the admiral, for he had taken stock and the respite was over. The British were now out of sight except that the dim outline of *Monmouth* could be seen by her fires, and *Glasgow* could be seen when she fired her own guns.

"Starboard searchlight crew to muster," was the repetition of the order passed on the decks of the two big cruisers. For a few moments the fire of *Gneisenau* and *Scharnhorst* was concentrated on the *Monmouth*, but then she was gone into the dark night and for the big ships the battle was over, at least for this moment.

"Clear the guns for the night," came the order through the two cruisers. There were no longer any targets in sight, and the chance of finding one of them in this night of storm and blackness was very slight. Just after 2000 hours, *Glasgow* fired her last shot, realizing that she was the sole remaining fighting unit of the British squadron, and taking the wise course of retreat.

On both big German ships the first officers made a rapid tour, and returned to the bridge to report to the captains. *Gneisenau* had suffered damage from four shells, but that was all. *Scharnhorst* had been hit only twice, and not a man had been wounded. The men, with glory in their eyes, began to batten the ship down for the night and to talk in shaky voices of what they had seen and done.

Monmouth turned away west, and for a few moments those with very clear vision might have seen the dim light of her fires through the filthy weather. In fifteen minutes of quiet she had extinguished the fires, and at 2015 she turned north, continuing the turn nearly sixteen points in order to present her stern to the high waves. She was down by the head and was making water badly forward. She needed every break that nature might give her at this moment.

A moment or two later, as the moon appeared above the driving clouds, Captain Luce in the *Glasgow* saw the Germans. They had not yet seen him, but they would see him in

204

a moment, for aboard the German ships life was not all repose, even though the *Scharnhorst* and *Gneisenau* were fastened tight for the night. The admiral still had orders for his squadron:

"Beide Englischen grossen Kreuzer schwer beschädigt. Ein Kleine Kreuzer anscheinend ziemlich intakt. Feind verfolgen, Torpedoangriff."

Both British heavy cruisers had been badly damaged—as the admiral said. *Good Hope* was much worse than damaged; she and her entire crew and the senior British naval officer had gone to the bottom of the sea. *Monmouth* was listing and taking water. Only *Glasgow* was apparently intact. The German light cruisers were to find the enemy and launch a torpedo attack!

And so out the *Leipzig* and the *Dresden* went in the heavy seas to do their duty: find the enemy and destroy him.

Seeing the Germans coming, *Glasgow* warned *Monmouth* to keep as much as possible to the northwest, and then speed off to the west herself, followed by *Otranto*. The flagship gone, *Monmouth* disabled, there was no other course save a suicidal attack. Captain Luce preferred to live to fight another day, and so *Glasgow* moved away.

Glasgow had been very lucky. Her captain estimated that the Germans had lobbed six hundred shots at her, and although she was nearly unarmored only six shots had done damage, five at the water line, which were dissipated by the coal in the bunkers, and one which wrecked the captain's cabin.

So *Glasgow* moved away into the dirty night sea.

As she did so, *Monmouth* turned northwest, to keep the sea at her stern, hoping to slip away.

Leipzig and the *Dresden* moved out in search from the point where the battle had been joined. Admiral von Spee took his big ships around on a great circle course, hoping to

205

come up behind the survivors and silhouette them against the moon.

Leipzig began to make eighteen knots, and soon steamed in a rolling sea past the spot where *Good Hope* had last been seen. On deck the *Leipzig* seamen were throwing ammunition boxes overboard and clearing the ship for further action, when they began to travel through debris. They saw broken boxes, spars, hammocks, and corpses of British sailors washing along the sides of their ship.

Soon *Leipzig* and *Dresden* came upon *Nürnberg*, and after an exchange of recognition signals they all went their separate ways. *Nürnberg* rolled through the seas, steaming southwest, trying to catch up with the British. At 2000 hours she turned sharply northwest and crossed the track just behind the *Glasgow*, at about 2015. Ten minutes later she turned sharply northeast in her search pattern. At 2030 a shout rang out from the crow's nest, and the ship's gunnery officer began shouting:

"Dampferplosion Schiff krängt (= left sich über) fünfzehn Grad nach Backbord."

He did not take his glass from his eye as he located the target on their port side, and assured Captain von Schönberg it was correct.

But what target? Was it the *Leipzig* or the *Dresden?* The captain was not about to open fire on anything that moved on a night like this when German ships were milling around in the storm. They must identify the target.

They moved in, the helmsman turning a point to port, and the signalmen readied their lights to give the recognition signals of the German ships. As they came within range, they saw the ship had a dangerous list to port and steam was escaping from her amidships. She seemed to be barely under way. To the *Nürnberg* this meant nothing, for the captain and his men had been totally out of the battle, because of that

206

wild goose chase earlier in the day after a plume of smoke along the Chilean coast. There was no way of telling in this filthy weather what ship this badly injured one might be.

Once, twice, three times, the signal lamp sent its beams across the water. The message arrived—they were so close it could not but have been read. It was not answered.

Captain von Schönberg ordered the searchlights turned on. In that light and at close range they saw the white naval ensign of the British navy, and all doubts were gone.

Seeing that she was trapped, *Monmouth* tried to run before the wind and reach the coast. But she could not move fast enough, and this became apparent. The German captain maneuvered so that the starboard guns could bear on the enemy—quickly because he had seen several plumes of smoke and he did not want to be caught by *Glasgow* while attacking *Monmouth*, as he now recognized his quarry to be. He came around the port side of *Monmouth*, for now her list was so pronounced that she could not fire the guns on that side.

Leutnant zur See Otto von Spee, son of the admiral, watched from his post on deck as the *Nürnberg* bore down on the helpless victim:

"To me it was dreadful to have to fire on the poor devil no longer able to defend herself," he wrote later, "but her flag was still flying."

Under the rules of naval warfare, as long as her national ensign was flying, a ship was in the fight and fair game to any enemy. *Nürnberg* had very little choice, even less choice than if Captain von Schönberg had been an admiral or a senior commander.

He came around.

"Die Steuerbordseite kommt ins Gefecht" ("Starboard side ready for action"), shouted the gunnery officer as the *Nürnberg* swept past the floundering *Monmouth* at point-blank range.

207

"*Salve—Feuerrrrrrrn!*" came the order, and the guns spoke but were scarcely heard in the howling of the wind and the pounding of the waves as the bow dipped and drenched the crew with spray.

The shells struck forward and along the middle deck of the British ship. Another run was made, and still the stricken British cruiser sat, neither fighting back, which she could not do, nor surrendering, which she would not do.

Captain von Schönberg stood off for a time, hoping that the British would haul down their flag. He ordered the spotlights again turned on the almost helpless hulk.

Then the captain of the *Monmouth*, or whoever was left alive on that unhappy ship's bridge, ordered one last desperation move. With her screws spinning, every ounce of steam brought forth to make her move, she began to swing around, bent on an attempt to ram her uninjured opponent. The flag flew proudly still.

Captain von Schönberg could take no further chances with the safety of his own ship. He moved off and fired again and again, and in a few moments the shells took their effect. Flags flying, steam escaping from a dozen wounds in her vitals, *Monmouth* slowly rolled over to port and capsized. Men could be seen sliding down the red bottom and into the sea—but nothing could be done for them, because even if *Nürnberg*'s boats had not been filled with water as fire protection, they could never have been launched in this raging sea.

Thus perished the *Monmouth*, with 540 officers and men dead or drowned, joining the 900 officers and men aboard the flagship *Good Hope*.

Nürnberg lost no time moving away from the dreadful scene. Smoke clouds could be seen to the southeast, and no one knew what they might be. (Actually the clouds came from the remainder of the German Squadron.)

At 2115 *Nürnberg* broke radio silence to call up the flag-ship:

"*Habe feindlichen Panzerkreuzer zum Sinken gebracht.*" ("I have sunk an enemy armored cruiser.")

"Bravo, *Nürnberg*," came the speedy reply from the *Kreuzergeschwaderchef*, the Admiral von Spee.

Now the reports of the sighting of flotsam and jetsam were brought together by the Squadron's intelligence officer, but there was no certainty about anything, except the sinking of the *Monmouth* and the disappearance of the *Good Hope*. The admiral ordered a search for the *Good Hope*, and the Squadron spread out to cover the waters. Meanwhile, *Glasgow* and *Otranto* swept around to the south, and made off, each alone on an unfriendly sea, to join the *Canopus* and prepare for any further action the Germans might instigate. They represented Britain's might, or what was left of it, on the west coast of the Americas, and they must be prepared to contest with the Germans, no matter the odds.

How little was known of the battle, how much was guessed at, and how the action disguised facts, was indicated by Admiral von Spee in a letter he wrote to his countess the next day, even as the Squadron moved northward. In the morning the decks had been scrubbed to remove the residue and odor of cordite. Fresh supplies of ammunition had been brought to the guns. The night glasses had been put away and the day glasses brought out. All damage had been repaired, and the crew had eaten a belated supper and then an early breakfast in the bright sun that welcomed a cloudless day. The wind had fallen and the sea was almost calm, so clear was the air that the distant coast of Chile could be seen through the slight haze. The admiral had been cheered from every ship, and the Squadron was heading north for Valparaiso to make a victory call and coal. The admiral had a little time to write and reflect over the action he had directed that stormy night before. He wrote:

Yesterday was All Saint's Day, and for us a lucky day. I was with the Squadron, traveling south along the coast when I got wind that an English cruiser had run into Coronel, a small coaling harbor by Concepción.

Since according to international rules a ship of a war power must run out again inside of twenty-four hours, I thought to catch it, and had the position so deployed that the *Nürnberg* should run before the harbor in order to see whether the cruiser was still in, while the other ships should be placed about outside. In order to save coal the ships steam at only fourteen knots, but we were specially on the outlook this time, all boilers either ready or nearly ready for more steam.

My ships also at 4:25 were somewhat removed from me, only *Gneisenau* really being in the vicinity, since it was reported that two ships were moving west-southwest. I gave the order for the other cruisers to come to me as soon as it was clear that it was the enemy, and indeed the armored cruiser *Monmouth* and the light cruiser *Glasgow* soon came into sight, and behind them the auxiliary cruiser *Otranto* and after a while the armored cruiser *Good Hope*.

The enemy sought a maneuver through which he, as I saw it, would come nearer to the coast and to the weather side, which would be very harmful to me. I had ordered *Scharnhorst* and *Gneisenau* to have all boilers in working order in a quarter of an hour. I ran out at twenty knots against heavy seas and ground swells, and came luckily so far that I was able to lie parallel to the enemy, but I was alone and must wait on the coming of the others. The enemy was charitable enough not to destroy me; the distance then was still about nine miles. When my ships were together at 6:10 P.M. [the admiral's time throughout is different from that of the British, whose timing was used in the narrative as the more accurate] except the *Nürnberg* which was still not to be seen, I began to diminish the distance and when it amounted to about five *Seemilen* [1 *Seemile* = 1.85 kilometers] that is to say 9.25 kilometers, I ordered the ships to open fire. The battle had begun. . . .

The sun was in the west. I had so outmaneuvered the enemy that it could not destroy me. The moon was in the east, still not full, but it promised to light the night well, even though rain squalls could be seen at different places.

My ships fired quickly and had good success on the large ships. *Scharnhorst* fired against *Good Hope* [flagship of Rear Admiral Cradock, whom the Graf and Gräfin von Spee knew well and liked]; *Gneisenau* against *Monmouth*; *Leipzig* against *Glasgow*; *Dresden* against *Otranto*. The last ship, after a time, left the line and escaped, so I think.

A great many fires broke out on *Good Hope* and *Monmouth*. On the first came a great explosion which looked against the dark sky like a brilliant fireworks display, white glowing with a greenish tinge at the stern—it rose up over funnel height. I believed that the ship must go under; it floated further and the battle continued. Darkness fell. The

211

distance between us dropped to 4500 meters, and then I turned wide so that it slowly increased again. There was further firing after that only at the glow of the ship as long as it could be seen, and then when our gunnery officer could not see her any more, the firing was broken off. The shooting of the enemy had stopped.

I ordered the small cruisers to take up the chase, but since the enemy, as it appeared, had extinguished the fires there was nothing to see. We traveled around the enemy line to get them in a favorable light but we saw nothing more.

The artillery battle had lasted fifty-two minutes.

At about 8:40 I saw on the northwest at a great distance some artillery fire—perhaps ten *Seemilen* away. I went there, in order to help if necessary. It was the *Nürnberg*, which had not been able before to make contact. Now it had pushed on the fleeing *Monmouth* and had found her there with heavy list. *Nürnberg* went close by and gave her the finishing stroke by artillery fire. *Monmouth* capsized and went under. Unfortunately the heavy seas forbade rescue work, in addition to the circumstances that *Nürnberg* believed *Good Hope* to be in the vicinity—which was certainly a mistake. She would have distinguished the big cruiser in the moonlight at a great distance.

I do not know what has become of the *Good Hope*. Lieutenant Grapow [a young deck officer on the *Scharnhorst*], who had time for observation, had recognized that she also had taken a heavy list and when I recalled the image I hold it certainly possible, but believe it was a result of the ship's movement in the heavy seas.

It is possible that she also went under; she was certainly incapable of battle.

Glasgow was scarcely seen at all; she should have also received a few hits but in my estimation, she escaped.

So we have on all sides triumphed and I thank God for that. We have been saved in wonderful ways: we have no losses to bemoan. A few lightly wounded men were on *Gneisenau*. The small cruisers were not hit. The shots which *Scharnhorst* and *Gneisenau* received did little or no damage. One 15-centimeter shell found itself a porthole and came through the side, then caused a lot of mess below; luckily it hit no one and is now just a reminder of the enemy. One funnel was hit, but not so badly damaged that it did not serve its purpose. Only small trifles occurred on *Gneisenau*.

I know not what perhaps unlucky circumstances occurred with the enemy, who suffered such results. . . .

If *Good Hope* has escaped, she must in my opinion, because of her damage, run to the Chilean coast. In order to determine that I will tomorrow run with *Gneisenau* and *Nürnberg* to Valparaiso, and see if *Good Hope* cannot be disarmed by the Chileans. Then I shall have eliminated two strong enemies. . . .

So the course was set, and Admiral von Spee, having secured an important naval victory, went off without knowing really how complete or important it had been.

213

13

THE VICTORS REJOICE

AT 2300 HOURS ON THE NIGHT OF THE BATTLE, when Captain Luce of the *Glasgow* saw *Monmouth* altering course for the northeast to head toward the Chilean shore, he also saw the enemy approaching, and signaled.

"Enemy following us," he said, and then sped away to protect his ship.

There was no reply from *Monmouth*; the last the men of *Glasgow* saw was a series of flashes from the guns of *Nürnberg*. They counted seventy-five.

Glasgow had headed south to meet *Canopus* and warn her of the change in the naval fortunes of Great Britain that night in the Pacific.

Glasgow could then begin to count her casualties and damage. Remarkably, for having been under fire for fifty-two minutes, as Admiral von Spee indicated, *Glasgow* was scarcely hurt. The hits on her had been surface wounds and only four men were wounded. She steamed west-northwest at first, then came around in a great circle and made her way to the Straits of Magellan and finally to Port Stanley in the Falkland Islands.

Captain Edwards on the *Otranto* had as difficult a time as he ever wanted to suffer; he was unable to fight to help his countrymen, and could only be a liability if he remained in the battle zone. At the beginning of the battle it became apparent that he was being used as a range finder so that the enemy gunners could calculate the distance to the *Glasgow*. Captain Edwards then worked out of line some 1200 yards and ran the gantlet of German fire to stand well away. When the flagship blew up, *Otranto* could see nothing of *Monmouth*, but soon Captain Edwards saw *Glasgow* crossing his stern, so he steamed full speed ahead for 200 miles to the west to throw off the enemy, and then went south, around Cape Horn, between the Falklands and the mainland, and into Montevideo.

The *Canopus* had intercepted a very early message—from *Glasgow* to *Good Hope* reporting the presence of the enemy. *Canopus* then had steamed full speed northward, and had dispatched her two colliers to Juan Fernández. She had hoped against hope that she might arrive in time for the fight. At nine o'clock in the evening, 2100 hours, she had received a message from *Glasgow* telling her that it was feared that *Good Hope* and *Monmouth* had been sunk. *Canopus* had turned around, picked up her colliers, and made for the Straits of Magellan via Smyth's Channel—the first battleship ever to navigate this tricky water. She reached Port Stanley without trouble.

The German Squadron—cocky and somewhat outraged because in England Winston Churchill was denying that there had been a battle of Coronel—was ready to show the world the force of German arms. On Tuesday, November 3, at daybreak *Scharnhorst*, *Gneisenau*, and *Nürnberg* entered the bay of Valparaiso. *Leipzig* and *Dresden* remained at sea to protect the supply train, for only three ships of a belligerent power might enter neutral waters at any one time.

215

Soon a Chilean torpedo boat came out to investigate the silhouettes of warships, and immediately turned back around the rocky point of Punta Caramilla to report the presence of the Germans. Shortly afterward a pilot steamer came out from shore and lay alongside the flagship, while a pilot went aboard. Arrangements were made for anchorage, and at 11:00 in the morning the Germans were anchoring in Valparaiso harbor. Admiral von Spee was careful to do all the naval honors: he fired a salute to the Chilean national flag, and he fired a salute to the admiral of the Chilean fleet, who was in harbor with several of that nation's warships.

As the German naval men looked about them they saw a number of German steamers, flying the national flag, but unable to go outside because of the strong force that Britain had shown in these waters until this time.

No sooner had the *Scharnhorst* pulled into harbor than the British embassy began making official protests about their presence in Chilean waters. The protests were embarrassing at first because the amount of Spanish spoken on the bridge of the *Scharnhorst* was extremely limited.

Soon, Spanish-speaking German officials came on board the *Scharnhorst* and undertook to answer the protests of the British. The Germans were entitled to twenty-four hours in Valparaiso under the rules of war and that was that.

It was imperative that Admiral von Spee be in touch with the Admiralty and he so told German Minister von Eckert and Consul General Gumprecht when they arrived on learning of the presence of the German warships in the harbor. For some time the officials were engaged in meeting Chilean naval and diplomatic protests about the violations by the Germans of the Chilean neutrality laws. The worst violation, of course, had occurred when the Germans lay in the harbor at Easter Island for several days. But it was hard for the Chileans to take a very firm line with the strongest fleet in Pacific waters—

at least the strongest fleet among the belligerents. Von Spee attempted by courtesy to overcome the distaste the Germans had aroused by doing what they must do for their own salvation.

Yet, in another way, the protests of the Chileans were helpful to Admiral von Spee, because he could use them in showing the German Admiralty what must next be done. A hard-headed realist, the admiral now realized that he could hope to survive only for a limited time in North and South American waters, because of the same old difficulty that had bedeviled him from the beginning: the shortage of coal. So far, the coal used by the Germans had come from existing stocks—that is, most of it was on the high seas at the time of outbreak of war. The disparity between the stories of *Leipzig* and *Dresden* on the American station was indicative of the problem. As long as the ships had coal, they could move without fear. But how much longer would they have coal? All the admiral had to do was look at the lines of silent ships in Valparaiso harbor and he knew the answer to his own question.

The admiral had now formulated the plan he intended to follow for the next few weeks. He would go around the Horn again and then, picking any targets of opportunity, he would proceed to the East. Finally, at some appointed hour in propitious circumstances, he would make the grand breakthrough into the North Sea, and join the High Seas Fleet, thus giving that fleet more strength with which to oppose the British Grand Fleet stationed at Scapa Flow.

The admiral's plan was based on many factors that could not have been foreseen at the outbreak of war—particularly the stubbornness of the neutrals of the Americas in the matter of twenty-four-hour stays and coaling, and the shortage of German supplies in an area where there were no German bases.

Chief among these shortages was a lack of ammunition.

During the battle just finished, *Scharnhorst* had fired 422 8-inch shells and had only 350 left. *Gneisenau* had used 244 shells and had 528 left. Another battle would empty the magazines of the big guns and make the two heavy cruisers useless as fighting craft. More ammunition was needed. But from where? It could not come from Germany in time. If Admiral von Spee kept his cruisers in South American waters while waiting for supply ships, he would be a sitting duck, and it remained only for the British to round up all available forces, find him, and destroy him.

There was a certain inevitability to Admiral von Spee's plan—it was in fact the only possible plan that would allow for the salvation of the East Asia Squadron.

Shortly after *Scharnhorst* anchored, Admiral von Spee went ashore. Nothing had been known about the battle as the Germans pulled into harbor, but the word spread quickly and by the time he stepped ashore a huge crowd, Germans and Chileans, had gathered to greet and cheer him. Newspaper reporters and photographers crowded about the admiral and fired questions and cameras at him as he walked along with the German civil officials.

The German colony wanted to arrange a huge celebration, but Admiral von Spee was a better diplomat than that and flatly refused to allow his presence on Chilean soil to become a propaganda matter. He made a courtesy call on the Chilean admiral, then went into the heart of Valparaiso to conduct his business of the day. He telegraphed to the German Admiralty an account of the battle of Coronel, sending the word by way of Count von Bernsdorff, the German ambassador in Washington. He went to the Deutsche Klub of Valparaiso with fifteen of his senior officers, Captain Fielitz, his chief of staff, the three ship's captains, and others who had official duties to perform in harbor. He spent a pleasant ninety minutes there,

218

in German surroundings, taking care of business that was no business of Chileans or others and enjoying himself.

Meanwhile, in the harbor, Germans and others were swarming aboard the warship. Of course care was taken to see that no English spies came aboard, and all but Germans were suspiciously scrutinized. But as for the German colony, men, women, and children came aboard. Women even braved the long climb up the Jacob's ladder, clutching their skirts about them, unconcerned about the sight they made in their eagerness to do honor to the heroes of their nation.

From the German ships in the harbor came scores of officers and men—all demanding that they be immediately enrolled in the German navy and taken aboard the warships to fight for their country. Anything, as one admitted to an officer of the *Gneisenau*, would be better than to continue to rot in harbor when there was a war on.

The first officers of the ships promised to sort out those who had skills that might really be useful to the Squadron, and the German volunteers went away.

Later in the day the officers of the ships were given shore liberty and a number of them took advantage of it, for they had not been in a real city for many weeks. *Scharnhorst* and *Gneisenau* had last called at Nagasaki. *Nürnberg* had last called at Honolulu.

A friendly German businessman offered to take *Korvetten-kapitän* Pochhammer and several other officers ashore and show them the sights of Valparaiso that day, and they were only too pleased to have the chance to stretch their legs.

The boats were put out from *Gneisenau* and the lucky officers and their hosts piled in, and were taken to the landing stage. First they passed through a line of Chilean warships, and the spick-and-span Germans were themselves impressed with the cleanliness and order of those vessels.

219

Ashore, the officers went shopping, as sailors always wish to do. They purchased Indian pottery and weaving and precious stones. They could not purchase much, because they had just jettisoned all the appurtenances of a peacetime navy, but the taste of victory was such that a few rules might be bent a bit this day, and they were.

They visited a German bookshop and saw there a war map, on which the fronts were shown by flags and lines of thread, changed according to the news reports. They saw and understood for the first time how impressive had been the German advance into France, but how on the opposite front, in the east, the Russians were still in territory the Germans called their own.

In honor of the great sea victory, the German-language newspaper of Valparaiso had issued an extra edition, and soon the Spanish-language newspapers were copying the report of the battle, as officers of the admiral's staff had given it to the German paper.

Wherever they went, the Germans were greeted with wide eyes and sometimes with smiles, sometimes even with cheers. Their host took them to a café for a meal, and they reveled in the soft seats of their chairs, the pretty women in the place, and the music.

They rode the funicular railroad up 400 feet to the height above the city, and gazed down on the happy sight of the harbor, dominated by their sturdy ships. They visited the German club for a few minutes, and their host took them to his factory where he insisted that the ships' officers take whatever machines and tools they might need aboard their warships. That night the lights burned brightly among the ships for the first time since war had been declared. They were in neutral waters, safe, and every porthole might be opened and every light turned on. Most were. Also, the rumors sped among the ships and throughout the city. The English had at first believed these gray warships were Japanese vessels assigned to help patrol the west coast of the Americas, and a small English contingent had come to the quay, only to be greeted by the unwelcome news that these were Germans. The English had also heard somewhere that *Leipzig* had been sunk by British warships, and they celebrated that—as much as they might—at the British club in Valparaiso that same evening.

Finally the lights were extinguished one by one, the last officers came back to their vessels laden with praise and satiated with food and drink, and the ships settled down for the night.

Next morning, bright and early, the officers and seamen of the civilian ships were again on board the warships, seeking interviews and enlistment in the cause of Germany. A hundred men assembled on the deck of the *Gneisenau*, for example, and that was typical of the other ships. First Officer Pochhammer walked up and down, stern and straight as a stick, and chose his men.

The engine room was the one place in which the ship really needed help. Under normal conditions the chief engineering officer had little trouble, given the staff set down in the table of organization for the ship. But *Gneisenau* had been steaming steadily for four months without a layup, and he could use some trained engineers and stokers to help keep the three big engines and the various motors and boilers in order.

Since there had been no casualties—with the exception of two men dead from dysentery—First Officer Pochhammer needed few men for the deck force, but he could use some. He could use prize crews, and so the biggest, sturdiest, cleanest, and most honest-looking applicants were enrolled in the ship's guard for this service. When not engaged in military duty, they would be deck scrubbers—but they were willing to accept this work. Many would have taken jobs as messboys just to get out of Valparaiso and into the war.

"Don't think that everything is always going to go as smoothly as it did at Coronel," warned First Officer Pochhammer. This warning came from the depths of his heart, for even as he had seen the easy victory the Squadron had scored at Coronel he had an uneasy feeling that the turn of the East Asia Squadron to take hits and fight fires would come all too soon. And the admiral shared this feeling. He had refused to allow any celebration of his victory. When hotheads had suggested that he drink to the damnation of the British navy, he had flatly refused to dishonor his enemies thus. And when, on the afternoon of the day before, the admiral had come back to his ship and had been presented a bouquet of red roses by a lovely lady, he had accepted them, but he had muttered that they had better be saved for his funeral.

"It's all the same to us, Captain," replied the men Pochhammer now selected. "We want to go with you."

And so several dozen men were enrolled, and even more because at the last moment "Uncle Hermann"—*Kapitänleutnant* Mezenthin—came rolling around a bulkhead, cast his grizzled and practiced eye on a half dozen of the men left over, and begged that they be taken too.

"They are the very best," he said.

First Officer Pochhammer did not feel like arguing with his prize officer, and so these half dozen, too, were enrolled in the ship's company, and soon it was swollen well above the 764-man quota of the *Gneisenau* under Berlin's organization chart.

Among the new men were carpenters, bakers, and other specialists, including torpedomen. Nearly all of them were reservists in either army or navy, and they came from many walks of life.

One of Admiral von Spee's first tasks when he arrived in

Valparaiso harbor was to order up provisions and coal. Somehow, through Chilean relaxation about timing or through British machinations (as the Squadron suspected) the barges were very late in arriving. Admiral von Spee could not secure all his provisions and also stick to the twenty-four-hour limit on his visit to Chilean waters, so reluctantly the men sent back the half-laden barges filled with potatoes and fresh vegetables, and at ten o'clock on the morning of November 4, just twenty-four hours after they had anchored, the pilot was aboard the flagship and she was weighing anchor to stand out to sea. One thing they had learned: the full extent of their victory. For *Good Hope* was totally unreported, and it was now certain that she had sunk as well as *Monmouth*.

In spite of the gaiety and presents that had come aboard from the German population of Chile, a Prussian *weltschmerz* had seized upon the senior officers of the Squadron. First Officer Pochhammer, for example, gloomily remarked about the presents from shore that those in Valparaiso "knew as well as we did that we were setting out on our last cruise."

Yet the weariness and sense of impending disaster in no way impeded the fighting qualities of the ships or of the crews. In a sense they were like the suicide forces of Japan in World War II, quite certain that they could not break through to Germany, quite certain that they would be engaged by the British in a major action very soon, quite certain that they would lose, that their ships would sink and they would die sailors' deaths in the deeps—and yet no more prepared to do anything to avoid that fate than had been Admiral Cradock and his brave men of the *Good Hope* and *Monmouth* who had known, hours before the fact, that they were going to their deaths unless fate somehow intervened.

The line of ships steamed out of Valparaiso in the sunlight, the wireless operators on the ships and ashore clacking furiously, as British, German, American, and other diplomatic and consular missions informed their counterparts elsewhere of the departure of the German Squadron for parts unknown.

On November 2, when the *Scharnhorst, Gneisenau,* and *Nürnberg* had gone into Valparaiso, the other ships of the Squadron had remained outside, given the task of rounding up colliers and meeting the ships which had been dispatched by the Germans in various ports to bring supplies and coal to the Squadron. *Leipzig* was detached and she went off cruising on her own along the seaways. At eight o'clock in the evening (2000 hours), the deck watch on *Leipzig* caught sight of a large sailing vessel which was scudding along the brisk sea on a following breeze, traveling northward well off the coast of Chile. *Leipzig* signaled with her lamps, making the usual demands for identification, and when Captain Haun was not satisfied, he put a shot across her bow, which brought the sailer around to lie to in the wind. She was the four-masted bark *Valentine,* carrying a cargo of Cardiff coal, the prize crew of the *Leipzig* was delighted to learn. The French captain protested that he knew nothing of a war, and pretended to disbelieve that the Germans had any right to capture him. Prize Officer Jensen explained to the captain that the Germans were just about to capture Paris.

"*Mon Dieu,*" said the Frenchman, and he subsided.

The admiral's orders to the Squadron had been to meet again at Mas-a-Fuera. Had the Chilean government known of this plan there would have been much resentment, because again the admiral was planning to violate the strict rules of warfare by making use of this deserted territory. It was his only hope—this use of uninhabited territory, without consideration for the rights of ownership or neutrality.

Leipzig towed her prize into the waters of Mas-a-Fuera. The collier *Baden* towed the Norwegian sailer *Helicon* into the harbor. *Scharnhorst, Gneisenau,* and *Nürnberg* arrived on

November 6, and the next day in came *Dresden* escorting the steamer *San Sacramento* which had been chartered by the German government at San Francisco and was loaded with 7000 tons of coal and 1000 tons of food for the Squadron.

In the harbor on November 8 were thirteen ships: the five cruisers; the armed auxiliaries *Titania* and *Prinz Eitel Friedrich*; the tenders *Santa Isabel, Baden, Amasis,* and *San Sacramento*; and the prizes *Valentine* and *Helicon*.

Now came the time-consuming process of coaling and provisioning once again.

Admiral von Spee came aboard the *Helicon* to inspect that prize. According to the laws of war and prizing the Germans were in the right in seizing her because, although a neutral ship she contained a cargo that was partly destined for the German enemy. She might even have been destroyed, as several of the officers of the Squadron suggested.

But the admiral was a more humane man than many of his subordinates. He ordered that *Helicon* be left with 800 tons of goods as ballast and then sent to the nearest port, but only after the coal was taken from her hold for the use of his fighting ships.

Gneisenau won the dubious honor of emptying the two sailing ships, perhaps because her black gang was largest and her record of coaling was best in the Squadron. The men discovered that coaling from a sailing ship was unlike anything they had ever done before; the sailers were brought up, one on port and one on starboard, and they sheered off and tugged up so hard at their anchors, then snuggled back so quickly, that one might step off the upper deck of the *Gneisenau* onto their rails at one moment, and find himself in a thirty-foot swimming trough if he tried it the next.

Then there was the question of the yards of the sailing ships. The swell was heavy, and the sailers rolled continuously, their braced yards pointing dangerously and describing what sometimes seemed to be totally elliptical figures, threatening the masts, funnels, cranes, and guns of the warships.

It was no sinecure, this job.

The weather grew so rough, the swell so persistent, and the wind so high that the sailing ships had to be removed from the sides of the warship at nightfall. And then Captain Maerker suggested that his men would coal on, even thirty-six hours at a stretch, if they would be allowed to bring up a steamer and finish the dirty job. The admiral concurred and this was done, although it meant ignoring Sunday and working six-hour watches, 0600 to 1200, 1200 to 1800, 1800 to 2400, 2400 to 0600.

The off-duty officers went aboard the *Valentine*, for she was one of those passing rarities of the First World War, a Cape Horn sailer. She was nearly new in 1914, built of steel with steel masts and yards. There was still a place for her in that world, carrying grain and coal, for the trip from the English Channel to the Cape and back again offered favorable winds, and coal and grain prices were such that a profit could be made. Her day was passing, and even as the Germans examined her old-fashioned lines and portholes, painted black on the white stripes of the two sides, the men could sense this change. She was manned by a crew of thirty well-trained sailors, and the men of the *Leipzig* remarked that when they had first brought her into sight, they had not really believed their eyes, because she was so clean and beautiful that they could not see how she could have remained that way and made her course around the dirty weather of the Horn.

Valentine was to be destroyed. No one wanted her destruction less than the admiral, who loved a good sailing ship. After all, he had trained in sailing ships and had been an instructor on them.

But what was one to do? She was an enemy and a valuable asset to the French.

So if she was to be destroyed, the Squadron should have everything aboard her. With that decision, the cannibalization began. First, the shining white sails were unbent, brought down, and cut up. A canvas shop was installed in Captain Maerker's dining room on the *Gneisenau*, a room which he had not used since the ship had been stripped for action, and which was occupied only by four 3.4-inch guns until the shop came into being. The sails were chopped and the mainsail was cut into some three hundred coal bags for use in giving the same life to the *Gneisenau* that the canvas had given to *Valentine*.

Two casks of wine were given to the crew of *Valentine* as they were unshipped from their happy home and transported to the *Prinz Eitel Friedrich*. As for the rest, this was a serious matter of disposition, and it was handled by a special representative from the admiral's staff. He split up the wine among the wine messes of the five warships, as equally as possible.

Then the rigging was brought down, the yards were lowered, and the other spars and masts were removed. Tools, tackle, fenders, charts, cables, and a dozen other commodities useful to men of the sea were found aboard her and split up among sailors turned scavenger, men brutalized by the exigencies of war.

All this equipment and 1000 tons of coal came out of *Valentine*. After she was emptied, she was moved to an anchorage behind the warships, out of harm's way, awaiting the inevitable moment when she would be sunk.

She did not wish to wait.

At night, when all the ships were quiet, suddenly a flash of flame burst from the windows of the main cabin of *Valentine*, and she stood out like a beacon in the night, threatening every ship in the Squadron with her light. Quickly the alarms were sounded aboard the warships and boats were put over the side. The damage-control parties moved swiftly, taking their fire extinguishers and making their way to the bouncing bark. But by the time the first boat pulled up to the ship, and men began swarming up the ladder, the fire was out. It was an easily explained fire, started by the men of the prize crew who had found the evening growing cold and had decided to warm themselves with the great stove in the cabin. They had not noticed that some official vandal had carefully undone the brass stovepipe to carry it off to one of the fighting ships.

The next day the remainder of the coal of *Valentine* was loaded aboard *Prinz Eitel Friedrich*. No more chances would be taken. That big auxiliary, once a luxury liner, needed coal badly if she was to carry on her task of raiding once the Squadron left her. She was a definite liability to Admiral von Spee, as great a liability as *Otranto* had been to Admiral Cradock. Without *Otranto* what might not have happened in the unequal war between squadrons? There was a moment— far more than that—when Admiral von Spee had called up his ragged ships and when the call had not yet produced the pack, when the neat two-cable line of British warships was broken only by *Otranto*'s sloppy performance into wind and wave, when the top speed of the British vessels had been cut by at least three knots. Might those three knots have enabled Admiral Cradock to steal the luff away from the Germans? No one would ever know, but no admiral of any nation ever felt completely at home in a mixed squadron of ships that were not all built for naval war. The converted merchantman, rusty tramp, or sleek liner was ever little but a headache to the admirals.

Not so to those lucky officers who were invited by Captain Thierechens to dine aboard *Prinz Eitel Friedrich*. They were now used to eating hastily between walls of painted sheet iron, the luxuries of their peacetime life all but forgotten. As a luxury liner, *Prinz Eitel Friedrich* had been outfitted with drapes and paneling, murals on the walls of dining rooms, shining silver, and damask table linens. Captain Thierechens had begun taking out the obviously inflammable materials but had been forced to give up the task—or prepare to rebuild parts of the ship. He lived in luxury, therefore, not because he wanted to, but because he was overtaken by events, and there was no time for proper conversion of the steamer to auxiliary warship.

The officers of the Squadron were always pleased to go aboard *Prinz Eitel Friedrich*. It was like getting into another world for a little while. The food and the wines still bore the traces of peacetime days, and although she was short of the materials of war, the ship was not short of luxuries.

On November 9, as the East Asia Squadron prepared itself for the troublesome times the admiral knew must come, *Dresden*'s sister ship, the *Emden*, met her doom in the Cocos Keeling Islands. She had sunk more than twenty enemy vessels in three months, including a Russian cruiser and a French destroyer. She had completely terrorized the shipping of the Indian Ocean, and nearly *four dozen* Allied warships were tied up in the search for her or were forced to alter their plans because of her. Due to a misreading of a radio transmission from a British convoy, she had come to believe that her enemies were 250 miles farther from her than they actually were. She had landed a party of armed men to destroy the Direction Island wireless and cable station manned by the British, and had been caught there by a heavy Australian cruiser, HMS *Sydney*. After a forty-minute fight that was even more mismatched than the struggle at Coronel, *Emden* was dismasted, holed, and destroyed, and Captain von Müller ran her aground on rocks to keep her from sinking under him and killing the members of the crew still living.

This news was not yet known to the Squadron when *Leipzig* and *Dresden* set out to take their turn at the pleasant trip to Valparaiso. They were to carry dispatches from the admiral to Berlin, and to pick up the official dispatches for the admiral from the Reichsmarineamt.

Admiral von Spee had received an old Admiralty order on his own visit to Valparaiso, which had warned him of the same situation that *Dresden's*, *Leipzig's*, and *Nürnberg's* captains had mentioned—the difficulties of securing supplies. That letter had also put into the admiral's head the suggestion that he return to Germany. Now he was awaiting the messages that should have come for him to Valparaiso, in order that he would know what course to pursue. In his own mind he was sure that he must try to break through to the homeland. Still, he waited.

He had some news—most of it disturbing. The German agents in Buenos Aires reported that if the Squadron was planning to come to southeastern waters it must bring its own coal, because the governments of Brazil and Argentina had embargoed supply ships for the Germans. Von Spee planned, then, to run down to St. Quentin Bay, and there to resupply himself from the colliers at hand and those he might expect to come from Chilean waters. Part of the reason for the trip of *Dresden* and *Leipzig* was to arrange for more coal to be sent to the Squadron.

After the two light cruisers left Mas-a-Fuera the Squadron became more nervous than usual. That night a ship suddenly appeared where no ship ought to be, and the admiral ordered *Gneisenau* to go out and inspect the suspicious vessel. It was only the *Baden*, whose windlass had been damaged so that she could not anchor until very late.

Then, from broadcasts, came bad news by the barrelful. Tsingtao had fallen on November 7 after a naval battle in

230

which the Squadron's old ship *S-90* had defended the harbor and torpedoed a Japanese cruiser.

And they learned of the destruction of their own *Emden*, two days later.

The *weltschmerz* was now forever with them.

14

SO FIERCE THE HUNT

ADMIRAL VON SPEE HAD VERY LITTLE ACCURATE information about the disposition of the British forces in eastern South American waters, and there was good reason for his confusion and lack of knowledge. The situation was in flux at the time of the battle of Coronel and it remained that way for several days.

The admiral wrote in his dispatches that he suspected a British battleship of the modern *Formidable* class to be somewhere in the vicinity, and he wondered why the British had not kept this ship in with the others of their squadron.

Of course there was no such strength in the Pacific. But following the defeat at Coronel, the British Admiralty moved with a speed unmatched to this point in the war. All the warnings of Admiral Cradock were now heeded. Too late it was recognized that the *Canopus* was useless for the job assigned to her.

The reshuffled British Admiralty board that met in November did not suddenly realize that Great Britain had just suffered one of the major naval defeats of her history, and had lost the most important naval action fought thus far in World War I. What was suddenly understood was that two inadequate squadrons had been assigned to defend the two shores of South America against the German East Asia Squadron. Either of these squadrons might be eaten up by "the great gray wolf," as the Graf Spee was now called in Germany.

The board took office twenty-four hours before Coronel and began to move at once.

The existence of Admiral von Spee and the East Asia Squadron was recognized by this new board as the most important single factor in the naval side of the war—before the news of Coronel was known.

Nervous British military and colonial leaders all slept uneasily in their beds. Wherever a sharp naval attack might wreck British hopes, the dream that Admiral von Spee was lurking offshore persisted, and brought either paralysis or excessive caution. If there was ever a "fleet in being" which terrorized an enemy by its simple existence it was the five-ship fleet of Admiral von Spee, led by one not-too-new heavy cruiser and her sister ship.

In London, the Admiralty took action to create forces all over the world that would have as their primary objective the finding and destruction of Admiral von Spee's Cruiser Squadron.

On the day that the new board had taken over from the old one, an attempt had been made to right the wrongs of previous weeks, and *Defence* had been ordered to Admiral Cradock—but too late to save that brave man's life and the situation in the Pacific. *Defence* did not arrive in Montevideo until November 3, two days after the British debacle at Coronel.

The first move of the British Admiralty was to order

Admiral Stoddart to concentrate his armored cruisers *Carnarvon* and *Cornwall* with *Defence* at Montevideo. *Canopus* and *Otranto* were also sent to that Uruguayan port. The light cruiser *Kent* from the Canary Islands Cape Verde station was also sent there.

The Admiralty's second move was to detach the heavy cruisers *Inflexible* and *Invincible* from the Home Fleet under Admiral Jellicoe. What a sign of panic that move represented! Nothing but the most severe of emergencies could cause any British sea lords voluntarily to weaken the Home Fleet, the guardian of British trade routes and the British shores. The detachment of these two big ships was a sure sign of the seriousness with which the Admiralty regarded the continued existence of Admiral von Spee's Squadron.

Vice Admiral Sir F. Doveton Sturdee was detached as chief of staff and given command of a new squadron whose basic purpose was to hunt out von Spee. He was more than a squadron commander—in the need of the situation he was named Commander in Chief of the South Atlantic and Pacific, with a northerly limit in the Atlantic of 5 degrees north—along a line from North Brazil to Liberia. But if the movements of von Spee caused him to come north, this command would expand to include any station he entered. He was directed to take *Invincible* as his flagship and then move to the Falklands, where Admiral Stoddart would be brought under his command.

Now in case Admiral von Spee decided to move north in the Pacific, rather than cross around the Horn and make a dash through the Atlantic, another plan was devised. The cruisers *Newcastle* and *Idzumo* were already off the west coast of North America. The *Asama* and the *Hizen* were at Honolulu watching the old-fashioned *Geier*, which had been ordered to take refuge there because she was too slow to fight. Admiral Patey was to be brought up from Australia and all the ships

234

named above would be brought to a point around San Clemente Island at the southern tip of California. The battleship *Australia* was to be brought up there too, and Admiral Patey would take command of the new squadron, which would move south and find von Spee.

The Japanese would send their First South Sea Squadron to patrol between Fiji and the Marquesas, in case Admiral von Spee suddenly broke back for the Pacific region, and they reinforced that squadron until it contained three heavy cruisers—*Kurama, Tsukuba,* and *Iwate*—which made it superior to the German East Asia Squadron.

Nor was this all that the Admiralty did to protect British might against five lonely ships. The British cruisers *Goliath* and *Dartmouth* were ordered away from the East African station to join the battle cruiser *Albion* at the Cape of Good Hope, in case von Spee headed for southern or southwest Africa. The British armored cruiser *Minotaur*, which the Germans knew so well from Tsingtao days, was ordered to reinforce the Cape squadron. A plan was laid to form an entirely new squadron of three British and three French ships, under a French admiral, which would protect the French and British West African colonies from *die grauen Wölfe*. The weak spot was the North Atlantic region, and here Rear Admiral R. S. Phipps Hornby was ordered to keep a sharp eye on the Panama Canal and be ready at all times with two of his fastest cruisers to shadow—but not engage—Admiral von Spee's force, if it came through the Canal.

These Admiralty actions were begun even though the results of the disaster at Coronel were very slow in arriving in Britain. The first indication of trouble had come to the Admiralty in London on November 4, when the consul general at Valparaiso reported on the visit of the German ships *Scharnhorst, Gneisenau,* and *Nürnberg*. His report stated:

Have just learnt from Chilean admiral that German admiral states that on Sunday (1st November) at sunset, in thick and wicked weather, his ships met *Good Hope, Glasgow, Monmouth,* and *Otranto.* Action was joined and *Monmouth* turned over and sank after about an hour's fighting. *Good Hope, Glasgow,* and *Otranto* drew off into darkness. *Good Hope* was on fire, an explosion was heard, and she is believed to have sunk. *Gneisenau, Scharnhorst,* and *Nürnberg* were among the German ships engaged.

Glasgow was in touch with the Port Stanley wireless telegraph station on November 2, but her report did not reach London until several hours after this consular message.

When this message arrived, First Lord of the Admiralty Winston Churchill and First Sea Lord Fisher sat down and began working out the detailed plans for the sinking of Admiral von Spee and his Cruiser Squadron, giving for the first time one British admiral command of one-half the British world.

Six hours after the news of Coronel reached the Admiralty, these plans had been worked out, and the battle cruisers *Invincible* and *Inflexible* were ordered to coal at once and proceed down the west coast of England to Plymouth, there to prepare for immediate foreign service.

Britain's naval dockyards were still operating on a peacetime basis, it seemed, for they reported that the ships would be ready for sea at midnight on November 13. Winston Churchill sent a message stating that the ships must sail not later than November 11, and that if necessary dockyard workmen must go along on the trip to finish their work. They would be sent home later from some port of call. When the dockyard authorities received *that* message they realized that

Churchill would brook no nonsense—and so the two ships *did* sail on November 11.

Admiral Sturdee was directed to go to St. Vincent, Cape Verde Islands, for coaling, and then on to Abrolhos Rocks, where he would rendezvous with Rear Admiral Stoddart. There were to be assembled *Invincible, Inflexible, Carnarvon, Cornwall, Kent, Glasgow, Bristol,* and the auxiliary cruisers *Macedonia* and *Orama.* Britain then would have a force of five armored cruisers and two light cruisers to throw against Admiral von Spee, not counting *Defence* which was ordered to the Cape of Good Hope.

Poor old *Canopus,* which Winston Churchill had stoutly defended as a fighting ship, was now sent to do a job for which she was suited: she grounded herself in Port Stanley harbor and turned herself into a fort for the defense of the islands. This was not wasteful; Captain Grant had reported that the attempt to reach the fighting at Coronel had caused him to make a speed of more than twelve knots, and that *Canopus* had strained her boilers so seriously that their safety was now doubtful. So Admiral Cradock was proved right beyond peradventure.

On their trip across the Atlantic, the big cruisers were warned to keep out of the way of shipping and above all to refrain from using their wireless. What the Admiralty wanted was secrecy, so that the Germans might be caught unaware. Instead of obeying orders, for some strange reason the cruisers did almost everything else. They stopped suspicious steamers and searched them on the way south—after they had passed the Equator. Obviously, in this way the news of their coming would get out, and it did. Worse for the cruisers, careless wireless operators at St. Vincent gossiped about the visit of the cruisers with their chums *in the clear,* so that all the world might learn of the voyage and destination of the big cruisers.

Meanwhile, *Glasgow* steamed to Rio de Janeiro, where she arrived on November 15, dirty and battered, having traveled 3000 miles since the battle of Coronel. In spite of their protests at Valparaiso about German entrance, the British at Rio took the position that they ought to be allowed much more time than the twenty-four-hour limitation. There was one clause under the rule of neutrality by which they could secure additional time: if a vessel was so badly damaged that it would be unsafe to move her out in that short a period, the stay could be extended and repairs made to get the ship to its nearest British port. Of course *Glasgow* was quite capable of steaming on, but here was an excellent opportunity for repairs, and a friendly Brazilian government was extremely lenient in its interpretations of the neutrality laws.

Glasgow was warped into the drydock of the Enrique Lage shipyard, and soon an army of Brazilian workers were at her sides, repairing the holes in her hull and scraping and painting—in short, giving the ship a general overhaul.

While *Glasgow* was in port, a most secret message was sent to Captain Luce, informing him of the voyage of *Invincible* and *Inflexible*. The secret was so grave that Captain Luce informed only the British minister in Rio de Janeiro. So Luce, the minister, and Intelligence Officer Lloyd Hirst were the only three men in Brazil who knew—or that is what they believed until Hirst overheard two British businessmen casually discussing the coming of the *Invincible* and *Inflexible* in the Club Central, an international club where Germans were at the moment in the room.

Horrified, Hirst asked the Englishmen to "keep it secret," and then learned of the wireless operators' gossip which had brought the story across the sea. The German intelligence network did know, therefore, of the coming of these big ships, but for some reason the news was never passed on to Admiral von Spee.

After five days in drydock, *Glasgow* coaled and took on a full supply of provisions. She was actually in better condition than she had been since the outbreak of the war, courtesy of the Brazilians. She steamed on November 16 for the rendezvous at Abrolhos and there met the other ships of the new squadron on November 26. For two days the ships transferred supplies and coal, and Admiral Sturdee learned of the local situation and of the battle at Coronel.

At this point the British were certain that Admiral von Spee would try to break around the tip of South America—going *somewhere*. They really expected him to steam up the middle of the South Atlantic until he reached the trade routes.

Glasgow and *Bristol* would go out as scouts, ferreting about Tierra del Fuego and the Chilean archipelago, and the big cruisers would remain at the Falklands until called for.

On November 28, the British force began to steam south to carry out this plan.

15

MOMENT OF GLORY

WHEN LEIPZIG AND DRESDEN CALLED AT VALPAraiso on November 13, they went through the same ceremonial entrance that had been made by the other ships of the Squadron: guns booming, bugles blowing, drums beating, and men standing at attention in salute of the Chilean national emblem and her naval force. Then, the honors finished, German Minister von Eckert came aboard at eleven o'clock and the real business of the trip was transacted. There was a certain amount of harassment from the British, who complained that the Germans had just brought three warships into the harbor. But there was no violation of the neutrality laws in what the Germans were now doing, so the complaints were little more than troublesome.

Again, reservists and volunteers applied to be taken aboard for the fighting they were sure was coming and they would soon enjoy in the service of the Kaiser. There was shore leave and the usual trips and purchasing by the officers, but the important business was to get the news and such dispatches as may have arrived from Germany.

The Germans had a telegram from Captain Boy-Ed, the German intelligence chief in the United States, telling Admiral von Spee to break through the British lines and come home to Germany.

The Admiralty had a number of important instructions for Admiral von Spee. He was to carry on *Kreuzerkrieg* as he moved east and north, and he must be prepared to supply himself with coal because of the pressure exerted by the British on neutral states. It would even be difficult to secure coal supplies from New York City at this point, the message reported.

All ships, of all kinds, that Admiral von Spee was able to collect would be placed under his general orders. He was to destroy any ships that were of marginal value and heavy coal consumption, such as the auxiliary cruiser *Kronprinz Wilhelm*.

The admiral was advised to take on enough coal in South America to reach the Cape Verde Islands. Then, when he was ready to make the final breakthrough, the German High Seas Fleet would steam out and engage or intimidate the British Grand Fleet so that the Cruiser Squadron could come home safely.

There was an air of urgency in the movements of *Leipzig* and *Dresden*. They had come into Valparaiso in the morning, but at midnight they were gone. The admiral was becoming restive, and there was no time for further play, or for supplying ships. From the colliers and the other freighters the ships were decently supplied—or as well as they were likely to be.

After instructing the German minister about their movements, they left. If colliers could be arranged, they were to be sent to meet the Squadron at St. Quentin Bay in the Gulf of Peñas, a thousand miles south.

Admiral von Spee then made ready to take his other

warships and supply train to the Gulf. One of his first moves was to eliminate the *Titania*. That armed freighter had given good service in the months since the Squadron left Tsingtao, but she had come to the end of the road. Her engines were limping and her boilers were weak. She could not be guaranteed to keep up, and the admiral must now travel fast. *Titania* came alongside the three cruisers and gave up from her bowels what supplies she had, and then went back to her anchorage. A party from the *Prinz Eitel Friedrich* went aboard and began to strip her of all that another auxiliary could use, especially of her armament. The crew was shared out among the other vessels: the wireless officer and commander going to *Gneisenau*, other officers going to *Scharnhorst* and *Nürnberg*.

On Sunday, November 15, Admiral von Spee issued through the fleet a list of promotions and honors for the enlisted men who had served especially well during the battle at Coronel.

It was a busy day. *Valentine* and *Titania* were moved into deep water and their sea cocks were opened. Luncheon was very festive, for the officers and men now knew that they would be leaving soon—Admiral von Spee had held a meeting of captains in the morning and had told them he planned now to move around to the southeast coast of South America to carry on the war. He did not say anything then about the plan to run home through the British gantlet, but that was because he had not received approval of this course of action from the Admiralty.

The atmosphere was still relaxed and easy. In Mas-a-Fuera there was a sense of being in friendly waters. All the Germans knew that unless a miracle occurred the British had no major strength in this area, and while they took regular precautions such as blackout and war watch, they were fairly at their ease and there was much visiting back and forth among the ships. At luncheon that day several officers from

Gneisenau dined on the *Scharnhorst*, and the first officer of *Scharnhorst*, Captain Bender, came to the *Gneisenau* with the captain of the *Prinz Eitel Friedrich* for a memorable meal. After church, the ships' bands played concerts, ending with *Die Wacht am Rhine* which everyone stood up to sing, and then the men adjourned below for beer while the officers had a cocktail and then a wine lunch in the officers' mess.

But after luncheon, the pace again quickened. Captain Schultz called for First Officer Bender to return to the *Scharnhorst*. Captain Maerker called First Officer Pochhammer to his cabin and told him that the admiral had ordered anchors weighed at 1600 hours. *Korvettenkapitän* Pochhammer saluted smartly, clicked his heels sharply, and went off to do his admiral's bidding. A fatigue party from the *Gneisenau* had been sent to help another ship coal, and it did not come back until the last moment, as Pochhammer paced the bridge fretfully, fearful that he would be late and would again be the object of the admiral's wrath. But at the last moment, as the ship was being made secure for departure, the labor party returned. The boat was hoisted quickly, and almost as it left the water the anchor windlass began to clank, and in a few minutes *Gneisenau* moved slowly forward.

The move out was quite correct. The Squadron was performing with its usual degree of spit and polish. Every man was doing his duty, and yet there was something dismal in the air this day; it was as if the officers and men of the Squadron knew that they had not yet finished with the British, and that the easy victory of Coronel must needs have its eventual accounting.

Admiral von Spee knew better than anyone else the odds they were facing. He did not have very accurate information about the British, but he did know that somewhere on the other side of the Straits of Magellan his enemies were congregating, with at least three armored cruisers, at least two light

243

cruisers, and the old battleship *Canopus*. He also knew of the combined British-Japanese squadron that kept him from moving north along the Pacific coast.

The Squadron and its train was for the moment sharply reduced. Besides the cruisers that accompanied the admiral's flagship, along came only the *Baden* and the *Santa Isabel*. All other ships had been sent away, either to find more coal and meet the Squadron at a later date, or to go their own ways.

The admiral spent several hours in conference with his staff, and prepared messages to be sent to various points regarding coal deliveries. One went to the German Admiralty's New York agents, another to those in the River Plate, ordering 10,000 tons of coal and three months' supplies for 1000 men to come to the rendezvous at Punta Santa Elena on the Argentine coast by December 5. He arranged for another 20,000 tons of coal to be held on readiness by New York and Pernambuco, for delivery in January to some as yet unstipulated place.

On November 18 *Leipzig* and *Dresden* joined the Squadron with their news. The fleet was stopped for a little while so that boats could run back and forth busily between the ships, bringing fresh fruits and newspapers to all the cruisers. *Dresden* had captured a British cargo ship, the *North Wales*, a 3600-ton steamer. She had only about 700 tons of coal aboard, and although she was a British Admiralty steamer, she did not have a wireless rig, much to the surprise of the Germans. Her captain and crew knew nothing of the defeat of the British at Coronel. Some coal was taken, the ship's charts were removed for what value they might prove to be, and the ship's log was appropriated. The crew was moved into *Dresden*, and then the *North Wales* was sunk, not far from the place where *Monmouth* and *Good Hope* had received their mortal wounds.

The Squadron then headed south again, through seas that

grew colder and rougher every hour as they progressed into the higher latitudes. At daybreak on November 21 they reached the mouth of the Gulf of Peñas, and secluded water where they were surrounded by glaciers, forest, and rocks. The glacier was so close that in the sunlight they could see its moraines and crevasses glistening.

Now there was time to read the newspapers. Some of the men learned of their own promotions thus, including *Kapitän zur See* von Lüdecke of the *Dresden* whose promotion had come through in October. Some learned of the deaths of relatives and friends. All learned more about the war effort, at least as it was seen in Chile, as translated by German observers.

Coaling began again, for in this bay a large German fleet was once again assembled. They had picked up the storeship *Rhakotis* which had run out of Valparaiso to bring supplies to the Squadron. In San Quentin Bay they found waiting for them the colliers *Seydlitz* and *Memphis*. Two days later the colliers *Luxor* and *Rameses* had also arrived, having come from Coronel and Valparaiso in answer to the admiral's requests.

Now again it was apparent that something was about to happen. Not only did they coal to capacity, but they were advised to take deckloads of coal onto the cruisers.

For men who had lived in the lap of luxury—in terms of such necessary but unpleasant labor as coaling—the German East Asia Squadron had done very well in learning to live without coolies. They had developed some advanced techniques of coaling that cut down on the labor and the dirt: on *Gneisenau*, for example, they had used sailcloth to line their cargo nets, and had made one coal net large enough to take a ton and a half of coal at one lift.

This development could only alleviate the unpleasantness of coaling, but at least it did that much. And this time the ships took more coal than ever before. It was piled up (in briquettes) on both sides of the middle-deck, so high that the deck of *Gneisenau* sagged and had to be supported with timbers. Between the third and fourth funnels, a space known for its openness, there was only room on the *Gneisenau* for the steam pinnace. The space behind the bridge was filled with coal. Every bit of extra deck was used for this storage.

The one positive advantage to all its dirty work, from the viewpoint of the men if not the officers, was that there was so much black dust on deck that it was useless to try to clean the ships after coaling, as they usually did.

In St. Quentin Bay the East Asia Squadron also made ready for the coming Christmas holidays. A large number of presents from Germans in Chile had been delivered to the various colliers and supply ships, and to the *Leipzig* and *Dresden* when they came into port. These were now put aboard the various supply ships and were kept for distribution at Christmas time. Further, all ships cut evergreen trees from the forests and laid them aside. In the cold they would keep fine, and no one aboard the ships knew how close to an evergreen forest the Squadron might be at Christmas time.

Cold as the weather was, at least in this bay it was protected and the sun was shining for a change. A special kind of warmth came to the Squadron one day as they lay in this haven: news from the German radio stations told them that the Kaiser had granted three hundred Iron Crosses to men of the Squadron. Admiral von Spee had received the Iron Cross First Class, and the Iron Cross Second Class. He ordered that the three hundred other crosses be given to the captains, first officers, gunnery officers, chief engineers and his general staff senior officers, and the wireless officers. These came, however, only to about 10 per cent of the total. So the remainder were distributed to the men, gunners first, engineers second, and specifically to any men who had distinguished themselves in action, although the fight at Coronel had been so unequal that it was difficult to single out men for individual acts of heroism.

The presentation ceremony was held on the decks of the ships on the afternoon of November 26. The admiral chose that day, because it was the day on which he intended to move out around the southern tip of South America, and he wanted to bring morale to a peak for this difficult passage.

The captains of the ships called their crews into their best uniforms for inspection that afternoon. The quarter-decks were shining and clear of coal, and the men lined up for the captains' stroll down the ranks. The captains commented here and there on some lack of spit and polish, but not with any seriousness, for their men were good fighting men and the officers were proud of them. Then each captain stood in front of his staff and read a note from Admiral von Spee, congratulating the men on the victory at Coronel, announcing the distribution on each ship of the awards, and urging them to ever higher acts of patriotism in the difficult days that would come.

"Three cheers for His Majesty" came the shout from the men.

And the three cheers were gladly given.

Even as the ceremony began the ships were made ready for sea, and immediately afterward they turned south, the heavy swell catching and pulling the ships, and the Cape Horn wind beating at them. They were on their way.

16

ONE LAST DEFIANCE

AT ST. QUENTIN BAY ADMIRAL VON SPEE HAD SE-cured a 17,000-ton supply of coal, which meant that he could make his way around the Horn and out of South American waters with one more coaling, provided he could keep Squadron and supply train together in the heavy weather they would encounter in the passage.

The admiral faced a new difficulty: the British had complained strenuously about German overstays in Chilean waters, and the Chilean government had become embarrassed and angry when the colliers had sneaked out of Valparaiso and Coronel without permission to come and supply the Squadron. Chilean waters were rapidly becoming unfriendly to the Germans, in spite of a long history of friendship which included even the development of the Chilean army along lines of the German. The admiral had other problems on his mind: not the least of these was his shortage of ammunition. He simply could not risk another important battle until he met an

248

ammunition ship. He had wirelessed Berlin about this on his arrival at Valparaiso, but he still did not know what the admiralty had done to alleviate his serious shortage.

There were also some good signs. He had a message from Punta Arenas stating that there were no British warships at the Falklands, and the information (which was erroneous) that all British units had left the South American coast because of a revolution that had broken out in South Africa. Since such a revolution was much to be hoped for by German standards it was not hard for anyone in the Squadron to believe this welcome news. (The fact was that on November 12 *Canopus*, for whatever she was worth, had actually arrived at Port Stanley, so the information was as faulty as if it had been prepared by the British for the admiral.)

There was no way that Admiral von Spee could get accurate news in these waters except by sending one of his light cruisers to a point at or near shore to be in contact with friendly radio stations. But the radio stations were growing less friendly, and he could not take the chance of running into port with a single small ship, not knowing where the British were, no matter how much he wanted to believe they had gone from these waters.

There were German centers at La Plata and Valparaiso, but he was out of touch with both. He had sent the collier *Amasis* to pick up coal and information at Punta Arenas and then proceed to a rendezvous some 400 miles southeast of the River Plate, and when he reached that point he hoped to have better information, but for the moment he was traveling in the dark.

At this moment on November 26, the British were spreading their nets wide to catch him, and German intelligence knew something of the facts, but what could be done?

By November 26 the German intelligence unit at La Plata knew of the whereabouts of *Glasgow* and *Canopus*, and also knew that three British cruisers had visited Abrolhos, but the only manner in which information could be offered to Admiral von Spee was to give it to the captains of two supply ships which were setting out from Buenos Aires and Montevideo to join the East Asia Squadron down the Argentine coast.

When the Squadron steamed away from St. Quentin harbor the five cruisers and three steamers with 17,000 tons of coal aboard accompanied them, while *Amasis*, *Memphis* and *Luxor* steamed away to various Chilean harbors to refill their bunkers and await orders.

As for the Squadron, the weather was all the admiral feared it might be. On November 27 the wind reached Force 12 on the Beaufort scale (which meant more that seventy-two miles an hour) and the waves were so high that the Squadron reduced speed to five knots. In the afternoon the weather abated slightly and the speed was increased to eight knots.

Again the next day the weather was so bad that the colliers could not keep up, and speed was reduced until about four o'clock—the same pattern as on November 27.

On November 29 the wind dropped to Force 8 but the sea was running higher than before. From the flagship, *Gneisenau* was *not visible* much of the time, although she was second in line, and one observer said that the seas ran thirty meters high—which would have been ninety feet. (It seemed hardly possible that the weather could have been as bad as that diarist reported, although it was terrible.) It was impossible to lay the tables. Furniture slid around, and lightweight articles crashed and broke. Much of the crockery in the wardroom fell out of its cabinet and smashed on the floor, in spite of retaining clips. Leaks developed in the ships as seams sprang. No one could go on deck unless secured by ropes.

On November 30 the weather let up and they were able

to steam at ten knots. The next day, when they reached Cape Horn, it was hailing but the weather was becoming more moderate. On December 2 there was definite improvement and they were able to sight two icebergs, which they gave a wide berth. One of these rose out of the water to a height of 200 feet, and seemed to be 650 yards long, all blue and frozen.

Hardly had the men of the crew been called up to see the iceberg, when a hail rang out from the crow's nest, on *Scharnhorst*:

"Sailer six quarters to port."

On his bridge the admiral trained his glasses, and soon made out a three-masted bark tacking against the westerly breeze, and lying near the shore. *Leipzig* was detached to investigate, and soon reported that the sailing ship was an Englishman.

"English ship, English cargo, coal," was the laconic message from Captain Haun.

She could not be allowed to escape and give away the position of the Squadron. (The admiral did not know that he had already been compromised; his fleet had been sighted off the entrance to the Straits of Magellan.) She must be sunk. But first her coal cargo should be taken off, because the admiral might need every black diamond he could find.

The sailing ship, the *Drummuir*, was taken in tow by the *Leipzig*, and the Squadron wheeled astern to find a quiet anchorage in the islands south of Patagonia. The weather could not have been finer for them; the storm had quite given way to a midsummer's night by the time they entered Beagle Channel, named after the ship on which Charles Darwin made his famous naturalist's voyage. They saw a large pack of seals who immediately dived off the rocks near Picton Island—and there they anchored at about five o'clock on the afternoon (1700 hours) of December 3. The coal of *Drummuir* was to be split between two ships, the colliers *Baden* and *Santa*

Isabel. Dresden, which had lost part of her deck cargo in the frightful weather north of Cape Horn, also coaled again from *Seydlitz* at the same time. All the other cruisers also topped off deckloads or bunkers.

Several days were spent at Picton Island, recovering from the blow around the Cape. Parties of hopeful hunters went ashore from several ships, praying for a shot at a bird or a running animal. But they returned to report plenty of evidence of previous tenancy by man: abandoned houses and abandoned pasturage, but little else. They did see smoke (and those on the ships saw it every day) from Tierra del Fuego, on the other side of Beagle Channel. But they saw no other men.

In truth, they needed no other men and were pleased to be alone. The presence of shepherds would probably have meant the presence of spies for the enemy. The admiral was well pleased that there were none to see his preparations. His plans had been changed by the untimely loss of *Dresden's* deck coal, for he had planned to steam to Egg Harbor on the Argentine coast, but against the sea and wind, with the loss of that extra supply, *Dresden* could not have made the trip, so the plan had been changed with this opportunity.

Admiral von Spee rounded up his sons and a few other officers and continued his studies of natural history, traveling from rock to island, picking up eggs, watching the seals, examining birds and nests and turning over rocks to see the squirming and scurrying life beneath them. In the evenings the admiral liked to play bridge, and he invited himself (since no one could really invite him) to the various cruisers for a rubber or two. One night he played with Captain Schultz of the *Scharnhorst*; the next, with Captain Maerker and two of his officers on the *Gneisenau*.

The lesser officers exchanged visits from wardroom to wardroom, singing and drinking beer and wine. A red wine punch was made up for the men one day from the French wine stores taken off the *Valentine.*

As he waited for the coaling to be finished, Admiral von Spee completed his plans. He had hoped to go to Egg Harbor, there to coal again, and then to speed his way to the North Sea and a friendly German harbor. Now delayed, he decided to make one last gesture of defiance at his British enemies. On Sunday morning, December 6, his captains were called to the *Scharnhorst* and he outlined his plan of action to them. The Squadron would attack this British colony, destroy the important wireless station there, burn the coal stocks from which the British navy replenished its stores, destroy naval installations, and capture the British governor as a reprisal for the British seizure of the German governor of Samoa.

All this plan was based on a bit of information the admiral had received earlier: that report from a British steamer picked up by the German intelligence net at Punta Arenas, to the effect that the Falklands were entirely undefended.

Some of the admiral's captains demurred: they wanted no part of political matters, but wanted to get on home to Germany. But the prospect of capturing a British territory proved too enticing to Admiral von Spee, and when Chief of Staff Fielitz and Captain von Schönberg of the *Nürnberg* agreed with him, the others were overruled. Messages went sent out to Punta Arenas, asking the local German organizations to mobilize volunteers of German settlers in Chile and Brazil to garrison the islands after the German force had captured them. The *Mera* and the SS *Elinore Woermann*, two German freighters, were to be loaded with entrenching tools, barbed wire, and other defense materials. They were then to be dispatched to the Falklands.

Noon was set as sailing time for the Squadron, but a few of the officers managed to get off to land for one more short visit, picking up rocks and other souvenirs of their stay at this very southern outpost of mankind. They also found a supply of wild myrtle, with small red berries, which helped relieve the naval green paint of wardroom and mess.

Precisely at noon the ships weighed anchor and formed into line, except *Leipzig* and *Drummuir* and *Baden*. *Baden* put a tow on *Drummuir*, and led the sailing ship out into deep water, outside the three-mile limit. Here sailors from *Leipzig* went aboard her, and put a charge of explosive deep into her vitals. The crew, of course, had been shipped onto one of the German colliers with the intention of leaving them at the first neutral port.

Drummuir sat stolidly in the water for a few moments, then she shook and at the same time an explosion was heard and smoke and debris arose from her. She sank very quickly.

The admiral moved on, beginning a new leg of his 15,000-mile journey across the oceans in defiance of his country's enemies.

17

THE WOLVES ARRIVE

ADMIRAL VON SPEE HAD DONE AS MUCH FOR THE war effort as any man in Germany, and more than most, by winning a major naval victory over a force of the greatest naval power in the world. Admiral Tirpitz, the commander of the German navy, did not expect more of von Spee than that, nor did anyone else. But there may have been in his mind an even greater plan than he announced to Berlin in his dispatches: if von Spee could capture the Falklands and then put in a garrison of loyal German troops, what damage could he not wreak upon the enemy in South American waters?

It was simply a question of assuring a coal supply, and the chances of that could be ascertained from the Falklands. Germany's problem, and specifically Admiral von Spee's problem, was that he had been forced during his 15,000-mile odyssey to rely on the most haphazard kind of fueling arrangements, conditions which made a conscientious commander sweat heavily in contemplation of the future. Perhaps a victory at the Falklands could resolve all that and make it possible for Germany to extend her *Kreuzerkrieg* rather than shrink it.

Nowhere were all these possibilities more resoundingly debated than at Port Stanley, the capital of the Falkland Islands. The colony entered the war very nearly defenseless. All the military force that could be mustered, at least on the day of the defeat at Coronel, was a handful of volunteers, and when the news of defeat at Coronel was wirelessed to the people of Port Stanley all this was emphasized to them; they were told that they might expect an imminent landing by the Germans. They were instructed to fight, and told kindly to keep out of range of the enemy's big guns.

This news had come to the islands on November 3, when the East Asia Squadron had appeared in Valparaiso with its alarming news. No one was quite sure whether he ought to believe it or not, for the first message had been unsigned. But then, on November 4, a message had come from Captain Luce of the *Glasgow* confirming the horror, and reporting that the *Glasgow* and the *Canopus* were making for the Falklands with all speed and—horror of horrors—were probably being followed by the Germans.

Then came four days of suspense to the people of the colony. Governor Allardyce did not take off his clothes for four nights running. Officers and former officers began organizing the ragged volunteers as a home guard, sweeping out of odd corners such weapons as they might find, from modern rifles to ancient fowling pieces. Men and women slept beside their telephones, awaiting the word to begin the impossible defense of their colony.

Early on the morning of Sunday, November 8, two warships had arrived, throwing a momentary fright into the community, but they had turned out to be *Glasgow* and *Canopus*. Even worse than their sudden arrival was their sudden departure on the evening of the same day, for the word had come from Rio de Janeiro that *Glasgow* could be accommodated there.

So here on November 8 was Port Stanley, hope having been given and hope having been taken away, facing the imminent (so the people thought) attack of their enemy, deserted by those who could defend them.

Governor Allardyce called a council of war.

The colony's elder and wiser statesmen met that evening and considered their problems.

There was no doubt but what they would be attacked, if only because the Germans would wish to destroy the coal supplies and naval facilities.

Should they resist?

Of course, said the majority. They must resist.

So a plan was made, such as it was. The women and children and old men must be sent away from Port Stanley to points of safety on the neutral mainland. All supplies must be removed from obvious places and hidden about the islands. Food and other necessities must be hidden in caves and places near the town. A hundred horses must be brought to Port Stanley from the outlying districts and placed within the "camp" they would construct, for every man must be mounted for the greatest effect and mobility.

The plan was put into effect that very night.

Books, papers, and money and stamps were removed from the Government offices. All official documents and seals were taken away. The offices of the Falkland Islands Company were also stripped in a similar manner, and what was not sent out of the city was buried carefully in the basements and gardens. At the governor's office, the official papers and code-books were buried every night and dug up again every morning. Even the governor's tablecloths, marked G. R. (*Georgius Rex*) were buried because it was feared they would be stolen by the Germans, and unfortunately they were buried in the same hole with the governor's silver, which was shielded in green baize. The hole grew damp, the baize faded, and the table linens were ruined, much to the chagrin of the defenders.

This state of tension continued—without an attack. Finally, the people grew tired of sitting up all night, waiting. They grew tired of nothing to do because the offices of Port Stanley were all closed tight and business was suspended. They were ready to declare business as usual, when from a lookout tower above the town a warship was sighted making straight for the wireless station, and then, when she neared the station, turning broadside on, just as would an enemy preparing to blast down the tower and wreck the buildings.

Bugles blew the call to arms. The men of Port Stanley rushed to the church and dockyard and began sounding the bells of the town to warn all the defenders. Men saddled their horses and mounted them. Noncombatants streamed out of the town into the "camp," for it had been impossible to evacuate everyone too old or incapable of fighting.

The volunteers lined up with their horses, waiting nervously for orders, for they were to resist the German landing party.

And then—the ship sent a signal. She was HMS *Canopus*, come to guard the colony.

Captain Grant came ashore and met with Governor Allardyce, and for the first time the people of Port Stanley felt some hope about their private war with a very specific group of Germans.

The Admiralty had finally come around to Admiral Cradock's view: Captain Grant was to scuttle the *Canopus* and make an offshore fortress of her to defend the wireless station.

The captain brought the *Canopus* around behind a sand

hill which stood between *Canopus* and the outside water (Port Stanley lay in a completely landlocked harbor). Quickly the topmasts of *Canopus* were housed. She was sunk in the mud. Her side was camouflaged so that she would look quite unlike a ship. From this berth *Canopus'* twelve-inch guns could command the approaches to the wireless station and the entrance to the harbor.

Engineering, torpedo, and gunnery officers put their heads together and devised a new type of "mine" made from old paint drums. These were quickly manufactured, in enough quantity to guard the entrance to the harbor. The light guns of the *Canopus* were landed and turned into coastal defense guns. A signal station was established on top of Sapper Hill, about 400 feet above the harbor, and on lesser points, and men were assigned to these stations to direct the fire of *Canopus* against any point in or around the harbor.

Then Governor Allardyce and the men and women of Port Stanley could feel a measure of relief.

All this was accomplished in mid-November. Then came the period of waiting, for attack was still expected—although every day new faces joined the group of doubters who said that von Spee was going somewhere else, that he would not bother himself with this little outpost in nowhere. Still, the women and children were evacuated, and life could scarcely have been called normal on the islands.

November passed into December. The tension grew less each day. The women and children were brought back, even though messages intercepted by the wireless station indicated that the Germans were still in the area. Then came Monday, December 7, 1914. The new, powerful cruiser squadron under Vice Admiral Sir Doveton Sturdee arrived at the anchorage at Port Stanley. Suddenly, instead of being a tiny colony defended by a group of sturdy volunteers and a sunken outmoded battleship whose assets were courage and those big twelve-inch guns, Port Stanley was the strongest point in the South Atlantic. Seven powerful warships were in the harbor.

That afternoon the officers of the ships came ashore to stretch their legs and take on a few fresh stores. No, they would not be in Port Stanley long. They were coaling. They would leave the next evening to begin their search for the German East Asia Squadron. Some of the optimists among the British officers said the search ought to take only a few days, for the Germans were most certainly hiding in the fjords and bays off Patagonia. Some said the search might take months—for no one could read Admiral von Spee's mind.

Since he could not read the admiral's mind, Admiral Sturdee decided that his first search sweep would be made around Cape Horn. Then he would run up to Valparaiso. If he did not find Admiral von Spee on that sweep, then he would have to reconsider the problem with the help of current intelligence.

In the anchorage at Port William, the outer harbor of the Falklands, lay the heavy ships of the British squadron. The two light criusers, *Bristol* and *Glasgow,* had taken on pilots, who guided them through the improvised mine field and into the inner harbor at Port Stanley. They coaled that first day. The other ships of the squadron were to coal beginning at dawn on December 8.

On that evening of December 7, officers strolled up and down the two streets of houses, walking by Government House and the "Cathedral"—an excessive title for a church built of timber and corrugated iron. It was a pleasant day, for it was midsummer and the ground of the hills and the yards was covered with sweet-smelling flowers. As evening came on, the temperature dropped into the 40-degree range, and the smell of peat fires straggled through the air.

As night came, the heavy cruisers *Carnarvon* and *Corn-*

wall were allowed to put out their fires, and so was the lighter ship *Bristol.* A few adjustments had to be made.

Then came dawn on December 8, the beginning of a perfect midsummer's morning. The colliers moved to the sides of the ships in the outer harbor, and soon began the sound of the rattling of winches hoisting coal.

18

"PREPARE TO WEIGH"

ON MONDAY, AS THE BRITISH SHIPS LAY QUIETLY
in Port Stanley's harbor, Admiral von Spee led the East Asia
Squadron along the southern coast of the Tierra del Fuego,
enjoying the fine clear weather that made it possible for them
to see and recognize the Argentine flag on land. They passed
the serrated coastline of Staten Island, and were soon in the
open sea. The Squadron took its new course from the flagship:
it would be northwest, toward the eastern tip of the Falkland
Islands, where Port Stanley lay.

The plan called for *Gneisenau* and *Nürnberg* to make the
landings, destroy the wireless station, destroy the port installations, and carry off the governor into captivity.

Monday night came up clear and fine and the visibility
seemed to be unusually good, particularly for an area where
it often rains three weeks out of four in December. At about
two o'clock in the morning, on Tuesday, December 8, the deck
watch of the Squadron was able to make out land masses on

the northern horizon. They were approaching the Falkland Islands.

At 0500 hours the signal came from the flagship and the *Gneisenau* and *Nürnberg* turned away from the Squadron on a sharp angle, proceeding directly northward at increased speed. They were to execute the landing, while the *Scharnhorst*, *Leipzig*, and *Dresden* stood guard outside in case the British arrived unexpectedly.

The landing parties were making ready. The men appeared on deck in white uniforms, wearing gaiters and ammunition belts, carrying gas masks. They went to breakfast at dawn, and then gathered on the forecastle and the upper deck to watch the coastline skid by.

All was serene. A finer day was seldom seen at sea. The bridge watch commented on the calm sea, the azure sky, the clear air stirred only by the slightest of breezes from the northwest.

Then they came upon Cape Pembroke, standing with its light at the outermost point of the harbor, and there from the bridge of *Gneisenau* Captain Maerker could see a slim plume of smoke rising high in the sky. His eyes widened, and he took up his glasses.

At first he could see nothing else. (The broad roadstead of Port William and the smaller protected harbor of Port Stanley are concealed from the southern approach by a long range of low hills and dunes.)

But as they approached, the dunes came alight with smoke and fires. Aboard *Gneisenau*, the officers believed it was the island watchers, destroying stores to keep them from falling into German hands. There were island watchers, the Falkland Island Volunteers, under Major Turner. But they were not burning stores; they were signaling with lights to announce to the strong British squadron the approach of the enemy.

263

Immediately, Captain Maerker saw mastheads above the hills. Two of these broke away and began moving slowly east toward the lighthouse and the open sea.

Gneisenau and *Nürnberg* increased their revolutions, hoping to catch a cruiser as it moved into the channel. There was no doubt in Captain Maerker's mind that he had cornered British warships.

Then, as the distance shortened, he could make out two, then four, then six ships. Swiftly he scribbled a message and sent it to the wireless room, and in a few moments Admiral von Spee had the word that six enemy warships were lying in the roadstead.

Admiral von Spee was distressed. At the moment the furthest thing from his desire was to encounter an enemy squadron of *any* strength. He was short of ammunition, and he might have to run through the North Sea with what he had in his magazines. He could not afford to stop to repair major damage to any ship. Consequently, although the first reports indicated that the enemy force was inferior to the force of the German East Asia Squadron, Admiral von Spee decided to avoid combat. He did not expect there would be much difficulty in that, since the ships he expected to find would all be inferior in speed to the ships of the East Asia Squadron.

The admiral gave the message and his clerk scribbled it down for the message center. *Gneisenau* and *Nürnberg* were recalled. They were to break off the operation and return to the Squadron. Von Spee gave a course and speed.

On board the *Gneisenau* the message came in, just as splashes appeared about the ship. From the sound and the splash it was apparent that the two German cruisers were under fire from heavy shore guns. They did not wait for a moment to investigate, however, but the telegraphs sounded, the engines turned faster, and they set out, northeast, to catch up to the Squadron and take their places.

Ashore, events were also moving rapidly.

The coming of the German East Asia Squadron had been discovered early in the morning by a lady named Mrs. Felton, the wife of a sheep farmer who lived near Point Pleasant on the south coast, about twenty miles from Port Stanley. Mrs. Felton sent her maid and houseboy to the top of a ridge to report what they saw. The boy ran back and forth between the ridge and Mrs. Felton, who was on the telephone. She gave the officials in Port Stanley reports of the ships as they passed.

Speeding more quickly than the rest of the Squadron, *Gneisenau* and *Nürnberg* had reached Pembroke Light at their estimated time—0930—and had for ten minutes before been aware of the existence of some kind of British fleet inside the harbor. But since 0735 hours various people in the harbor had been aware of the approach of vessels.

At 0745, *Canopus* received the message: "A four-funnel and a two-funnel man of war in sight from Sapper Hill, steering northward."

Canopus sent a flag message to *Glasgow*, and that light cruiser put up its flags: "Enemy in sight."

It was 0750.

Invincible, the squadron flagship, was busy coaling, and the admiral was busy shaving, having just gotten out of bed, when the flags were raised.

No one on *Invincible* saw them.

Captain Luce, the commander of *Glasgow*, waited for a few moments, impatiently. Then he grew desperate. He ordered a gun fired. That brought men running to the decks of *Invincible*, and they looked up to see the flags waving in the northwesterly breeze.

It was 0756.

On hearing the gun, Admiral Sturdee's flag lieutenant rushed out of his cabin, looked up at the *Glasgow*, and sped to the admiral's cabin to interrupt the good man just as he was taking a stroke with the razor.

"*Glasgow* signals enemy in sight, Sir."

The admiral looked up calmly in the mirror, at the young officer clad only in his pajamas.

"Well," said Sir Doveton dryly, "you had better go and get dressed."

As the flag lieutenant went scurrying back to his cabin and scrabbling for his uniform, Squadron Intelligence Officer Lloyd Hirst was climbing the bridge of *Glasgow*, rubbing the sleep from his eyes. Lieutenant Commander Barry Bingham, mate of the upper deck and assistant to the first officer of the *Invincible*, was sipping his third cup of coffee after a leisurely breakfast, having just supervised the transfer of some 400 tons of coal from a collier to the bunkers of the *Invincible*.

In a moment, they too were on the way to the upper decks.

Intelligence Officer Hirst arrived on the bridge of *Glasgow*.

"Mr. Hirst," said the captain. "Go to the masthead with the Silhouette Book and identify those ships."

The intelligence officer was down off the bridge, on the main deck, and then up the foremast climbing tree. Halfway up he shouted out: "*Scharnhorst* or *Gneisenau* with a light cruiser."

On top, he had leisure to open the book.

"*Gneisenau* and *Nürnberg*," he corrected.

At this moment, the British squadron began to move toward action. It was eight o'clock, a good hour and a half before *Gneisenau* and *Nürnberg* would approach the harbor.

Admiral Sturdee needed that hour and a half, for the British squadron had been caught completely by surprise. Who would expect "the gray wolf" to walk into their parlor?

As the squadron was constituted, the old armored cruiser

266

Kent, 9960 tons, built in 1901, was stationed at the mouth of the harbor as guard ship. The heavy cruisers *Invincible, Inflexible,* and *Carnarvon* were coaling. *Bristol* and *Glasgow* were in the inner harbor, with their engines opened up for repairs. The admiral had issued orders that every ship was to be ready to move within two hours, but *Bristol* could just barely make that, her captain indicated. The heavy cruiser *Cornwall* had not coaled. *Macedonia,* the auxiliary, was anchored at the entrance to the harbor.

Actually, the British cruisers were very much at a disadvantage, although Admiral von Spee had no way of knowing that fact.

Shortly after eight o'clock Admiral Sturdee had finished shaving and put on his shirt, and the messages began to flow thick and fast from the flagship. At 0810 *Kent* was ordered to weigh anchor and reconnoiter the entrance to the harbor. Four minutes later the signal came to the squadron: "Prepare to weigh."

At 0820 the signal station reported more smoke off to the southwest. A quarter hour later *Kent* passed down the harbor, and it was her masts moving that were first seen by Captain Maerker and the men on the bridge of the *Gneisenau.* At this time *Gneisenau* and *Nürnberg* were eight miles away from port and the remainder of the German ships were twenty miles away.

Bugles aboard the ships made the call to action. The captains were concerned lest they be caught at anchor and shelled or torpedoed. The stokers in the holds of the ships were working at top speed, sweat dripping down their backs and flanks as they fed the red maws of the furnaces, but the steam gauges were rising with disconcerting slowness. *Macedonia* was recalled into the inner harbor, and that was the second set of masts that Captain Maerker saw moving about.

The *Canopus* was making ready to begin the battle from

her stationary position on the mud flat. She had observers out at all the peaks on the south shore, and her gunnery officer had gone to a point of observation. She asked for permission to open fire with her twelve-inch guns on the approaching cruisers, and permission was given. They began to move into range.

It was 0852.

Now came the puzzling smoke that Captain Maerker and his officers had seen and had identified as burning coal stores. The smoke was the smoke of the frantic vessels in the harbor, trying to make steam and go out to engage their enemy.

At 0915 the two German cruisers eased down and from the shore it could be seen that they were making ready for action. Captain Maerker, at that moment, had identified *Canopus, Kent, Glasgow,* and another of her class and had asked for permission to attack. Then came the triple shock of being fired on from shore (*Canopus* had opened fire). Captain Maerker identified tripod masts, which meant heavy battle cruisers of the *Dreadnought* type—battleships—and Admiral von Spee ordered him to cease his observations or any attempt to attack, and to come and rejoin the Squadron.

The first two shells fired by *Canopus* were 800 yards short—nearly half a mile. They sent up huge columns of spray, fifty yards high, but they did not threaten the German ships, or the German crews, except to surprise them with the size of the splashes and the guns that had fired those shells.

In a moment came another salvo from the guns of the fore turret of *Canopus.* Again they were short, but not by much. By that time the admiral had recalled his ships, and the *Gneisenau* and *Nürnberg* were speeding toward the Squadron, to overtake her in an hour.

At 0945 all ships of the British squadron reported that they had steam up—except *Bristol,* which reported that she would not be ready until 1100.

268

Glasgow went out to the roadstead at 1010. *Kent* moved in behind her. The remainder of the squadron weighed anchor and began to move through the mine fields, *Inflexible* first, then *Invincible*, then *Cornwall*, which carried Admiral Stoddart and his flag. *Glasgow* and *Kent* were told to keep after the German cruisers and notify position at regular intervals to the squadron.

At 10:15 the big battle cruisers came out around Cape Pembroke, visible to Admiral von Spee and his Squadron for the first time, and now the admiral realized that he was facing a situation far more serious than the difficulty with which he had confronted Admiral Cradock on the other side of Cape Horn such a short time before.

As the ships came out and were identified by the officer in the crow's nest of the *Scharnhorst*, the picture began to be laid out. From Admiral von Spee's point of view, it was anything but a pretty one.

19

THE LAST BATTLE

FROM THE CROW'S NEST OF SCHARNHORST, AS SHE led the Squadron away from the Falklands, the intelligence officer of the Squadron read the bad news as it came out of the harbor, ship after ship. As the word was passed about what lay ahead for the Germans, faces and hearts began to fall.

For here was the story:

SHIP	TONS	SPEED, KNOTS	ARMAMENT
Invincible	17,250	26	8–12″, 16–4″
Inflexible	17,250	26	8–12″, 16–4″
Carnarvon	10,850	22	4–7.5″, 6–6″
Cornwall	9,800	23.6	14–6″
Kent	9,800	23.5	14–6″
Glasgow	4,800	25.8	2–6″, 10–4″

Six British ships against five German ships. But what a difference!

To bring the comparisons down: *Invincible* was faster, bigger, and her guns were twice as large as those of *Scharnhorst*. The flagship, then, could neither run away successfully nor battle the British flagship successfully. So was the case with *Inflexible* as compared to *Gneisenau*.

Carnarvon, while an older ship, was far more than a match for any of the light cruisers. So was *Cornwall*, a ship of the same class—in tonnage almost three times as large as the German light cruisers. (*Dresden*, the heaviest German light cruiser, weighed only 3544 tons. Even *Glasgow*, the smallest of the British ships, was more than a thousand tons heavier than *Dresden*.)

The German Squadron suddenly found itself in a position where it was outmanned, outgunned, and outsped by its enemy.

In such a situation, the only hope for any naval squadron was to run for it, and to hope that bad weather—a squall, a storm, a hurricane—would save it from the enemy.

But today?

Relentlessly the golden sun climbed in a cloudless bright sky, and out came the British ships, flashing from the harbor, into the very slight, only cooling northwesterly breeze, without incident save that *Inflexible* rammed a sailing pinnace belonging to *Cornwall*, a boat half full of stores which was on her way through the mine field to rejoin her ship.

Cornwall was the last of the line to come out, for the auxiliary *Macedonia* was not needed for this work and she was ordered to stay behind with the unhappy *Bristol* whose fires were still unlit and her boilers cold.

At 1030 the last of the line cleared the harbor. Off on the horizon, hull down, could be seen the German East Asia Squadron, steaming off to the southeast, hoping to escape. The word was escape now, for every man in the Squadron knew that they faced two of the frightful *Dreadnought* class ships—battle cruisers they were called—which could blow the proud *Scharnhorst* and *Gneisenau* out of the water in very little time, quite out of range of those ships.

The reaction of the Germans that day was not a reaction of fear; it was simply surprise and horror. The uneasiness of *Korvettenkapitän* Pochhammer and the others had come home, but now it was no longer uneasiness; it was quiet desperation and resignation.

Invincible made a signal as the squadron came out of the harbor and began to move. "General Chase" said the flags.

So first out went *Glasgow*, charging along at twenty-five knots, her mission to keep the German Squadron in sight, to keep out of range, and to keep in constant wireless touch with the flagship.

It was one thing to know that the Squadron was being chased by the huge battle cruisers, quite another to see what they could do. Few men and not many officers were very familiar with these ships, but soon they were to learn, as First Officer Pochhammer of *Gneisenau* recalled later:

> . . . It was not long before we became aware of its real strength. Two vessels soon detached themselves from the number of our pursuers; they seemed much bigger and faster than the others, as their smoke was thicker, wider, and more massive. All glasses were turned inquisitively upon their hulls, which were almost completely enveloped by the smoke. . . . Were they Japanese?

This question did bother the underofficers of the Squadron because they had no idea that a heavy British cruiser was within 5000 miles of them. But soon even the younger officers realized that the ships were British battle cruisers, and they began to feel quite numb.

This was bound to happen one day or another. Why not today rather than tomorrow? What have we to say then? We are the champions of our country. Our lives belong to her. It is our duty not to save them, but to risk them. We had no more claim to be treated with a velvet glove than those who were fighting in Europe, and the old law of naval warfare which ordains that the less powerful and less swift ships should be vanquished in free waters in fine weather was again to be exemplified in our case.

It would have been vain to harbor the slightest illusion in this respect for the sky remained clear; there was not the slightest cloud presaging bad weather to be seen, nor any wisp of fog to throw over us its friendly mantle and hide us from the enemy's sight. Consequently at the muster of the crew held at the end of the morning, the men were warned that the fighting would be warm, and we awaited the following hours calmly and animated with the firm intention to fight and die like true Germans.

The muster was held on all ships. The seriousness of the situation was neither camouflaged nor dwelt upon. It was stated, and that was all that was necessary. The ghostly quality that had dogged the Squadron since Coronel seemed now to overshadow it. Here were two thousand five hundred men who knew they were about to fight and that most of them were about to die, and yet there was not one thing to do about it except to wait, to watch a steam gauge that would never gauge again, to clean a gun barrel that would never fire past this day, to check a compass that would be shattered or soon be a mass of rust, and to do it bravely and without thought for the piece of steel that would blow out a man's vitals or the gagging final taste of salt water that would mark the blackness that would come to him.

There was never any hope. Soon there would be anger to replace fear, and discipline to replace desperation. But at this moment, as the long chase continued, there was only numbness.

The light northwesterly breeze scarcely ruffled the surface of the blue sea as the ships sped along, pursued and pursuers. To the west lay the low gray-green islands of the Falklands colony. Rushing east and south was Admiral von Spee's Squaddron. He charted a narrow course, trying to keep within roundup distance of the fleet of supply ships in case he should escape this net, yet trying to stay far enough away so as not to compromise them if he did not escape.

Between the Squadron and the islands charged the British—*Glasgow, Invincible, Inflexible* leading. How confident were the big ships, basking in their superiority of three knots speed, four inches of projectile capacity, and a fine day that brooked no escape for an enemy only fifteen miles away.

At 1050 Admiral Sturdee noticed that the battle cruisers were outdistancing the remainder of his fleet, and the line was growing more ragged than more regular. He reduced speed from twenty-five knots to twenty-four knots. At 1115 he saw that the "county cruisers," *Cornwall* and *Carnarvon*, were not catching up, and reduced speed to twenty knots. There was plenty of time. At the same time he ordered *Glasgow* to remain three miles ahead and scout.

Now came a moment of respite for the crews of the British ships, most of whom were still in their coaling gear, filthy and uncomfortable—and also subject to infection in case of battle injuries. The captains of the ships sent the men below

274

to wash and change their clothing and to prepare for battle, as the ships sped along. At 1130 Admiral Sturdee also ordered a meal served, for there might not be another chance this day.

At 1145 the German Squadron was also ordered to eat a meal. Neither German nor British sailors and officers found it possible to remain long below, and the decks of all ships were soon crowded with men in white, meals in hand, watching and waiting. Closest to the East Asia Squadron was *Glasgow*, but all eyes were fixed on the shapes of *Invincible* and *Inflexible*, off the port quarter, some 18,500 yards away. Admiral von Spee turned again in a southeasterly direction, but the big battle cruisers turned with him, and by eight bells it was apparent that the action was about to begin.

Aboard the *Scharnhorst* the Admiral ordered the battle flags broken out. On every German cruiser the bugles began to blow and the drums to roll. The officers and men scurried to find their action stations, but today there was one difference from the past, as noted on the *Gneisenau*:

". . . a brief handshake here and there, a manly farewell between particularly close friends. . . ."

The first officers of the ships went to the bridges, to receive the last fast-to-face orders from their commanders. They knew that they would soon be far too busy in their special battle duties to confront one another again until the end of the fight, whenever that might be. The commander took the bridge and directed the fighting of the ship. The first officer went below and directed damage control.

For the last half hour Admiral Sturdee had simply been waiting for his men to clean up and for the struggling cruisers to close in. *Carnarvon* was the problem. Her maximum speed seemed to be slightly below twenty knots this day and she was dropping behind. At 1217 Admiral Sturdee caught a flutter of the mast of *Scharnhorst*, as the battle flags were raised, and he decided to wait no longer before beginning the action.

275

He ordered full speed ahead, and the battle cruisers seemed to leap in front of the other ships in the British line.

They were making twenty-five knots.

Admiral von Spee moved into battle formation. *Gneisenau* and *Nürnberg* were on the left of the line. *Scharnhorst* and *Dresden* were on the right, with *Leipzig* trailing on the starboard column.

"Action" was the bugle call aboard the British flagship, and the pennons fluttered from her rigging.

Another signal was run up the *Invincible*'s yardarm.

"Open fire!"

The range was more than 16,000 yards even to *Leipzig*, and she became the target of the first shot of the action, fired by *Inflexible*.

"Wham!" went the huge rifles in salvo.

The shells screamed across the nine miles of water, each projectile weighing 840 pounds, and when they hit, not far behind their target, the columns of water spurted 150 feet in the air.

Aboard all the ships of the East Asia Squadron men winced when they saw the power of their enemy.

The speed of the two battle cruisers was now increased to twenty-six knots, and they were sighting carefully. That first salvo had come from the fore 12-inch turret of *Inflexible* at exactly 1255. For the next quarter hour *Inflexible* and *Invincible* fired sighting shots at the end-on enemy, without any visible effect. On *Leipzig* the effect was profound, however. One projectile landed so close to the ship that the men at the after guns were deluged with water.

At 1315 Admiral von Spee made a new signal.

"*Leipzig* proceed independently," it said. The admiral saw those two huge battle cruisers coming up, up, up on the Squadron, and he saw the columns of water edging in on *Leipzig*.

A few moments later the admiral made another signal to the entire Squadron, and laid out what plan of battle he was at liberty to make:

"The armored cruisers will engage the enemy as long as possible. The light cruisers are to use every endeavor to escape."

Leipzig had already turned away to starboard—south—moving out of the line of fire, and the British battle cruisers were shifting their fire to *Nürnberg*. Now both remaining light cruisers turned south, to starboard, hoping to escape as the enemy concentrated on the *Scharnhorst* and the *Gneisenau*.

Admiral Sturdee was not to be so easily thrown off the track. He had discussed with his captains the various moves that the Germans might make when they came to grips, and now his battle orders were remembered. In any pursuit, if Admiral von Spee were to dismiss his light cruisers, then *Kent, Cornwall,* and *Glasgow* were to take after the lighter ships, leaving the heavy ships to the battle cruisers. They began speeding after *Leipzig, Dresden,* and *Nürnberg*.

Admiral von Spee then signaled *Gneisenau* to follow him and turned the flagship sharply, helm hard over, to port. The battle was about to be joined, and as this move was made, and as the German commander threw the gantlet to the enemy, how eerie was the sight that struck his eye. There, coming along under full sail, making slow way in light wind, but beautiful with all canvas set and working, came a three-masted schooner, silent and serene.

Scharnhorst and *Gneisenau* lined up again after the turn, and Admiral von Spee hoisted the signal to begin firing. The range was 15,000 yards, a little long for the Germans' 8.2-inch guns. He must close, and he kept his course, so that the British closed for him. Or at least that was what he hoped would happen.

20

"WHAT IS THE *SCHARNHORST* DOING?"

"SHE IS SINKING."

WITH EVERY ADVANTAGE HIS TO COMMAND, ADMIRAL
Sturdee had no intention of fighting Admiral von Spee's
battle. The *Scharnhorst* turned 80 degrees to port, and
Gneisenau followed, which brought them into line ahead, with
Gneisenau leading as the ships opened fire on the British.

At twenty-six knots Admiral Sturdee was walking into
their range. But not for long. Immediately—just after 1330—
Admiral Sturdee ordered speed on his battle cruisers cut to
twenty-four knots and then he turned away from the Germans, to port, bringing the *Invincible* ahead, and the British
battle cruisers onto a course parallel to that of the Germans,
and still at a range of 14,500 yards, which was long for good
shooting by the Germans, but a very decent range for the
12-inch guns of the British.

The German gunnery was good—better than the British
by far, as could be seen by the stern chase against the light
cruisers. But Admiral Sturdee was not worried. This was not

a day when gunnery counted for much, given any skill at all. The extreme range of the German guns was 16,500 yards and Sturdee's task was to keep as close to that range as possible and in a slow, leisurely fashion blow his enemy off the water.

On the *Scharnhorst* the guns were pointed almost as high as they would train. The chains of ammunition groaned along the passageways and up the hatches from the magazines. Overhead from the interior of the ship could be heard the thump of shells and cordite and the grunt of men as they lifted the heavy weights onto trucks and sped them along the decks to the guns. *Scharnhorst* was making twenty-one knots.

Throughout the ship the speaking tubes were rattling as officers ordered and men obeyed. Punctuating the steady level of noise was the crash of the guns as they fired in salvos, well-spread salvos, with an interval of 200 yards between the shells. The British gunners, watching these shells hit, saw that they were shooting against experts.

As Admiral Sturdee edged away to open the range again, the *Scharnhorst* went into the lead of the German line, and both ships began firing on *Inflexible*. They scored no hits. They changed to *Invincible* as the target. At 1345 the *Scharnhorst* scored its first hit on the British flagship.

Four minutes later Admiral Sturdee turned away, to increase the range again. This action was not totally to his benefit, because the oil-fired furnaces of the two big battle cruisers had been prepared less than carefully that morning, and both ships were making excessive smoke in their efforts to maintain speed and maneuver promptly. The wind, coming from his port beam, was blowing this smoke and the smoke from the guns along the sighting line of both battle cruisers.

At this point in the action Admiral von Spee and his commanders began to take heart; the British were scoring so few hits even with their superior armament. *Gneisenau* suffered two direct hits at about this time: one grazed the third funnel and exploded on the upper deck above the eight-inch casemate of the after starboard battery. Pieces of shrapnel penetrated the casemate and even went in the coal bunkers. A deck officer was horribly wounded; both forearms were torn off. A seaman was down with a serious wound. Others were wounded lightly. A stoker was killed in the corridor where he was stationed for damage-control warning. Inside the casemate, others grasped rubber bandages and tied up the dangerous wounds. The call went out for stretcher bearers, and those who could not walk were carried to the aid stations where the white-coated doctors got to work. The dead man was laid aside in the ship's forge. He would be accompanied by many others before the afternoon was over.

The shell had destroyed an iron ring which kept the coal chute in position. The platform of one of the amidships 8-inch guns had been bent and the gun could not be aimed.

First Officer Pochhammer rushed to the scene with his damage-control men, and began chopping away the debris. Another party rushed to the third funnel, to patch up the outside and give back to the engines the draft for their boilers.

The second shell crashed through the port bulwark above the middle deck, almost at water level, piercing the armored deck and coming to rest in a magazine! Fire threatened.

The damage-control parties were at the scene in seconds, flooding the magazine (which contained ammunition for the smaller guns) and repairing the hole in the deck.

At 1400 hours the range was 16,450 yards, which made it almost impossible for Admiral von Spee to fight, so he turned away at 1410, in what appeared to the British to be an attempt to escape. The maneuvering continued until 1445, when the range was again down to 15,000 yards. Sturdee then turned slightly to port and reengaged the German heavy cruisers.

In the first round both *Scharnhorst* and *Gneisenau* had scored a number of hits on the enemy, not all of them effective because of the heavier armor plate of the British ships and the inferior penetrating power of the 8.2-inch shells as opposed to the 12-inch shells. But it must be said that the honors for shooting had gone to the Germans in the first round. *Scharnhorst* had suffered little and *Gneisenau* had only her two hits.

This time the British gunners improved.

At 1453 the Germans turned to port again, trying to close with the battle cruisers and do more damage. Again Admiral Sturdee hauled around to a course that paralleled that of the Germans. Suddenly Admiral von Spee turned sharply, as if to cross the British line, startling Admiral Sturdee; but according to those in *Gneisenau* who could see clearly, a British shell had caused serious damage to the port screw and steering mechanism, and it was some moments before the *Scharnhorst* could move back onto her course. The German secondary guns were able to fire as the range dropped to 13,000, 12,500, and 11,500 yards. Admiral Sturdee did not like this development at all. He turned away once again. He would follow the old dictum: ammunition is cheaper than human life. He would move out to maximum range and pick off the Germans at his leisure. There was plenty of time before dark.

The damage done to the Germans by coming to close quarters was far worse than that done to the British ships. At close quarters the British gunners were hitting far more often than at the longer ranges. At 1500 hours *Scharnhorst's* first funnel was gone. Her third funnel was badly hit. Shells kept striking her sides and breaking through, to reveal raging fires beneath the main deck.

The action slackened for a few minutes at 1515, when the smoke made by the British battle cruisers' guns and fires became to intense that the gun pointers could not see the target for minutes at a time. Admiral Sturdee turned away. Both German cruisers now showed the effects of the battle. *Scharnhorst* was in serious trouble. *Gneisenau* had suffered a number of hits and had a distinct list. Yet the Germans continued to shoot, and to shoot accurately.

Admiral von Spee copied the British move at about 1325, and then all four cruisers were steaming west by south, and about 12,000 yards apart. So many were the fires aboard *Scharnhorst* now that when some of them were extinguished by 12-inch shells falling short, others almost immediately broke out. She was lying very deep in the water and heeled over to port. There was a large hole in the fore end and one on the quarter-deck. Flames guttered in the portholes.

Yet, four minutes later, Admiral von Spee brought her completely around, to engage the enemy with his other broadside, and to fire torpedoes should he have the chance. But now the British were shooting well and the big shells went home, one after the other. Fifteen minutes later the decrease in *Scharnhorst*'s fire was noticeable. At 1600 hours her mainmast and three funnels were all shot away and she was ablaze from stem to stern.

Here is an eye-witness description of *Scharnhorst* by an English officer aboard *Invincible*:

"Masses of steel were twisted and torn as if growing out in all directions like the roots of a tree, clouds of steam were going up sky high, and she was blazing fore and aft."

At this moment, still firing from his starboard batteries, and *still firing in salvos*, Admiral von Spee sent a message to *Gneisenau*: "If your engines are still intact, try to get away."

That was the last word. After sending the signal, Admiral von Spee, like a great gray wolf at bay, turned the *Scharnhorst* directly toward the side of the *Invincible*, trying to torpedo and even perhaps to ram. But then the British shells reaped their final harvest. The engines seized and stopped and *Scharnhorst* was dead in the water.

Admiral Sturdee signaled her to surrender.

There was no reply.

282

The British shells continued to pour into the helpless ship, and her list grew more and more pronounced.

On the *Gneisenau,* officers and men took precious moments of life from their fighting with the *Inflexible* to look at the flagship. Water had risen to the fore upper deck, but the admiral's flag floated proudly in the wind from the foremast and so did the battle flags from the mainmast and the gaff. Still she heeled over to port and her bow kept going down. Her fore turret was only six feet above water, and still it fired one last shell.

Then the screws came out of water.

"What is the *Scharnhorst* doing?" asked First Officer Pochhammer from the bowels of the ship.

"She is sinking," came the captain's reply.

A few survivors could be seen on deck, moving about as in a daze. And then, at 1617, she plunged, and suddenly she was gone, down into the deeps.

Now came *Gneisenau*'s turn, for she was the new target of both the British battle cruisers.

While the battle was reaching its height, the older cruiser *Carnarvon* came up and, just before 1600, began to fire, first on *Scharnhorst,* and then on *Gneisenau.* So the pride of the Kaiser's navy, the greatest gunnery ship of the fleet, was beset by not one but three enemies, two of them her masters in any contest of weight and power.

No move was made by the British ships to save the men struggling in the water from the wreckage of *Scharnhorst,* and no move could be made by the *Gneisenau,* if she hoped to fight.

"Three-quarters starboard," Captain Maerker told his helmsman. He was going to move in closer to try to engage his enemies.

The men of the *Scharnhorst* struggled and drowned in the water, no one coming to their aid.

At 1615 the *Invincible* opened fire on the *Gneisenau*, and *Gneisenau* shifted her fire to the British flagship. She had fire from both the battle cruisers, and a steady hail of shells from *Carnarvon* which stood behind her stern and poured 7.4-inch shells into her.

The damage to *Gneisenau*—the punishment she was able to take—was nearly unbelievable to the British. There was some confusion; at one point First Officer Pochhammer came upon a man standing at a drinking fountain when he should have been at his action station. The first officer pulled out his pistol and shot the man dead.

But there was little mutiny and little panic as the officers and men of the *Gneisenau* fought on for Kaiser and for country.

The middle-deck was wrecked: angle irons stuck through the broken deck plates. Both boats were smashed in their cleats, and the stern of the longboat was shot away. The water that had filled the boats had poured onto the deck, and then had rushed through a shell hole into the officers' mess, putting out a fire. Shrapnel had torn up the officers' mess, and a shell had exposed to the deck the only partly cleared table with its white cloth. The last of the little black pigs from Easter Island lay wounded and rolling on the deck in pain untill Pochhammer shot him to death. Still some livestock remained among the wreckage. A goose sat among scattered potatoes and hissed. Pigeons flew down to the mantlepiece of the officers' mess.

In the other parts of the ship there was no leavening of the horror, however. Men fell and died, and others fell and bled, their gore running out on the hot steel in little pools until they were picked up automatically and put aside, to be out of the way of their living comrades.

A shell fell into the storeroom between the 12-inch ammunition casemate and the crew's kitchens. First was heard a loud muffled report, and the noise of bursting steel. Smoke and steam came gushing out. The shell had also penetrated a gun position. The battery chief was flung to the deck along with his two assistants. When they arose they were in one huge room, the iron bulkheads of the storeroom had completely disappeared, and so had those into the kitchen. Saucepans were smashed into crazy patterns, some handles met the lips, some bottoms were burned out like sunblazes. Throughout the room lay dead men, mutilated men, men flung aside by the shock of a direct hit, their clothing burst at the seams or torn from their bodies. Among all this, except for three men, only the guns were unhurt. As if nothing had happened the three men went back to serving their gun.

Throughout the ship powder-blacked men served their guns, wiping their faces with dirty hands, and moving aside the corpses of the dead, putting flags over them where the flags were easy to find, trying to keep away from the bulkheads splattered with blood and brains.

As the three English ships poured their rain of death into *Gneisenau*, the ship's ensign was shot down from its lofty spar. Another was hoisted. This too was shot down. *Gneisenau* was not giving up. Another was hoisted, and again another had to be sent aloft.

From his command post on the bridge, Captain Maerker spoke often and softly into the speaking tubes, and was heard throughout the ship. No sign of fear, no sign of consternation came from him. He gave orders in a calm, level voice, as if they were out in the East China Sea on gunnery practice once again, as they had been so many times before, to gain the skill to win the Kaiser's trophy.

How strange that under such a hail of shot and shell, the men of the *Gneisenau* could move on calmly! They knew there was no chance. Those on deck had seen the stricken looks of their comrades from *Scharnhorst* as the sister ship moved away to fight and the men went down, down, and down again, to drown—even though they had escaped shot and shell and the dreadful suction of the flagship as she sank.

Yet there was no panic.

The coal was shoveled. The guns were manned. The fires were fought. The floods were staunched. The debris was cut and pulled away. The bodies were rolled away from the walkways. The surgeons cut and staunched and patched as the shells blasted around them. And the captain remained serene, he above all knowing how desperate their situation had become.

Gneisenau was fighting well.

At 1625, when she turned her attention to the *Invincible*, she began straddling the British flagship with her 8-inch shells; no mean feat, even at 10,000 yards. Admiral Sturdee moved away. During the next quarter of an hour, even though harried by three enemies, *Gneisenau* hit the flagship no less than three times with armor-piercing shells.

First Officer Pochhammer described the new carnage thus:

> . . . We were now being hit much more fre-
> quently than before. Owing to the great range of
> the fight, the shells fell aslant and consequently hit
> the thin armored deck more often than the strong
> side plates. Thus they found their way more easily
> into the ship and wrought considerable destruction,
> even in the lower compartments.

How dispassionate an account of what was occurring!

A shell destroyed the wireless station, next to the 6-inch casement amidships on the starboard side. A deck officer's head was blown off and rolled on the deck. A shell fell into the after dressing station, killing nearly fifty wounded men, killing *Oberstabsarzt* Dr. Nohl, killing Chaplain Rost.

The middle stokehold filled after a direct hit—and so rapidly that most of the stokers were drowned.

The starboard guns of the *Gneisenau* were put out of action one after another. The after turret was struck by a direct hit and every man inside was killed, the gun put out of action. A shell exploded on the upper deck just above the base of one of the 8-inch guns, sweeping the men away as if with a broom, down into the 6-inch casement below, where every man, too, was killed, except the battery chief and the lieutenant in charge of the gun. The battery chief was buried under a pile of corpses and had to dig his way free.

Suddenly, the firing ceased. It was 1647. The British noticed that *Gneisenau* had struck her colors, or so it seemed. She was not firing.

But the fact was that she had not struck her colors; they had been shot away again and she had no flag left to hoist.

In this respite, the captain and the gunnery officers left alive began to try to repair some guns for firing. The British moved slightly toward her to keep from sliding away.

First Officer Pochhammer went on a tour of his ship, glad for the quiet moment, at least. He found water dripping here, gushing there, bodies and debris everywhere below decks. Above, from the British point of view, *Gneisenau* seemed scarcely hurt at all. Below, it was carnage.

Gneisenau now had a very bad list to starboard, and she could barely maneuver. The port guns could be made to fire, and she was turned, and they did begin firing. So once again the British ships opened fire on her.

Now the *Gneisenau* suffered another problem, one which did not bother the flagship because she had not lived long enough: the guns began to run out of ammunition. There was ammunition for the big guns at the after turret, but to get it meant to run a gantlet of death. So firing stopped. Then, one

287

more shell was found for the fore turret, and it was fired: to strike squarely in the hull of *Invincible*.

The British firing increased, even as the German firing stopped. Shells hit in the forward dressing station. A shell carried away the first funnel.

First Officer Pochhammer left the central damage-control station, and climbed onto the main deck. He saw that the blockhouse and bridge were intact but that the fore funnel was down, and the other three were holed. The wireless rod had slid down the mast as far as the truck and had torn their last flag to ribbons; the battle flag on the foremast was gone. Rubble and broken equipment was everywhere on deck and the men were clambering over it.

Yet there was no panic.

It had come time to abandon ship and there was no panic at all.

The men were moving to the port side of the ship, the starboard side sinking all the time. Others were climbing out of gaping holes, coal-blackened and shot-blackened men coming out of caves like so many prehistoric men emerging from their hillsides. But they were quiet and disciplined. The officers stood near the bulwarks, handing out spars and hammocks and buoys to help the men to save themselves.

From the bridge the captain called for the attention of the men—even as the three British warships bore in from three sides, firing as they came.

"His Majesty the Emperor," Captain Maerker shouted.

"*Hoch! Hoch! Hoch!*" replied the men.

"Our good and brave *Gneisenau*," he shouted.

"Hoch! Hoch! Hoch!" returned the men.

The crew began singing, although it was hard for one to hear another above the sound of the English guns.

"*Deutschland, Deutschland über alles,*
Über alles in der Welt . . ."

They continued through to the end, and somewhere a black, red, and white flag was found to float from the mainmast.

At 1745 *Gneisenau* fired her last shot, and then even the British stopped firing, for it was apparent that she was finished.

Fifteen minutes later, *Gneisenau* heeled over.

"All men overboard," shouted the captain.

All men went overboard.

Gneisenau stood on her beam ends for a few moments, some men clambering along her sides. Then the stern sank. The bow remained in the air for a little longer, and then she foundered.

Now four hundred men were in the water, survivors. How long would they survive, and for what?

They clung to broken spars and to flotsam and to one another.

Almost immediately the sea birds set about seeking prey. They swooped down, gulls and albatrosses to pluck at the eyes of the dead and the dying. The men defended themselves as best they could with clubs and fists.

And then, slowly, the British ships began to send out boats.

21

THE STERN CHASE

WHEN ADMIRAL VON SPEE SENT THE SIGNAL TO
Leipzig to detach herself from the Squadron and to make a
run for safety, Captain Haun lost no time in doing exactly as
he was told, as fast as he could go, which at best was twenty-
three knots. If he was to escape, he needed a great deal of
luck, because *Glasgow* was nearly three knots faster than
Leipzig.

Soon, however, Admiral von Spee detached his other light
cruisers, *Nürnberg* and *Dresden,* and all three headed off to the
southeast, with *Glasgow, Kent,* and *Cornwall* in hot pursuit.

At 1320 *Glasgow* was making twenty-six knots, one knot
over her contract speed, but Captain Luce wanted to be sure
that he did not lose his enemy this day, so he ordered the
engine room to give him everything she had. Soon he was
doing twenty-seven knots. *Kent* and *Cornwall* followed, making about 23.5 knots.

The Germans formed into a triangle: *Dresden* at the apex, *Leipzig* on her starboard, *Nürnberg* on her port.

Now began a stern chase, every engine room outdoing itself in keeping the fires even hotter and the steam ever flowing.

At 1445 *Cornwall* and *Kent* were eleven miles astern of *Leipzig*, but *Glasgow* was only four miles away on her starboard quarter. Fifteen minutes later, *Glasgow* opened fire on *Leipzig* at 12,000 yards, hoping to shoot over her bows and force her to change course or otherwise lose speed. Captain Haun was not to be intimidated. He kept on course, and he returned *Glasgow*'s fire, although he could thus only show his intentions: the range was too great for his guns.

With *Glasgow*'s superior speed, she was able to overhaul *Leipzig*, but at 10,000 yards *Leipzig* and *Nürnberg* both turned to bring their guns to bear for broadsides, and *Glasgow* bore off. *Leipzig* and *Nürnberg* resumed their southerly course.

These maneuvers served to lengthen the distance between *Dresden* and the pursuers, and fortunately for the Germans the sky in this area was beginning to patch over with rain squalls and clouds.

Captain Luce was the senior officer of those English officers present, which meant that he had to make the command decisions. His *Glasgow* was the fastest ship, and both *Leipzig* and *Nürnberg* were faster than *Kent* and *Cornwall*. Should he take the chance that these two ships could catch the two slower German cruisers before nightfall, while he went after *Dresden* for what might be a clean sweep?

He decided not. He decided it was too risky to leave the slower British ships to do the job, and that he must fight *Leipzig*, *Nürnberg*, or both.

"Are you gaining on the enemy?" Captain Luce signaled to *Cornwall* and *Kent*.

"Yes," they replied.

And they were gaining, but scarcely fast enough, given the threatening condition of the skies, Captain Luce decided as he cocked an eye upward. If he were to go after *Dresden* (and he was the only one who could catch her) he would have to make a wide detour around *Leipzig* and *Nürnberg* to stay out of their range. In any event, the captain indicated as he looked at the ship's chronometer, he could not catch *Dresden* until 1730 and this was getting too late for safety.

So Captain Luce in *Glasgow* redoubled his efforts to destroy *Leipzig* and *Nürnberg*.

Just before 1500 hours, *Glasgow* secured one hit on the ventilator head of *Leipzig*, forward of the third funnel. Thus fell the first man of the *Leipzig* in battle, *Matrose* Nicholas, the "talker" of the third 4.1-inch gun. His body was moved out of the way and covered with a flag, and the fight began in earnest. Miraculously, in this explosion Lieutenant Pöpperling was thrown from the upper to the middle deck, but was unhurt. He picked himself up and straightened his hat, and went about his duties.

"Hard aport," shouted Captain Haun—and for a moment they escaped the straddling of the British gunners.

The *Leipzig*'s maneuvering lost her distance, but for the moment brought a respite in the shooting. Then the shells began falling again, and now men began dropping.

Shortly after 1500 there was another break used as any respite would be for the rest of the afternoon by the medical corps men to take dead and dying into the aid stations for examination, and for whatever help might be given them.

Leipzig was shooting well, even with her smaller guns. (All the German ships shot well that day.) She had on several occasions straddled *Glasgow* with her salvos.

But *Glasgow* was shooting well and scoring hits, even though the German 4.1-inch gun was superior in range to the British 6-inch guns of the older model. The trouble—from

Leipzig's point of view—was that each time she wished to fire against the enemy, she must turn her broadside on, port or starboard, thus cutting the margin of distance between ships.

This became a serious matter because *Cornwall* and *Kent* were pouring on the steam and had managed to achieve twenty-four knots, quite unbelievable to anyone who had ever argued their merits from the depths of a club chair.

At 1535 Captain Ellerton of *Cornwall* made a signal to *Kent*, for both armored cruisers were coming into range.

"I will take the center target [*Leipzig*] if you will take the left hand one [*Nürnberg*]. . . ."

At 1617 both big cruisers opened fire. *Cornwall* moved in close to *Leipzig*; her guns had not the German's range. *Nürnberg* turned more eastward to avoid *Glasgow*, and *Kent* turned after her.

Captain Haun, seeing that *Cornwall* was coming at him swiftly, ordered the guns to switch targets and fire on the larger cruiser, but that did not mean that *Glasgow* had quit firing on *Leipzig*. Now she was the target of two cruisers, and she was being hit steadily.

One shell struck the Number 1 starboard gun. Two gunners were killed and the observer on deck behind the command post for the port gun saw his left arm smashed to a pulp by a splinter.

So rapidly was *Leipzig* firing at her enemies that the linoleum baffles between the guns burst into flames, but luckily so many were the splashes of water around *Leipzig* that the flames were extinguished.

Leipzig had taken one bad hit, which was to prove very important: a 6-inch shell had fallen into the clothes press between decks and had started a fire there, so fierce that the fire-control party was having difficulty in getting close enough to fight the blaze. The problem was smoke, compounded by the blazing garments in the area.

Dresden had turned sharply and suddenly away to starboard and was three or four miles ahead of *Leipzig* and *Nürnberg* when the fighting became intense.

Captain Haun looked off at her wryly.

"When one is naked, that's the time to get away," he said, quite without rancor, if a little wistfully.

They saw *Dresden* once again, at about 1630, far away to port and speeding southwest. But in between and afterward, the men of *Leipzig* were far too busy to give more than passing thought to *Dresden* or any of their other comrades.

Leipzig, in her zigzagging to stop and fire and then run some more, had inclined to port until she was now heading south-southeast and *Cornwall* had broken away to follow her. When *Cornwall*'s shots began to straddle *Leipzig*, Captain Luce in *Glasgow* swung around to starboard to join *Cornwall*. His idea was to produce a maximum effect through two ships firing on the same side.

The chief engineer reported to Captain Haun that hits below the *Leipzig*'s water line and hits coming through the decks had reduced his capacity to make steam, and from this point on the ship could only expect to have enough revolutions to make twenty knots.

This news, of course, meant disaster—but Captain Haun had been expecting it.

Chief Engineer Karl Hahn was doing everything! He was personally heaving coal out of the bunkers so the stokers could get at it more quickly. He was running from one end of his department to another, doing what must be done to keep the ship fighting.

The British fire was now proving to be deadly accurate. The *Leipzig*'s guns were being hit and knocked out of action. A shell fell into the small-arms magazine, and machine-gun bullets began popping away like firecrackers. Gunners and officers were killed at their posts as they aimed shells at their enemies.

The fires on the *Leipzig* were growing more noticeable and more smoke was rising from the interior of the ship. The damage-control parties rushed from one fire to the next, and for a moment nearly all action was suspended on the ship when a fire threatened one of the main magazines.

But *Leipzig* was doing damage too. *Glasgow* had become her secondary target with the coming of *Cornwall* to a point within range, but *Glasgow* was hit three times between 1600 and 1800 hours. One shell passed through the foretop without exploding, but it took off the hand of a young signalman. Another shell, which hit the mast just below the top, knocked out the electrical system and killed a stoker petty officer. *Leipzig* was firing regularly and in salvos, hitting *Cornwall* heavily. *Leipzig's* men were moving constantly and throwing ammunition boxes over the side (the British believed these were mines and at one point *Glasgow* swerved suddenly to avoid them).

Mist and a drizzle had set in over the battle scene, and this did not help the gunners. Between 1712 and 1730 the battle slackened off—the range was becoming too short, and the German shooting was too good. The British moved away to take advantage of their longer range guns, and to cut down on the casualties to personnel.

But at 9000 yards the men of the *Leipzig* could still shoot. Finding the range on *Cornwall*, she put *ten shots* into that cruiser within a matter of moments. *Cornwall* again altered course, moving away, firing a broadside, and moving away again.

At 1746 the British ships checked their firing; the weather was getting worse and they were finding sighting difficult because of their own smoke. Just then, *Cornwall* was hit in the paint room forward, a shell that did little damage except to her paint supply.

Leipzig was badly hurt but she was still fighting. Her speed was slowed to eighteen knots, as hits had flooded the fourth boiler and had created havoc elsewhere. One hit in a bunker had started a coal fire. Her fore topmast was shot away, a hit that also killed a gunnery officer.

At about 1800 hours more troubles developed aboard the little German cruiser. From the main magazine came the message: *"Die Munition ist achtern gleich zu Ende!"*

The ship was running out of ammunition!

This news Captain Haun had not expected. He had begun the battle with 1800 shells for his 4.1-inch guns. Now he had only 200 shells, and the after guns were almost completely out of ammunition.

Oberleutnant Giseke, the chief gunnery officer, was completely downcast. He had been hoping for a lucky hit which would take at least one of his enemies out of action, and then he was confident that he could deal with the other. But without ammunition . . .

There were those 200 shells, but they were all forward, and the firing position was now aft and must remain so. The sighting and communications mechanisms for the forward guns had been knocked out. The after guns could still fire, or at least three of them were still in working condition.

There were no spare men to put on the strange task of moving shells from forward to aft, and had there been, it was a dangerous job that called for volunteers. The volunteers were Lieutenants Jensen, Johnke, Pöpperling, and Riedeger, who carried the shells although at every moment they were under fire.

The firing against *Leipzig* became stronger and more effective at about 1815, when the British began using lyddite instead of common shells. This powerful explosive had far more force, and soon *Leipzig* was afire again. The British thought the reason for *Leipzig's* slow return fire was the increased effect of their hits—while actually it was because of the ammunition problem—and the *Cornwall* moved in to 7000 yards to deliver a broadside—taking several hits in the process.

One fire on *Leipzig* began forward; it quickly knocked out the ship's communications system, and then the emergency system.

At 1900 hours the last shell was fired by *Leipzig*. Now the entire ship was on fire, and the flames danced in the lowering light from stem to stern. *Leutnant* Schiwig, the torpedo officer, wanted to get in for a shot, and Captain Haun agreed that this was their best course at the moment. *Glasgow* was still standing off, shelling, but *Cornwall* was prowling back and forth, staying out of range of these guns, but gathering courage as they failed.

The trouble with making a torpedo run was that speed was now cut down to fifteen knots, and the ship was scarcely maneuverable.

"That's it," said Gunnery Officer Giseke. "Down the drainpipe we go."

Leutnant Schiwig was checking his tubes. The starboard tube was usable, although he had no working direction finders, no working apparatus for estimating distance, no communications with the bridge.

He and Giseke estimated the range at about 5000 yards at this point, for *Cornwall* was closing in.

The British cruiser stopped firing for a few moments at 1910, hoping that the Germans would surrender. On *Glasgow* signalmen were sent aloft to watch *Leipzig's* flag. Darkness was falling, so Captain Luce queried by searchlight and by flag if she would surrender. But Captain Haun had no intention of surrendering the ship without a few last shots.

Aboard *Leipzig*, *Leutnant* Schiwig was organizing a

human chain of communications, leading from the torpedo command post to the bridge. *Cornwall* closed in to 4700 yards, turning 16 points in order to keep out of torpedo range, and gave *Leipzig* several more salvos of lyddite shells with her starboard guns.

Even in this light, without his mechanical aids, *Leutnant* Schiwig managed to get away two torpedoes against *Cornwall*. Both missed, and she circled warily. Another torpedo was fired against *Glasgow*, and it, too, missed the mark.

The British firing became more insistent as light failed. The fires aboard *Leipzig* leaped higher. At 1920 came the cry from the bridge: *"Schiff versenken. Alle Mann an Deck."*

The men came pouring out of the vitals of the ship like children leaving a school, almost with pleasure at the thought that they would not be trapped below.

Then, at 1943, a tremendous explosion took place. Three minutes later a British shell took down the mainmast, and killed Gunnery Officer Giseke and *Leutnant* Johnke. On deck now stepped *Korvettenkapitän* Kretschmar, the first officer of the *Leipzig*, and he ordered three cheers for the Emperor. They were given.

Cornwall and *Glasgow* were circling, firing occasionally as some gun or piece of munition exploded aboard the burning *Leipzig*. They were flying flags asking the *Leipzig* to surrender, but not one word came from her. (Actually, in the growing darkness the men of the *Leipzig* could not read the British signals.)

With this call to the deck, more than a score of men tried to get into the port cutter, to lower her for escape, because *Leipzig* was no longer capable of action. Her battle was done. But a British shell struck the cutter as the men were clustered in and around the boat, leaving a welter of splintered wood and maimed bodies on the deck. Other men rushed to the other side of the ship, hoping to make use of the starboard cutter, which was in its cleats, half filled with water. But the ship's list was now too profound, and as Captain Haun told the men when they came to ask permission to try to use the boat, the cutter was holed besides.

Captain Haun looked at the British, still circling and firing, and wondered aloud why they would continue to massacre a defenseless foe. (In reality, it was a tribute to the East Asia Squadron that the British were so relentless—they were afraid not to be relentless with this enemy.)

Dr. Schaafhausen, the ship's surgeon, shook his fist and cursed at the circling British ships.

Leipzig suffered one tragedy after another, as the list to starboard deepened. *Leutnant* Schiwig was asked to try to keep the stern into the enemy, so *Leipzig* would present a stern-on target, and some of the men might escape the shelling. Schiwig did so, and to their credit, the men in the engine room responded, and so did men in the after steering compartment who were handling the manual steering, after the message system was shot out. In both areas men were trapped, locked in by twisted metal without a chance to escape and save their lives. But to the last they did their duty.

Perhaps a hundred men were left alive on deck. Most of these seized hammocks, and life jackets or spars, and went into the water, hoping to escape the shelling and the suction of a ship that must soon sink. Soon the captain, a half dozen officers, and a dozen seamen only were left on board the foundering vessel. She was going down steadily, filling with water.

Glasgow came to within 500 yards of *Leipzig*, but still could not understand whether or not she would surrender. *Leipzig*'s flag could not be reached by the survivors because the mainmast was ringed by fire and the men could not get inside to reach the lanyards and pull down the ensign.

The ship heeled over further. Captain Haun told his

officers and men to jump before they were caught in the sinking ship or the suction. They asked him to come with them, but he said he would wait until his ship had sunk—then swim to save himself.

Just before nine o'clock *Leipzig* heeled over and the officers and men aboard her jumped into the cold sea. Thick clouds of steam came up from the vessel, as she lay on her port side. Then, at 2121, as the boats of *Glasgow* and *Cornwall* searched the icy waters, an explosion rocked the *Leipzig*. Her stern went up into the air, and two minutes later she sank in deep water, latitude 53 degrees 55 minutes south, longitude 55 degrees 12 minutes west.

22

ONE BOAT WAS LAUNCHED

AT 1630, AS CORNWALL AND KENT BEGAN OVER-hauling *Leipzig* because of her delaying actions, it was agreed that *Kent* would branch off in pursuit of *Nürnberg*. *Kent's* speed was never supposed to be more than 23.7 knots and *Nürnberg's* was 23.5, so given any luck at all *Nürnberg* might have been able to escape. But the men of *Kent* were determined that she should not, and they urged their eleven-year-old ship to a speed of twenty-five knots, while *Nürnberg*, which was overdue for a refit, could not make her maximum speed.

So the British armored cruiser overhauled the German light cruiser, and the end was in sight at 1700 hours, when *Kent* came close enough to the light cruiser to open fire with her 6-inch guns.

The fighting of *Nürnberg* followed much the same pattern as that of the *Leipzig*—the Germans scoring hits early with their superior marksmanship and training (but not as often as *Leipzig*) and the British scoring as the battle progressed with their determination and improving marksmanship. There was good reason for this in both cases, and on the bigger cruisers: the Germans had been trained as a fighting force; the British were getting their training "on the job."

Before 1730 *Nürnberg* had taken two bad blows: her after steering flat had been hit, killing all the men in it but one.

At 1735 two of *Nürnberg's* boilers burst, either as the result of gunfire, or from the excess pressure forced into them in the ship's attempts to flee. Her speed fell to nineteen knots, and the end was in sight.

Now, from Captain von Schönberg's point of view, it was simply a case of going down fighting. The tale was almost the same as that of *Leipzig*, except that the action began later and ended earlier. *Kent* was using lyddite shells, which caused far more damage than the old explosives. By 1800 hours *Nürnberg* was afire near her mainmast, and soon her topmast toppled. Many of her 4.1-inch shells exploded on the armor of *Kent* but did not penetrate—the short range and low deflection worked to the advantage of the British in every way.

At 1820 *Nürnberg* was a wreck, "riddled like a watchman's bucket," one Englishman reported, her funnels torn and twisted—which meant that the moments of the engines were ending. Only two guns on her port side were firing.

By 1836 she had stopped firing altogether and at 1857 her flag was hauled down to stop the British fire on the mangled hulk that was burning so fiercely. Captain von Schönberg called the handful of survivors of this ship together, called for the three cheers for the Kaiser, and dismissed the men to escape as best they could. He returned to his bridge to await death.

One boat was launched from *Nürnberg*, and into it were put the wounded who might have a chance of survival. On launching, the boat sank, her seams opened by the terrible pounding the ship had received for an hour and a half.

Kent put boats into the water at 1927—exactly the moment that the *Nürnberg* chose to turn over on her starboard beam and then slip quietly down without an explosion. Just before she sank, by searchlight, the men of *Kent* saw a group of German seamen standing on the after end of the boat waving a flag. Then she was gone, and the boats went out into the cold water to search for survivors.

23

THE SUMMING UP

THE BATTLE OF THE FALKLAND ISLANDS HAD continued all day long, from that moment when the shepherd's wife on the hill in the south had warned Port Stanley that the Germans were coming, until the sinking of the *Leipzig* long after dark. When it was over, it was apparent that of the five German ships only one had escaped.

Dresden had made her getaway, beneficiary of the sacrifice of the others, particularly of *Leipzig*, which had fought an action very much like that of a rear guard on land for the first hour of contact with the British cruisers.

Although not as complete as in the battle of Coronel, the loss of life among the men of the defeated ships was appalling. Not one man of *Scharnhorst's* crew was saved. Admiral von Spee and his entire staff went down.

Once *Gneisenau* was sunk the British ships began to rescue as many men in the water as possible. The nearest of the three cruisers, however, was seven miles away so it was some time before the ship's boats could be brought into the middle of the debris. By this time many men, particularly the wounded, had died. Nearly two hundred survivors were picked out of the 40-degree water, but wounds and exposure began to take their toll, and all night long men of the *Gneisenau* died in the arms of the late enemies.

As the men of *Gneisenau* were being rescued, unbeknownst to the British squadron, *Nürnberg* was receiving the shattering blows that would soon send her to the bottom. The captain of HMS *Kent* was much heartened at this time to have the news from *Invincible* that *Scharnhorst* and *Gneisenau* were gone, but he could not respond even to tell Admiral Sturdee that he had engaged the enemy because one of *Nürnberg's* early shots had knocked out the *Kent's* wireless sending station.

At 1857, when *Nürnberg* hauled down her flag in her total helplessness, the men of *Kent* looked to their boats, knowing that they would soon be called to attempt rescue. Every one of *Kent's* boats was holed, and only two could be patched together to become seaworthy even for a time. Unlucky men of *Nürnberg*! For even though the British tried, they were long in launching the boats, and the water was cold and rough. Twelve men were picked up, and in a few hours five of them died of exposure or wounds.

When the men of *Leipzig* saw the ship sinking lower and lower, and took the opportunity to try to save themselves, Captain Haun gave them his blessings. He sat with his men on the helpless hulk, sharing out the contents of his cigarette case until the last. Unhappily those few who had remained on board the sinking ship could see their shipmates drifting *away* from the British enemies. The British ships would not stop shooting or lower boats until the *Leipzig's* flag came down. The flag could not come down, because there were fires ringing both masts, and no man dared go inside the rings. So the men who abandoned ship for the new danger of cold water were the victims of their ship's own long-livedness. They drifted and froze and were attacked by the vicious albatrosses.

After the hulk sank, and the few men struggled from it in the water, the boats came out to help them. Six officers and nine men were saved—so high a contingent of officers because they had chosen to stay with the ship until ordered off at the last moment by their captain.

By the time the men of *Leipzig* were rescued, night was well settled in, and aboard the *Invincible* Admiral Sturdee could begin to sort out the events of the day. He and his staff worked long into the night to establish just what had happened, and it was many hours before they learned from *Kent* the final part of the story.

Dresden's escape was not due to any laxity on the part of Admiral Sturdee, but more to the luck of *Bristol*'s having her engines down and being unable to steam out of Port Stanley with the fleet, and also to the fateful decision of Captain Luce that two birds in the hand were better than one in the bush.

Almost at the moment that *Gneisenau* was sunk, Admiral Sturdee began sending wireless signals to his ships, asking where *Dresden* was last seen, and in what direction she was heading. The most accurate information that could be obtained came from *Glasgow*, which had seen the German cruiser heading south-southwest. Ominously, nothing at all was heard of *Kent*, and would not be until she would limp into Port Stanley the next day.

Unable to secure accurate information about *Dresden*, Admiral Sturdee headed back to Port Stanley to assess the day's work and damages.

There was one more bit of work to be considered: the supply train of the East Asia Cruiser Squadron.

When Admiral von Spee had approached the Falklands, he had ordered his colliers to remain off Point Pleasant, and it was here that Mrs. Felton, the shepherd's wife, had spotted them and known the Germans were approaching.

At 1127 on the day of battle, while Admiral Sturdee was plunging after *Scharnhorst* and *Gneisenau*, the shore station had informed him that three enemy ships were lying off Port Pleasant, and he had seen a way at last to make some use of *Bristol* and the auxiliary cruiser *Macedonia*. They were told to "destroy the transports."

The transports were scattered, the British found, as they approached. *Seydlitz* had cleared out when she smelled trouble, but *Baden* and *Santa Isabel* were slower to get away. *Bristol* went out to the southeast and intercepted them, removed the crews, and sank both by gunfire.

Seydlitz had run east, and even though preoccupied with his own fate Admiral von Spee had instructed the collier to return to Picton Island or St. Quentin Sound, so she ran east, and then south, and moved into the Gulf of San Mathias, where a few days later she was interned and the crew of the *Drummuir*, which she had carried all this while, were landed and freed.

On the night of December 8 reports began to come in from the various British ships as to damage sustained. *Invincible* had been hit twenty-three times. The shooting had been good, but the angle bad—meaning that since the Germans were firing at an extreme angle, their shells did not often penetrate the heavy armored decks of the *Invincible*—but they had wrecked much of the ship's upper works. In the wardroom the grand piano had been destroyed by a direct hit. Another direct hit had struck the paymaster's money chest, scattering a thousand gold sovereigns about the ship. An unexploded shell even found its way into the captain's mess storeroom, and was discovered the next day sitting alongside a Gorgonzola cheese. But one hit on the water line had made a hole seven feet long and three feet wide and had flooded two bunkers. *Invincible* was not invincible.

Inflexible had suffered a few hits but not many; *Invincible* had been the main German target all along.

Cornwall was hit eighteen times by the excellent *Leipzig* gunners, but she was well protected by her armor against the 4.1-inch shells, and had only one serious bit of damage, a flooded bunker which gave her a list to port. *Glasgow* was hit only six times, because she had fought a long-distance battle with *Leipzig*, and had suffered no serious damage. *Kent* had been hit thirty-seven times by *Nürnberg*'s 4.1-inch shells, but, again, she was an armored cruiser and was protected against most damage. Her worst effects were the destruction of her wireless sending station and a 6-inch gun casement, when a shell came in through the gunport.

The difference in casualties was immense. *Kent* suffered four men killed and twelve wounded (one of whom later died). *Glasgow* had one dead and four wounded. *Invincible*, *Inflexible*, *Carnarvon*, and *Cornwall* had no casualties.

Scharnhorst carried more than 850 men, including the admiral's staff of a dozen. *Gneisenau* carried more than 850— and how many men had joined the ship as reservists at Valparaiso was not known except in the Squadron records that went down with the ships. *Leipzig* and *Nürnberg*'s complements were about 350 each, but they too had added reservists. To the British six dead one might better compare, not the German dead, but the German survivors.

When all the dying men had died on the night of the

battle and in the few days following, and when all the heads were counted, here was the total of German survivors:

SHIP	SURVIVORS
Scharnhorst	none
Gneisenau	25 officers, 132 men
Leipzig	7 officers, 11 men
Nürnberg	7 men

Vice Admiral Maximilian the Graf von Spee, commander of the crack German East Asia Squadron, pride of the German navy, first victor in a major naval battle in World War I, was dead, and dead with him were his two sons: Heinrich, who had gone down on the *Gneisenau*, and Otto, who had died in the last throes of the *Nürnberg*.

Germany's finest cruiser admiral was gone, and so were most of her cruisers, except for a handful that could now be regarded as bandits of the sea and hunted down individually. For all practical purposes, the German Admiralty's dream of *Kreuzerkrieg* was dead.

EPILOGUE

AS SOON AS THE GNEISENAU HAD SUNK, ADMIRAL Sturdee had set out to find the *Dresden*, but without success, because she was speeding along in bad weather, out of sight of the British squadron leader and his searching party. The admiral headed south toward Staten Island with *Invincible*, *Inflexible*, and *Bristol*. The force was strong enough to make any light cruiser captain shudder. It would have been stronger had the admiral had his way, because when *Glasgow* and *Cornwall* had finished off *Leipzig*, he ordered them to come along with him. They could not. They had fired nearly all their ammunition and *Cornwall* was down to 250 tons of coal. So those ships returned to port, but the hunt went on.

By 10:30 on the morning of December 9, Admiral Sturdee was within fifty miles of Staten Island. Then the weather became quite hopeless: thick fog and heavy seas. Admiral Sturdee turned and swept north-northwest, and *Bristol* was sent to sweep the western Falklands. For twenty-four hours

311

more the search continued, and then on December 10 it was abandoned and the ships returned to Port Stanley. *Dresden* had made her escape.

Arriving in Port Stanley on December 11, the admiral and his officers gave themselves a little respite and had time for speculation. Where had *Dresden* gone? With the eyes of an old sea dog cast at the weather, Admiral Sturdee considered it most likely that the German cruiser had headed for Punta Arenas or Cape Horn.

And he was quite right.

At first Captain von Lüdecke had thought about making for Picton Island where Admiral von Spee had set up a rendezvous earlier. He changed his plans when repeated calls on his wireless for supply ships elicited no answers from that area. He could not chance such a landfall—he must have coal—and he must find some German collier in all this waste of British seapower.

The only place he could be sure of receiving a friendly reception and the coal he needed was Punta Arenas, inside the Magellan straits. Yet, as von Lüdecke reasoned it, the British admiral must come to the same conclusion, and he was quite sure that by the time he arrived at least one of the British warships would be lurking at the entrance to the Straits.

What to do?

Captain von Lüdecke decided that brave, bold action was his only salvation, and so, in the thickening weather he moved into Cockburn Channel, a virtually uncharted body of water and certainly not one that a warship would choose under any normal circumstances. This narrow, tricky waterway would lead him to Punta Arenas by a back route, and whatever else might happen to him, he was unlikely to be surprised and captured by his enemies in this water.

Captain von Lüdecke gave the order to turn into the

Cockburn Channel early on December 10, and slowly, with leadmen in the bow, the ship made her way through the threatening waters until 1600 hours that day, when anchor was dropped in Sholl Bay, still some sixty miles south of the haven of Punta Arenas. There was very good reason for anchoring at Sholl Bay. The *Dresden* was nearly out of fuel. She had depleted her bunkers and her deck supplies. Now she must make out under emergency conditions.

Here men were sent ashore in the ship's boats to cut down trees from the evergreen forests, and the green wood was brought back to the ship to stoke the *Dresden*'s fires. There still remained 160 tons of coal in the bunkers, but this was just enough to make the green wood burn. It was not even certain that coal would be available at Punta Arenas. What if the British warships were there before her?

As if Captain von Lüdecke did not have enough trouble at the moment, the Chilean gunboat *Almirante Condell* came alongside on the night of December 10, and her captain informed Captain von Lüdecke that he must respect the Chilean neutrality and be out of these waters in twenty-four hours.

The captain *almost* complied.

At 1000 hours on December 12, Captain von Lüdecke had enough green lumber to serve his purposes, and he brought in his boats and raised anchor. Now he went straight to Punta Arenas, chancing the coming of the British squadron, for he must have *real* fuel.

At Punta Arenas lay the United States collier *Minnesotan* filled with coal that belonged to the German government. She had been chartered by the Germans, too, but the American captain would not give *Dresden* a bag of coal. He said he was a neutral, in neutral waters, and he had no right to turn over coal to a belligerent warship.

Fortunately for Captain von Lüdecke there also lay in Punta Arenas harbor the German Roland liner *Turpin*, which had been at anchor there since the war began. From *Turpin* the captain received 750 tons of briquettes.

On December 11 all the paperwork was handled by the pursers and paymasters of the two ships, and immediately the coaling began. There was not a moment to waste, for Captain von Lüdecke *knew* the British would soon be upon him, now that he had been sighted twice in Chilean waters.

How right he was!

At 0230 on December 13 an urgent wire reached Admiral Sturdee at Port Stanley from Montevideo. The *Dresden* had arrived at Punta Arenas on the afternoon of December 11, said the message, and was coaling.

Inflexible, *Glasgow*, and *Bristol* were immediately ordered to raise steam and move out.

It took time. More than a hundred men of *Glasgow*'s crew were ashore on overnight permission, and they had to be rounded up by the shore police. Steam was up and the men were aboard when the admiral ordered the three ships to have bills of health made out by the colonial surgeon. It was 0915 before the three ships were all out of harbor, trailed by good-luck signals from the *Invincible*, on their way to find and destroy the last ship of the German East Asia Squadron.

During the afternoon the British wireless rooms picked up fragments of an Argentine message about the *Dresden*, which seemed to indicate that her captain had sought asylum in Punta Arenas and that the ship would be interned there for the rest of the war by the Chilean government.

The report was not true. *Dresden* had coaled at amazing speed, for every man knew what might happen and what his responsibility was. At 2200 hours on the night of December 13 she had raised anchor and steamed south down the Straits of Magellan.

The next afternoon the British ship *Bristol* arrived at Punta Arenas and learned of the *Dresden*'s visit. She was

314

ordered to steam south and find the German ship, and she left. A few hours later, *Glasgow* pulled into harbor there. The British officers bullied the port commander who had allowed *Dresden* to coal in Chilean waters for the second time in less than three months, and left it at that. *Glasgow* then steamed south to try to find the German ship.

Dresden was in serious trouble. She could scarcely show herself at civilized places—and yet the 800 tons of coal she possessed, plus her load of wood, would not take her far or long.

For the moment, she must hide from her enemies, and fortunately for men of daring this hiding was not too difficult a process. The Straits of Magellan are filled with narrow tortuous waterways which at that time had never been charted. Indeed, in 1914, most of the charts that existed had been made by the scientists of the *Beagle*. Captain von Lüdecke decided to hide in these waters, and to secure his supplies by coming out to raid his enemies. He hoped that he would find some of the many German colliers attached to or sent to the Squadron, but he could only hope. He would be in touch with German authority as much as possible—in fact, on December 14 he was in touch with the German officials in the Argentine by radio, much to the disgust of the British. But he must be very careful if he was to survive.

He must simply wait for the colliers to find him.

It was easier said than done. The British were knocking off his colliers right and left. *Memphis* was interned at Coronel. *Luxor* was confined in the Peruvian port of Callao. *Patagonia* was arrested by the Argentines for breaking neutrality regulations. *Mera* was interned at Montevideo. *Josephina* was captured by the British.

On leaving Punta Arenas, Captain von Lüdecke steamed south, through Magdalena Sound and Cockburn Channel, then through narrow, rocky fjords, to Hewett Bay at the southwest end of Barbara Channel. The messages had produced their results. Here *Amasis* was waiting for her, with life-giving coal!

Dresden hid in this place until after Christmas. But she could not hide there forever—she must be off about the Kaiser's business, there was no point in simply hiding. On December 19 the collier *Sierra Cordoba* was sent her way by the German authorities on land, and she also sent *Amasis* into Punta Arenas to try to take off the coal from the *Minnesotan*. The Chilean authorities were quite thoroughly pro-Allies at this point—the German naval might had been destroyed—and *Amasis* not only failed in her mission, but she also was interned for trying to breach neutrality regulations.

The British squadron was very active in this area. *Bristol*, *Kent*, *Glasgow*, *Inflexible*, *Invincible*, steamed back and forth around the Cape and through the Straits. They investigated some channels. They called at every known port. They went through Baker Channel on a raw morning, to enter St. Quentin Sound, quite expecting to find *Dresden* there, and disappointed when they did not. They searched Mas-a-Fuera, Juan Fernández, San Felix, Vallemar. The Japanese cruisers *Idzumo* and *Hisen* were sent to help them. The battleship *Australia* came into these waters. The cruiser *Newcastle* came south. *Carnarvon* was detailed to watch the Straits of Magellan at all times.

The British grew very eager. On December 22 they sighted a "cruiser" and *Kent* gave chase, funnels streaming black smoke as she ran. It turned out to be a Chilean steamer.

By Christmas time the hunt slowed down. The Japanese ships were ordered off to other duty. *Inflexible* went home. *Australia* went home.

The German freighter *Sierra Cordoba* steamed into the Straits of Magellan, but she was spotted by the British and was afraid to move in to the place where *Dresden* lay, so she hid in Magdalena Sound.

316

INDEX

The day after Christmas the Germans were betrayed into action. Actually, they betrayed themselves.

On Christmas and for a day or so before that time the men had been sent into the forests again to cut wood to keep the fires going, so as not to consume the valuable coal. On December 26 the wood parties went out again, and they encountered the French motor sailer *Galileo* which hailed the *Dresden's* boat. In the conversation that followed the Frenchmen accused the Germans of being Germans, and they denied it. The Frenchmen then pointed to tattoos on the arms of some of the German seamen (*Mutter, Gott Mit Uns*). The Frenchmen were unconvinced.

The ship's boat made its way back to the *Dresden*, and the leader of the landing party told Captain von Lüdecke of their encounter. The captain grew very worried and very restless, because he realized that *Dresden's* secrecy was now compromised.

What to do now?

He decided that the only action was to take more of a chance. He sent the ship's steam pinnace into the channel that led to Christmas Bay at the top of Stokes Bay, and he literally felt his way along the bottom, following the soundings of the pinnace. He was now moving along what the British Admiralty charts of the day had designated as solid land!

At the end of the day Captain von Lüdecke was as safe as he could be. The British searchers were most unlikely to come looking for him in an area where their charts showed no water existed. He could afford to breathe deeply again.

As Captain von Lüdecke suspected, the French sailing-ship captain rushed to Punta Arenas as quickly as his vessel could go and reported having seen the German cruiser. He gave her position very accurately to British Consul Milward at Punta Arenas. The consul took the story to the admiral. The admiral's advisers looked at their charts and scoffed. The man was either drunk or trying to spoof them. The charts said there was not a decent channel in the area. It was mostly shallows and dry land.

So the whereabouts of the *Dresden*, although known perfectly to the British, were quite secret from them because they believed in their charts.

Dresden continued to hide in the channels that did not exist, down at this far end of the Americas. *Sierra Cordoba* evaded her pursuers and delivered coal to the German cruiser. The Chilean steamer *Esplorador* was chartered by Germans in Punta Arenas, loaded with sausages and provisions and luxuries, and sent to join the cruiser. She too found her way into the maze of channels and to the side of the last ship of the German East Asia Squadron.

January moved along. Through the wireless station at Punta Arenas, Captain von Lüdecke was in touch with Berlin, and the Admiralty advised him to come home. He was not to use the normal channels, but the old sailing-ship route which came north up the middle of the Atlantic.

Colliers would be arranged, off the Brazilian coast.

It seemed like a good idea, on paper in Berlin. From Captain von Lüdecke's position it seemed a terrible idea. The Admiralty was asking him to steam 5000 miles without coaling. How could he do it? He could not.

So Captain von Lüdecke said no. He would go into the Pacific and raid enemy commerce there.

The Admiralty said no. "Further coal supply for Pacific and Indian oceans is impossible," said the message. "Voyage home by sailing-ship route recommended. Collier awaits you in 5° S., 36° W."

How appealing a message: "Collier awaits you." But how bleak the prospect.

On January 28 a local German otter hunter directed Captain von Lüdecke to a new hiding place, and a few days later the German pilot of the *Esplorador* confirmed it. So on February 5 Captain von Lüdecke had new shelter of which his enemies knew nothing: a deep channel south of Santa Ines Island and north of William Island. He anchored here and *Sierra Cordoba* anchored with him.

What to do? What to do?

He could not do as the Admiralty asked. He must do as the Admiralty ordered him *not* to do: he must become the same kind of corsair that Captain von Müller of the *Emden* had been, working his way across the Pacific Ocean, taking his coal from captured enemies. He must make his way by raiding; there was no reasonable alternative.

Oh, yes, he could steam bravely into a Chilean port and demand that his ship be interned. But Captain von Lüdecke, even though not as daring or as bold or as purposeful as many of the officers of the cruisers of the Kaiser, was a good sailor and a good subject of his emperor. He was not in action to give up.

He sent a letter by messenger to Punta Arenas, asking the Admiralty to arrange a collier to rendezvous with him at latitude 37 degrees south, longitude 80 degrees west, west of Coronel, 200 miles south of Mas-a-Fuera. Then he made his preparations for the breakthrough into the sea.

On February 14, after two months of successful hiding in uncharted waters, *Dresden* steamed for the rough waters of the Pacific Ocean, followed by *Sierra Cordoba*.

Captain von Lüdecke then set course west, moving out 200 miles away from the coast, to give the British cruisers a wide berth. He planned to work the sailing-ship routes.

Sierra Cordoba was posted 100 miles ahead as lookout ship, for she was as harmless-looking a vessel as sailed the sea, with her one funnel and concealed wireless. Then the ships waited.

Not long before, the channels had been filled with sailing

319

ships, but now there seemed to be none at all. On February 27, however, von Lüdecke captured the British bark *Conway Castle*, carrying barley to Valparaiso. He sank her and transferred her crew to a Peruvian sailing ship that came along a week later.

He had sunk a ship at long last, but he had not secured any coal. Finally he had to send *Sierra Cordoba* on a desperate mission to Valparaiso for coal. She steamed in on March 3, managed to appear innocent enough to secure 1200 tons of coal, and steamed out.

So desperate was the *Dresden*'s need for coal that she was constantly on the wireless, sending messages everywhere, and everywhere that Germans were located attempts were made to help her.

From Montevideo on the night of February 20 was dispatched the German collier *Gotha* with instructions to meet the *Dresden* about 200 miles south of Mas-a-Fuera, as earlier indicated. The British intercepted the message and knew where the meeting would be held. But did they believe it?

Consul Milward, very much annoyed at having been disbelieved, chartered a motor sailer, and with a skilful Chilean pilot went into the waters where the *Dresden* had been—into that "dry land" that showed so plainly on the Admiralty's charts. And eventually the British learned that there were waters in the interstices of the Straits that their chartmakers knew nothing about. The naval men became believers.

So finally, some credence was given to the message that *Dresden* would be meeting *Gotha* at the rendezvous, and HMS *Kent* was ordered to be there and to destroy *Dresden*.

Kent steamed toward the rendezvous.

At 1550 on March 8 a seaman on the bridge of *Kent* suddenly spotted a three-stack cruiser, and finally the British knew they were on the track of *Dresden* again. She was nine miles away when she came up through the mist. But, of course, when the British saw *Dresden*, so did Captain von Lüdecke see *Kent*, and the chase was on.

Dresden was stopped at that moment, trying to conserve coal. It took her fifteen minutes to get going, but then she sped away and the British ship never came to within 12,000 yards, which was the range of her outmoded guns.

Dresden then signaled *Gotha* to meet her at Juan Fernández, and after dark she proceeded there. But the British had broken her code; they, too, had the message that night.

All through the night Captain von Lüdecke drove the *Dresden*, with a growing feeling of despair. So long had he been afloat without a refit that the ship could now travel at only twenty knots, which made her fair game for any British cruiser, new or old. He could never make it into the Pacific to fight. He could not carry on much longer.

So now he headed into Cumberland Bay in Juan Fernández, and early on the morning of March 9, 1915, he anchored about 500 yards from the shore. It was in his mind to have the ship interned, although he had not decided upon this at the moment of anchoring. But what else was there to do? He could not run the gantlet to Germany. He could not carry on successful *Kreuzerkrieg*, without spare parts, with rusty tired boilers, and a bottom fouled with barnacles. He had only eighty tons of coal left in his bunkers, not even enough with which to make a fight if he was cornered, and he had received a message during the night in which the Admiralty gave him permission to intern himself if he wished.

But he did not.

After the *Dresden* anchored, the lighthouse keeper, who was also governor of the island, came aboard the ship and told Captain von Lüdecke that he must either leave within twenty-four hours or be interned. The captain said he wanted only to make his ship seaworthy, and then he would leave—and the governor was satisfied.

So it was von Lüdecke's hope to make the try, to get the coal, to repair his boilers, to cant his boat and scrape at least a part of the bottom. And then to go somewhere and do something to bring honor to his ship and to himself.

The code broken, the message deciphered, the British sent *Glasgow* and *Kent* also to Juan Fernández, and they arrived off Cumberland Bay on the morning of March 14. Captain von Lüdecke did not have enough coal to raise steam for his ship to move and fight. He ordered steam in the second boiler, which ran the auxiliary machinery.

Dresden was flying the German flag and the German naval ensign, which meant she was a German warship, ready for battle.

The British came into range, and opened fire. Then it became apparent to Captain von Lüdecke that to fight would simply mean the loss of the lives of his men, without a chance of damaging the enemy seriously or of winning a victory or even of escape. So the white flag was brought out and run up, and the crew began leaving the ship, except for a final party that set charges in the main magazine.

At noon the charges went off. At 1215 *Dresden* was under water with her flags still flying. In the five minutes of bombardment seven men of *Dresden* had been killed, fourteen seriously wounded, fifteen slightly wounded, and one man had simply disappeared, probably the victim of a direct hit.

There was argument between Captain von Lüdecke and the British about whether or not he had intended to have himself interned—but really it made no difference. There was also argument between the Chilean fishermen of the area and the British about the damage done to a Chilean schooner and the death of about a thousand lobsters. Both were settled in short order: the lobsters were interned by the British navy, and the Germans were interned by the Chileans.

As the British ate their lobsters they could contemplate the knowledge that the seven seas were as very nearly freed from German warships as possible. The German High Seas Fleet existed in the North Sea, a constant threat against the Home Fleet, but outside the North Sea there was very little to worry Britannia. It would be many months before the British Admiralty would learn of it, but the *Karlsruhe* was to threaten no more; she blew up while traveling at high speed, victim either of her boilers, or of faulty munitions, or a stray mine. On the East African coast the *Königsberg* was bottled up in the Rufiji River delta and would never escape. The heavy cruisers *Goeben* and *Breslau* had made the most miraculous escape, steaming through the British fleet in the earliest days of war, through the Mediterranean to the Bosporus, and were safely locked up in the Black Sea, nominally at least to become the property of Germany's ally, Turkey. It made no difference to whom they belonged; they were no threat to British sea might.

So far as World War I was concerned, the armed navy cruiser passed out of existence as an offensive weapon of the type envisaged in the master German war plan. Had Admiral von Spee won his victory at the Falklands the result in terms of strategy would have been the same. The best he could have hoped for would have been to scurry homeward, doing more damage as he ran, hiding and scheming, and raiding for the coal that must keep him going. There was the rub—the perennial shortage of coal for the German raiders—and there was absolutely nothing that could be done about it. As the war progressed the Germans would not abandon the strategy of the raider, not at all, but they would make radical changes in their tactics, and already had begun to do so as Admiral von Spee and his men went down. Successor to the cruisers, and to

Kreuzerkrieg, would be the twin tactics of raiding by armed merchant raiders and by submarine. The merchant raiders were very successful, particularly the *Wolf*, *Moewe*, and *Seeadler*, which accounted for hundreds of thousands of tons of Allied shipping during the war. The submarine tactic was so successful that it replaced the concept of *Kreuzerkrieg*, and both the use of merchant raiders and submarines transcended World War I and were standard German tactics in World War II.

As for the cruiser, it persisted in the development of naval vessels, although it changed a little in form, and the concept of its use changed, too. The light, unarmored cruiser of the *Nürnberg* type was replaced by the big destroyer, but the heavy cruiser persisted and the Germans developed it into what would be called a "pocket battleship" in World War II. One of these ships, the *Graf Spee*, would quite fittingly come to the Western Hemisphere as a commerce raider. A national naval strategy dies hard, and the concept of *Kreuzerkrieg* was no exception. Just as the Kaiser's before him, Hitler's naval high command had hoped to wreak havoc with British might by use of strong, fast, heavily-armed vessels, and given the powering of modern naval vessels by oil rather than coal the admirals believed they might succeed. But the result was the same: the pocket battleship *Graf Spee* was tracked down in the South Atlantic, not so very far from Admiral von Spee's watery grave, and she was run to ground in Montevideo harbor, and scuttled there by her German crew. It finally became apparent that there was no place at all for cruiser warfare of the Graf von Spee's type in the modern world of airplanes and instant communication by radio, and so, twenty-five years after the Graf Spee's death, his concept of *Kreuzerkrieg* gave its last gasp.

Abrolhos Rocks, 151, 237, 239, 250
Abyssinia, 167
Admiralty (British), 134, 135, 146, 158, 167, 178, 179, 182, 183, 186, 232–236, 244, 258, 317, 320, 323
Admiralty (German), 10, 20, 144, 153, 216, 217, 218, 230, 241, 242, 244, 309, 318–319, 321
Africa, 10, 12–13, 21–22, 85, 117
Ahlers, 115, 123, 127, 130, 166
Albania, 14, 15, 44
Albany, USS, 54, 135
Albermarle Island, 137
Albion, HMS, 235
Alexandria, 62, 78, 99
Algerine, HMS, 54, 78
Allardyce, Governor, 256–259
Allies, 116, 229, 316, 324
Almirante Condell, 313
Amasis, 138–140, 167, 174, 225, 249, 250, 316
Amazon River region, 147
Americas, 117, 120, 145, 149, 181, 209, 217, 221, 324
Ammunition, 63, 198, 216–217, 248–249, 279, 287, 311
Amur River, 58
Ann-Marie Port, 161
Annapolis, USS, 54
Antarctic, 168

Anubis, 174
Apia, 124–127, 134, 135
Apolima, strait of, 126
Aranco Bay, 190
Argentina, 86, 244, 250, 252, 262, 314, 315
Arkona Island, 29, 33
Asama, 234
Asia, 11–13, 19, 22
Askold, 60, 81
Atlantic Ocean, 85, 155, 178
Australia, 59, 60, 86, 91, 111, 117, 122, 134, 150, 229, 234, 235
Australia, HMS, 59, 63, 79, 91, 92, 125, 126, 316
Austria-Hungary, 14, 37, 44, 48, 55, 144, 145

Baden, 150, 154, 174, 175, 224, 225, 230, 244, 251, 254, 307
Baghdad, 15
Bahia, 149
Bahia Blanca, 152
Baja California, 49, 61, 120–121
Baker Channel, 316
Balkan power, 14
Ballena Bight, 104
Bankfields, 139
Barbara Channel, 316
Beagle, 315
Beagle Channel, 251, 252
Belgium, 93

327

Belgrade, 48
Bender, Captain Alfred, 41, 243
Bengal, Bay of, 134, 157
Berlin, 12, 15, 16, 44, 68, 70, 111, 153, 166, 222, 249, 318
  See also Germany
Bernsdorff, Count von, 218
Berwick, HMS, 144, 145
Bingham, Lieutenant Commander Barry, 266
Bismarck, Prince Otto von, 9–10, 20
Black Sea, 323
Blanc, Admiral von, 21
Blanquet, War Minister, 144
Boers, 85
Bora Bora, 129–130, 161
Born, Kapitänleutnant Waldemar, 35, 110
Bosporos, 323
Boston, 146
Boxer Rebellion, 21, 22, 23, 27
Boy-Ed, Captain, 241
Brandenburg, SMS, 67
Brasseys Naval Annual, 194
Braun, Marine-Stabszahlmeister, 175
Brazil, 149, 150, 234, 238–239, 253, 318
Bremen, 10
Bremen, 142
Breslau, 81, 119, 323
Bristol, HMS, 144, 145, 178, 237, 239, 260, 261, 267, 268, 271, 306, 307, 311, 314, 316
British Admiralty. See Admiralty (British)
British-Japanese squadron, 54, 244
British West Africa, 235
Brüninghaus, Captain, 36
Buenos Aires, 147, 152, 230, 250

Burma, 86
Busch, Kapitänleutnant Johann, 176

Cabedello, 150
California, 235
California, Gulf of, 120, 136
California, USS, 54
Callao, 138, 140, 315
Cameroon, 22, 67
Canada, 78, 86, 94, 97, 122, 146
Canadian Pacific Line, 71
Canary Islands, 149, 234
Canopus, HMS, 157, 178, 179, 182–186, 192, 193, 209, 215, 232, 233, 237, 244, 249, 256, 258–259, 265, 267, 268
Cap Trafalgar, 152
Cape of Good Hope, 235, 237
Cape Verde Islands, 237, 241
Capuana Mission, 65
Caribbean, 146
Carnarvon, 178, 237, 260–261, 267, 270, 275, 283, 284, 308, 316
Caroline Islands, 39, 40, 46, 56, 73, 116
Carranza, Venustiano, 50, 51, 53
Central America, 137, 146
Chalientao lighthouse, 26
Chamorros, 39
Charron, Ensign, 132
Chikuma, 116
Chile, 22, 78, 111, 137, 141, 158, 159, 171, 173, 174, 178, 179, 183, 184, 187, 190, 191, 197, 207, 209, 213, 214–230, 239, 240, 245–246, 248, 250, 253, 313, 314, 315, 316, 318, 319, 320, 322, 323
China, 11, 16, 21, 22, 23, 24, 27, 56, 89, 174

China Squadron (British), 27–29, 60, 85, 91, 116
Christmas Island, 117, 121, 122, 317
Churchill, Winston, 48, 183, 215, 236–237
Ciphers, 63, 81, 183, 184, 321
Citriana, 51, 52, 53, 61–64
Club Central, 238
Coal, 53, 55, 62–63, 68, 71, 76, 78, 79, 96–97, 103–105, 111–112, 121, 128, 130, 136, 138, 149, 152, 188, 209, 214, 224, 227, 228, 230, 239, 241, 244, 245, 247, 248, 250, 251, 255, 261, 286, 312, 313, 314, 315, 317, 320, 321
Coaling, 31, 40, 64, 72, 97–99, 106–109, 122, 130, 136, 140, 154, 167, 173, 185, 225, 245–246, 314
Cockburn Channel, 159, 160, 312–313, 315
Cocos Keeling Islands, 229
Codes. *See* Ciphers
Colnett Strait, 35
Colombo, 123, 134
Colombo-Calcutta steamer route, 134
Concepción, 210
Constantinople, 14
Controleur Bay, 160
Conway Castle, 320
Cordillera Mountains, 184, 192
Cornwall, 178, 237, 267, 269, 270, 271, 277, 290–291, 292–298, 308, 311
Coronel, 172, 183–187, 209, 215, 222, 229, 233, 235–237, 243, 244, 245, 247, 248, 256, 273, 315, 319
  battle of, 197–208, 218, 232, 238, 239, 242, 304

Corrientes, SS, 149, 150
Cradock, Rear Admiral Sir Christopher, 135, 140, 145, 146, 148, 157, 158–160, 167, 171, 178–179, 180–187, 192, 193, 195–197, 211, 223, 228, 232, 233, 237, 258, 269
Cruiser Squadron. *See* East Asia Cruiser Squadron (German)
Cuba, 148
Cumberland Bay, 321, 322

Danish West Indies, 144
Dar es Salaam, 10
Dardanelles, 135
Dartmouth, HMS, 235
Darwin, Charles, 251
Defence, HMS, 135, 157, 158, 179, 182, 233, 237
Destremau, *Lieutenant de Vaisseau*, 131
Deutsche Klub (Valparaiso), 218
Diaz, Porfirio, 50
Dieterichs, Admiral von, 22
Direction Island, 229
Djokadj Rock, 46, 47
Dreadnought, HMS, 268, 271
Dresden, SMS, 141, 142–145, 157–159, 166–167, 172, 174, 178, 190, 191, 193, 195–197, 201, 205, 206, 211, 215, 225, 229, 230, 240, 241, 244–246, 252, 263, 271, 276, 277, 290–294, 304, 306, 311–322
Drumcliffe, 147, 148
Drummuir, 251, 254, 307
Dupleix, 58, 92
Düsseldorf, 67
Dutch East Indies, 86
Dysentery, 172, 221

East Africa, 19, 21, 235, 323
East American station, 142
East Asia Cruiser Squadron (German)
   accomplishments of, 323–324
   Admiral von Spee appointed to command, 23
   Admiralty plans for, 241
   ammunition shortages of, 63, 198, 216–217, 248–249, 279, 287, 311
   captains of, 69–70
   off Chile, 177–180, 187–188, 214–230, 240–247
   in China waters, 16, 19–33, 56–57, 75–77, 115
   coaling, 32, 41, 64, 72, 97–99, 106–109, 122, 130, 136, 154, 167, 173, 185, 225, 245–246, 314
   compared to Allied ships, 59–60, 194–198, 270–272
   Coronel, battle of, 189–193, 197–208
   creation of, 10–11
   defeat of, 304–305, 308–309
   drill of, 49
   Falkland Islands, battle of, 275–277, 278–303
   first ships of, 21, 23
   gunnery skill of, 32, 45, 91, 131–133, 194–195, 199, 215, 271, 278, 285, 301
   in Indian Ocean, 88, 111, 116, 135, 231
   in Mexican waters, 50–54, 104–105, 121, 135–136, 145
   morale in, 27–29, 42–43, 47–48, 81, 94, 184–185, 223, 231, 242, 247, 252, 273, 284, 286, 288
   neutrality, violations of, 96, 99, 187, 210, 216, 238, 316

   provisioning, 52, 72, 75, 80, 90, 99, 112, 115, 130, 139, 158, 161, 164–165, 175–176, 223, 225, 244
   results of, 323
   at San Francisco, 54, 78, 79, 99–102, 103, 120
   off South America, 137–141, 142–155, 166–167, 172–180, 187–188, 214–230, 240–247
   in South Seas, 39–48, 63–64, 71–74, 77–99, 105–115, 117–119, 123–127, 128–134, 160–166, 168–171
   specifications of ships in, 59–60, 194–198, 270–272
   superiority of, 194–198
   survivors of, 309
   volunteers for, 219, 221–222
   at war's outbreak, 39
   and weather problems, 79, 91, 158, 169, 171, 176, 196, 199, 201–202, 226, 246, 250–251, 271, 311
East Asia Squadron (British), 85–86
   Admiralty confusion over strategy of, 134–135, 156–157, 232–236
   off Chile, 171–172, 182–186
   Coronel, battle of, 189–193, 197–208
   Falkland Islands, battle of, 275–277, 278–303
   and defense of Far East, 134
   a "fleet in being," 117
   inferiority of, 194–198
   in Mexican waters, 144
   reinforcements for, 178–179, 233–236
   specifications of ships in, 59, 60, 194–198, 270–272
   unreadiness of, 92–93
   victory of, 304–305, 308

and weather problems, 196, 199, 201–202, 226, 246, 250–251, 271, 311
See also China Squadron (British)
East Asia Squadron (French), 126
East Asia stations, 21
East Asia waters, 134
East China Sea, 35, 285
East Indian waters, 59
Easter Island, 166, 167, 172–176, 178, 216, 284
Eckert, Minister von, 216, 240
Ecuador, 137
Edmunds, Mr., 173, 174
Edwards, Captain, 199, 215
Egg Harbor, 252, 253
El Dorado, 173
Elinore Woermann, SS, 253
Ellerton, Captain, 293
Elsbeth, 41, 57, 92
Elsinore, 137
Emden, SMS, 23, 24, 28, 33, 55–57, 58, 60, 63, 69, 70, 75, 76–77, 80–82, 88–89, 90, 94, 111, 112, 123, 134, 142, 143, 157, 229–230, 231, 319
Emmich, General von, 93
England. *See* Great Britain
English Channel, 226
Eniwetok, 94, 105, 111, 112
Enrique Lage shipyard, 238
Espionage, 98, 184, 185, 187, 238, 249
Esplorador, 318, 319
Essex, HMS, 144
Eten Island, 40
Europe, 11, 13, 14, 26, 149

Falkland Islands, 168–170, 172, 178, 179, 215, 239, 249, 253, 255, 260, 262, 263, 270, 304, 307, 311, 323

battle of, 275–277, 278–303
Falkland Islands Company, 257
Fanning Island, 121, 129, 134, 161
Far East, 27, 45, 58, 59, 71, 86, 134
Farallone Islands, 79, 94, 97–98, 120
Fare-Ute, Point, 128
Felton, Mrs., 265, 307
Ferdinand, Archduke Franz, 37, 43
Fielitz, Chief of Staff Otto, 47, 68–69, 70, 87, 218, 253
Fiji, 235
First South Sea Squadron (Japan), 116, 235
Fisher, Lord, 186, 236
Fleischacker Zoo, 100
Formidable, 232
Fox Bay Settlement, 168–169
France, 12, 14, 15, 19, 20, 26, 38, 45, 56, 57, 58, 59, 85, 86, 91, 126, 127, 129, 136, 145, 146, 181, 220, 224, 227, 229, 235, 317
Freshwater Bay, 137
Friedrich Wilhelm harbor, 92
Fueling. *See* Coaling
Fukoku Maru, 40–42, 63–64
Fylgia, 150

Galápagos Islands, 137, 138, 167, 186
Galileo, 317
Garapan settlement, 39
Geier, 234
General Gueraro, 53
German Admiralty. *See* Admiralty (German)
German Intelligence. *See* Intelligence (German)
German New Guinea, 92, 134
German South Sea colonies, 117, 127

Germany, 233, 241, 253, 255, 256, 320, 323
Gill Bay, 153
Giseke, Gunnery Officer, 296, 297, 298
Glasgow, HMS, 140, 151, 157, 168, 171, 178, 183–187, 190–192, 195, 197–201, 204–207, 209–211, 213–215, 236, 238–239, 249, 256, 257, 260, 265–272, 274, 275, 277, 290–298, 306, 308, 311, 314–316, 322
Gneisenau, SMS, 22, 24, 28–29, 32–37, 38, 39–42, 44, 45–46, 49, 56, 57, 59, 60, 63, 64, 69, 72, 73, 76, 79, 80, 89–90, 92, 94, 96, 107–110, 113, 114, 123, 124–125, 128–129, 131, 153, 159, 160–167, 171, 173–178, 182, 188, 191, 194, 196, 197, 199–201, 203–205, 210, 211, 213, 215, 217, 218, 220, 222, 224, 225, 227, 230, 235, 236, 242, 243, 245, 250, 252, 262–265, 266–268, 271, 272, 275–289, 304–305, 307–309, 311
Gneisenau, Field Marshal, 94
Goeben, 81, 119, 323
Golden Gate, 94, 95, 97, 100
Goliath, HMS, 235
Good Hope, HMS, 140, 157, 158, 160, 166, 171, 172, 178, 183, 191–192, 193–195, 198, 200–203, 205–206, 208–213, 215, 223, 235, 244
Gotha, 320–321
Göttingen, 115, 166, 174
Gouverneur Jaeschke, 80, 112
Graf Spee, 324

Grand Fleet (British), 217, 241
Grant, Captain, 237, 258–259
Grapow, Lieutenant, 212
Great Britain, 11, 14–15, 19, 20, 38, 45, 48, 56, 58, 61–64, 71, 75, 80, 85, 86, 111, 117, 122, 126, 127, 136, 145, 146, 148, 151, 154, 158, 215, 216, 233
See also Admiralty (British); Intelligence (British)
Greece, 15, 123
Guayaquil, Bay of, 139
Guaymas, 51, 52–53, 105, 120–121, 134, 135, 137
Guianas, 146
Gumprecht, Consul General, 216
Gunnery, 91, 131–133, 194–195, 198, 199, 215, 271, 278, 281, 285, 301

Hague Convention, 97, 135
Hahn, Chief Engineer Karl, 294
Hamburg, 10
Hamburg-Amerika Line, 144, 149
Hampshire, HMS, 59, 92, 157
Hanover Island, 155
Hapsburg Empire, 14, 37
Haun, Captain Johannes, 25–26, 30, 50, 52, 53, 61–62, 70, 78, 79, 94–98, 103–105, 120–121, 135–138, 140, 141, 224, 251, 290–293, 296, 297, 299, 305
Hawaii, 30, 31, 104, 116, 118
Heinrich of Prussia, Prince, 67
Hela, 68
Helicon, 188, 224, 225
Heltorf, 66
Herford, 69
Hewett Bay, 315
High Seas Fleet (German), 86, 143, 217, 241, 323

Hintze, Rear Admiral Paul von, 145
Hirst, Commander Lloyd, 183
Hirst, Intelligence Officer Lloyd, 168–171, 238
Hisen, 316
Hitler, Adolf, 324
Hiwaoa, 161
Hizen, 234
Holmwood, 152
Holsatia, 80, 166
Home Fleet (British), 11, 85, 234
Hong Kong, 12, 13, 92, 116, 119
Honolulu, 24, 31, 37, 52, 54, 71, 100, 110, 111–113, 118, 119, 121, 153, 166, 219, 234
Horn, Cape, 154, 158, 182, 215, 217, 226, 234, 247, 251, 252, 260, 269, 312, 316
Hornby, Rear Admiral R. S. Phipps, 235
Hoste Island, 154
Hostilius, 148
Howard, Rear Admiral, 54
Huerta, President Victoriano, 50, 51, 53, 142–143, 144
Huguet, Vice Admiral, 126
Hyades, 150, 151

Ibuki, 116
Idzumo, 54, 61, 95, 96, 104, 119, 120, 234, 316
Iltis, 21
India, 86
Indian Ocean, 86-90, 111, 116, 123, 134, 135, 229
Indochina, 12
Inflexible, HMS, 235–238, 267, 268, 270, 271, 274–276, 279, 283, 308, 311, 314, 316

Intelligence (British), 92, 145, 317, 320
Intelligence (German), 58, 95, 184, 187, 238, 241, 249–250, 253
Internment, 321, 323
Invincible, 234, 236–238, 265, 267, 269–272, 274–276, 279, 282, 286, 288, 305, 306, 307–318
Italy, 15, 37
Iwate, 235

Jaguar, 23
Jaluit, 114
Jaluit Company, 56
Jamaica, 145
Japan, 12, 20, 26, 34, 38, 40, 45, 57, 59, 61, 71, 73, 76, 83, 85, 86, 91, 95, 97, 111, 114, 116, 117, 133, 220, 223, 231, 235, 315
Jebsen and Company, 105, 121, 135, 136
Jellico, Admiral, 234
Jemtschug, 58, 60
Jensen, Lieutenant, 98, 100, 137, 224, 296
Jericoacoara, 149
Jerram, Admiral Sir Thomas, 27, 32, 60, 91–93, 116, 117, 134, 135
Johnke, Lieutenant, 136, 296, 298
Josephina, 315
Juan Fernandez Islands, 111, 166, 180, 182, 184, 188, 215, 316, 321, 322

Kaiser Prize, 198, 285
Kaiserliche Marine, 66
Karlsruhe, 143, 144, 146, 148, 323
Karnak, 174
Katherine Park, 152

333

Kauai, 31
Kent, HMS, 234, 237, 266, 268–270, 277, 290–292, 301–303, 305, 306, 308, 316, 320–322
Kiaochow colony, 11, 14, 16, 19, 21, 22, 76, 83, 97
Kingston (Jamaica), 144
Kinneir, Captain D. R., 155, 157
Knorr, Korvettenkapitän von, 26, 76
Kohler, Captain Erich, 142–144
Kongo, 117–119
Königsberg, 134, 323
Korea, 12, 34, 40, 60
Korea, 31
Kormoran, 75, 111, 114–115
Kraft, Chief Gunner, 176–177
Kretschmar, First Officer, 79
Kreuzergeschwader. See East Asia Cruiser Squadron (German)
Kronprinz Wilhelm, 241
Kurama, 235
Kyushu Island, 35

La Paz, 54, 61, 62
La Plata, 147, 148, 151, 249
Ladrone Islands, 116
Langar Island, 46, 56
Latin America, 111, 142, 145
Laushan, 33
Lauterbach, Oberleutnant zur See Julius, 75, 80, 89, 90
Leipzig, SMS, 23, 25–27, 30, 37, 49–51, 52–54, 59, 61–64, 70, 71, 76, 78–79, 88, 94, 97–98, 103–105, 119–121, 134, 135, 136–140, 152, 159, 166–167, 172–174, 178, 184, 186, 187, 190, 191, 196, 197, 199–201, 205, 206, 211, 215, 217, 221, 224, 226, 230, 240, 241, 244, 246, 251, 254, 263, 276, 277, 290–301, 304, 305–306, 308, 311
Liberia, 234
Lobos de Tierra, 139
London, 151, 167, 179, 183, 184, 233
    See also Great Britain
Longmoon, 80, 91, 107
Luce, Captain, 183, 184–185, 187, 204, 205, 214, 238, 256, 265, 290, 291, 292, 293, 297
Lucerne, Switzerland, 67
Luchs, 23
Lüdecke, Fregattenkapitän Fritz Emil von, 142–155, 157–158, 245, 312–315
Luther, Martin, 188
Lutz, Funkentelegraphic-Meister, 46
Luxor, 245, 250
Lynton Grange, 147

Macedonia, 178, 237, 267, 271, 307
Madero, Francisco, 50
Maerker, Captain Gustav, 34, 49, 69–70, 94, 110, 112–113, 128, 163, 164, 176, 226, 227, 243, 252, 263, 264, 267–268, 283–289
Magdalena Bight, 62, 104
Magdalena Island, 61
Magdalena Sound, 315, 316
Majuro Atoll, 112, 114
Maler, Major, 53
Manchuria, 12, 40, 76
Manila, 112
Manzanillo, 51
Marianas Islands, 20, 35, 38, 39, 40, 75
Marie, 121, 136–138, 138–140
Mark, 80, 115

Markomannia, 76, 77, 80–81, 89, 90
Marquesas Islands, 123, 133, 160, 161, 163, 166, 172, 174, 235
Marshall Islands, 9, 90, 93, 105, 111, 112, 116, 117
Mas-a-Fuera, 155, 182, 185, 224, 230, 242, 315, 318, 320
Mas-a-Tierra, 184
Mazatlán, 105, 120–121
Mazatlán harbor, 49, 51, 54, 64
Mediterranean Fleet (British), 85
Mediterranean Sea, 323
Memphis, 245, 250, 315
Mendocino, Cape, 97
Mera, 253, 315
Merlet, 173
Metalinim, 47
Mexico, 24, 25, 37, 49, 50–52, 61, 78, 104, 121, 134, 135, 142, 145, 154
Meyer-Waldeck, Governor, 28, 75, 76
Mezenthin, *Kapitänleutnant* Hermann, 89, 94, 222
Milward, British Consul, 317, 320
Minnesotan, 316
Minotaur, HMS, 27–30, 32, 58, 92, 235
Miquelon Islands, 146
Moeller, Consul, 136
Moewe, 324
Moltke, 67
Monmouth, HMS, 140, 157, 168–170, 172, 178, 183, 187, 190, 192, 194, 195, 198, 200–202, 204, 205, 207–212, 214, 215, 223, 236, 244
Montcalm, 59, 126, 127
Montevideo, 178, 215, 234, 250,

314, 315, 320, 324
Moore, Rear Admiral, 118
Moorea Island, 131
Morale, 184–185, 223, 231, 242, 247, 252, 273, 284, 286, 288
Mount Aconcagua, 184
Mount Fuji, 30
Mulinu Peninsula, 125
Müller, Captain Karl von, 55–58, 60, 63, 64, 69, 70, 75–77, 81, 87–89, 143, 229, 319
Mutiny, 284

Nagasaki, 34–35, 219
Nanking, 12
Naval warfare, rules of, 207, 210
Nelson Straits, 155, 157
Neu Pommern, 92
Neutrality, rules of, 96, 99, 187, 210, 216, 238, 316
New Guinea, 92
New York, 146, 147, 241
New Zealand, 59, 91, 117, 126–127, 134
Newcastle, HMS, 59, 92, 234
Newfoundland, 146
Newport, 152
Newport News, 147
Nohl, *Oberstabsarzt* Dr., 35, 286
North America, 71, 135, 146, 234
North Atlantic Ocean, 86, 150, 235
North China waters, 36
North German Lloyd Company, 24, 79, 118
North Sea, 68, 217, 253, 264, 323
North Wales, 244
Norway, 188, 224
Nuku Hiva Island, 160

Nürnberg, SMS, 23, 24, 37, 49–
51, 52, 54, 57, 59, 63–64,
70–73, 79, 105, 107, 109,
110, 112, 113, 117–119,
121–123, 134, 153, 159–
161, 166, 173, 175, 179,
190, 191, 193, 196, 206–
215, 219, 224, 230, 235,
236, 242, 253, 262–265,
268, 277, 290–294, 301–
303, 305, 308, 309
Nuu Tere, Point, 128

Oahu, 31
Olinda, 150
Orama, 178, 237
Orange Bay, 154, 158, 159,
168–171
Oregon, 62, 173
Oroluk, 44
Ortega, 154–155, 158
Otranto, HMS, 141, 157, 178,
183, 186, 187, 190, 192–
193, 195, 197, 198, 205,
209, 210, 211, 215, 228,
234, 236
Ottawa, 146
Otter, 23

Pacific coast, 52, 98
Pacific islands, 57
Pacific Ocean, 14, 19–20, 21,
24, 35, 40, 61, 71, 79, 96,
116, 128, 135, 167, 173
Pagan, 36, 73, 75, 76, 78, 79–
81, 84, 88, 89, 92, 93
Palaus, 92
Panama, 50, 86, 136
Panama Canal, 139, 154, 186,
235
Papeete, 128, 132–133, 134
Patagonia, 251, 260
Patagonia, 315
Patey, Rear Admiral Sir George,

91, 92, 117, 123, 126, 134,
135, 234, 235
Patricia, 25, 27, 45, 68, 70
Pearl Harbor, 118
Pegasus, HMS, 134
Pelikan, 68
Pembroke, Cape, 263, 269
Pembroke Light, 265
Peñas, Gulf of, 155, 241, 245
Pernambuco, 150, 151, 244
Persia, 14
Persia, 150
Peru, 138–140, 315, 320
Pescadores Islands, 140
Petites Iles Sous-le-Vent, 129
Picton Island, 251, 307, 312
Pittsburgh, USS, 95
Plate River, 152, 157, 179, 244,
249
Pleasant, Point, 265, 307
Plymouth, 236
Pochhammer, *Korvettenkapitän*
Hans, 41, 108–110, 112–
113, 163–167, 174, 182,
200, 201, 218, 221–223,
243, 272–273, 280, 283,
288
Pocket battleship, 324
Pommern, 118
Ponape, 23, 46, 47, 48, 54, 56,
63–64, 71, 72, 153
Pontoporos, 123
Pöpperling, Lieutenant, 296
Port Arthur, 12, 34
Port Low, 112
Port Stanley, 169, 215, 236, 237,
249, 256–260, 262, 263,
265, 304, 306–307, 311,
314
Port William, 260, 263
Port-au-Prince, 144
Portugal, 15, 19
Preussen, *Kontreadmiral* Prinz
Heinrich von, 22
Princip, Gavrilo, 43

336

Prinz Eitel Friedrich, SMS, 76, 77, 80–81, 90, 115, 184, 225, 227–229, 241, 243
Prinz Waldemar, 80, 107, 109
Protz, Dr., 31
Provisioning, 52, 72, 75, 80, 90, 99, 112, 115, 130, 139, 158, 161, 164–165, 175–176, 223, 225, 244
Prussia, 150–151
Puenta Parina, 139
Puerta Mexica, 144
Puerto Monte, 186
Punta Arenas, 153, 158, 159, 171, 249, 253, 312, 313–314, 316–319
Punta Caramilla, 216
Punta Santa Elena, 244

Quelpart Island, 34, 57

Radio Apia, 127
Radio Callao, 140
Rainbow, 78, 94–95, 97, 119, 120
Raleigh, USS, 54, 99
Rameses, 245
Reichsmarine, 68, 70
Reichsmarineamt, 110, 142
Reimer, Dr., 54, 62, 95–97, 98, 105
Reuters News Agency, 81
Rhakotis, 245
Riedeger, Lieutenant, 296
Rio de Janeiro, 151, 238, 257
Rjasan, 63, 64, 74–76
Rocas Reef, 149, 150
Rodik, German Consul, 118
Roggeveen, Dutch Admiral, 173
Rost, Chaplain, 77, 94, 188, 286
Rota Island, 39
Routledge, Mrs., 173, 174
Royal Naval Reserve, 61
Rufiji River, 323
Russia, 12, 14, 15, 20, 33, 37, 38, 44, 45, 48, 55, 56, 58, 60–62, 81, 83, 91, 145, 147, 181, 220, 229
Russo-Japanese War, 58
Ryukyu Islands, 35, 77

S-90, 23, 77, 119, 231
St. George, Gulf of, 153
St. Lawrence River, 146
St. Louis, USS, 99
St. Lucas, Cape, 49, 120, 136
St. Petersburg, 14
St. Pierre, 146
St. Quentin Bay, 230, 241–242, 245, 246, 248, 250
St. Quentin Sound, 307, 316
St. Thomas, 144
St. Vincent, 237
Saipan, 39
Samoa, 10, 20, 21, 39, 40, 63, 64, 100, 104, 117, 123, 124, 126, 157, 253
San Blas, 51
San Clemente Island, 235
San Diego, 78
San Felix, 316
San Francisco, 51, 52, 54, 61, 62, 71, 78, 79, 95, 97, 100, 103, 111, 120, 136, 137, 225
San Juan, 145
San Luis de Maranhao, 149
San Mathias, Gulf of, 307
San Roque, Cape, 149, 150
San Sacramento, 225
Sanders, General Liman von, 15
Santa Elena, Cape, 139
Santa Ines Island, 319
Santa Isabel, 152–154, 158, 225, 244, 251–252, 307
Santa Maria Island, 186
Sapper Hill, 259
Sarajevo, 37
Sausalito, 99

Scapa Flow, 217
Schaafhausen, Dr., 299
Schack, Vice Consul von, 95–97, 98–99, 120
Scharf and Kayser, 161, 164–165
Scharnhorst, SMS, 22, 24, 28–30, 32, 33, 35, 37–39, 41–46, 56, 57, 59, 63, 64, 69, 72, 73, 79, 87, 90, 92, 94, 96, 107, 110, 112, 114, 119, 123, 124–125, 127–133, 153, 160–162, 166, 167, 171, 173, 175, 182, 189, 190, 191, 194, 196, 197, 199–205, 211, 213, 215–230, 235, 236, 242, 243, 251–253, 263, 266, 269–272, 275–277, 279–283, 285, 304, 305, 307, 308
Schiwig, Lieutenant Walter, 26, 31, 97, 101, 139, 297–299
Schönberg, Captain Karl von, 52, 70, 71, 111, 116, 118–119, 121, 206, 207–208, 253, 301
Schultz, Captain Felix, 49, 57–58, 69, 72, 89, 197, 243, 252
Second South Seas Squadron (Japan), 116
Seeadler, 324
Serapis, 98
Serbia, 14, 44, 48, 85, 144
Sevilla, 152
Seydlitz, 245, 307
Seymour, Admiral, 22
Seymour Expedition, 27
Shanghai, 12, 13, 24, 34
Shantung peninsula, 11, 19, 21
Shearwater, HMS, 78
Shih-kai, President Yuan, 24
Shimonoseki Strait, 26
Sholl Bay, 313

Siamese Prince, 151
Siberia, 57
Sierra Cordoba, 316, 318–320
Simpson harbor, 92
Slavs, 14, 37
Smyth's Channel, 155, 215
Society Islands, 128
Solomon Islands, 19
South Africa, 85, 152, 249
South America, 86, 88, 117, 134, 135, 140, 146, 153, 154, 157, 158, 167, 168, 173, 178, 184, 217, 218, 232, 239, 241, 242, 247–249, 255
  See also Americas
South Atlantic, 145, 239, 260, 324
South China, 12
South Dakota, USS, 95
South Pacific, 32, 93, 129, 184
South Seas, 24, 40, 88, 161
Southwest Africa, 19
Spee, Admiral Maximilian Graf von, 23, 24, 27–30, 32, 35, 37, 38, 40–44, 46–49, 54–57, 59–60, 66–76, 80, 83–84, 86–93, 110, 113–117, 120–121, 127, 128, 131–135, 155, 157, 158, 160–167, 171–175, 178, 179, 181–186, 189–193, 195–197, 199, 203, 205, 207, 209, 211, 214, 216–218, 222–223, 228, 230, 232–243, 246–248, 250, 252, 253, 255, 260, 262, 264, 267, 269, 275–282, 290, 304, 307, 309, 312, 323, 324
Spee, Countess von, 181, 211
Spee, Leutnant Heinrich von, 72, 160, 309

Spee, *Leutnant zur See* Otto von, 72, 160, 175, 309
Staatssekretar Kraetke, 80, 112
Steiermark, 152
Stoddat, Rear Admiral Archibald, 178–179, 237, 269
Stokes Bay, 317
Straits of Magellan, 153, 182, 215, 243, 251, 312, 314–316
Sturdee, Vice Admiral Sir F. Doveton, 234, 237, 259–260, 264, 266–267, 274, 275, 277–279, 281, 282, 286, 305, 306, 311–312, 314
Suffolk, HMS, 145
Sunda, 24
Suvarov Island, 127
Swan of the East, 48
Sweden, 150
Swiftshire, HMS, 59
Sydney, 128
Sydney, HMS, 229

Tagus Cove, 137
Tahiti Island, 127–129, 131, 158, 160, 161
Taku, 21, 27, 34
Tellez, General, 53
Thierechens, Captain, 228–229
Tientsin, 27
Tierra del Fuego, 171, 239, 252, 262
Tiger, 23
Timor, 112
Tirpitz, Admiral, 22, 255
Titania, 23, 40, 41, 48, 49, 73, 79, 81, 89, 107, 113–115, 121–123, 166, 173, 188, 225, 242
Togoland, 152
Toloas Island, 40
Torgau, 53
Trans-Siberian Railway, 33, 34
Trinidada, 151–152

Triple Entente, 14–15, 26
Triumph, HMS, 59, 92, 116
Truk, 39, 40, 44, 46, 71
Tsingtao, 12, 13, 21, 23–28, 30, 32–35, 40, 41, 44, 45, 55–57, 62–64, 68, 75, 80, 83, 85, 89, 92, 97, 115, 116, 118, 119, 230, 242
Tsingtau, 23
Tsukuba, 235
Tsushima Strait, 57, 60, 63
battle of, 20
Turkey, 14, 15, 119, 323
Turner, Major, 263
Turpin, 313–314

Union of Death (The Black Hand), 43–44
United States, 19, 20, 31, 50, 54, 78, 86, 88, 94, 98, 111, 118, 121, 223, 241
Upolu, 126–127
Urakas, 35
Uruguay, 234

Vaea Mountain, 124
Valentine, 224–228, 242, 253
Vallenar, 183, 184, 316
Valparaiso, 111, 112, 128, 154, 157, 159, 171, 174, 184, 209, 213, 215, 218–222, 230, 235, 238, 240, 241, 245, 247–249, 256, 260, 308, 320
Vaterland, 23
Vera Cruz, 50, 52, 144
Villa, Pancho, 51, 52–53
Vladivostok, 12, 34, 57
Vogt, Captain, 41, 49

Walküre, 133
Weather, 79, 91, 158, 169, 171, 176, 196, 198, 199, 201, 202, 226, 246, 250–251, 271, 311

Weihaiwei, 12, 32
West Africa, 21
Westphalia, 69
Wied, Prince zu, 15
Wilhelm I, Kaiser, 9, 10, 19, 49, 57, 67, 240, 246, 284, 319, 324
William Island, 319
Wireless, 61–62, 74, 81, 83, 93, 110, 122, 126, 140, 149–150, 157, 167, 169, 172, 176, 182, 184, 185, 190, 192, 193, 223, 236, 238, 242, 244, 258, 262, 314, 320
Wittelsbach, 68
Wolf, 324
World War I, 226, 233, 309, 323, 324
World War II, 223, 324

Yangtze River, 12, 23, 24, 39, 56
Yap Island, 71, 80, 83, 92–93, 111
Yarmouth, HMS, 59, 92, 157
Yatau, Cape, 26
Yokohama, 26, 30, 31, 52
Yokosuka naval base, 26
Yorck, 79, 123, 166, 174
Yunnuisan, Cape, 77

Zanzibar, 134
Zelee, 130–131, 133
Zuckschwerdt, *Korvettenkapitän*, 114

ABOUT THE AUTHOR

Edwin P. Hoyt was born and educated in Portland, Oregon. During World War II he served as a member of the United States Army Air Force. Following his discharge he joined the Office of War Information as an editor in the Psychological Warfare Division. Mr. Hoyt, who lives in Bomoseen, Vermont, is the author of many well-known books, including *A Matter of Conscience, The Vanderbilts and Their Fortunes,* and *Paul Robeson: The American Othello* (World). Among his previous books on naval affairs are *The Last Cruise of the Emden* and several naval adventure stories for young people.